Richard Usborne was born in 1910 in India. After Oxford, he began a career in advertising, and was a writer and journalist. He was, for three years from 1948, assistant editor of the *Strand Magazine*, in which, from 1910, most of P. G. Wodehouse's short stories appeared.

Long regarded as the leading authority on Wodehouse, he was, with eleven other eminent admirers, a contributor to *Homage to P. G. Wodehouse*, the Festschrift presented to the author in 1973, and, in 1977, he edited *Vintage Wodehouse*, a selection from his works. Mr Usborne is equally noted for pioneering the critical evaluation of three other of his boyhood favourites – Dornford Yates, 'Sapper' and John Buchan. His entertaining, nostalgic, yet unblinkered study of the recurrent characters in their fiction, *Clubland Heroes*, was much praised on first publication in 1953, and is now recognized as a classic. He recently revised it for publication in a second edition.

Richard Usborne has written for *Punch*, *The Times*, *Guardian* and *Sunday Times*. He has been a book-reviewer for B.B.C. radio, the *Times Literary Supplement* and other journals.

14

RICHARD USBORNE

WODEHOUSE AT WORK
TO THE END

PENGUIN BOOKS

Penguin Books Ltd, Harmondsworth, Middlesex, England
Penguin Books, 625 Madison Avenue, New York, New York 10022, U.S.A.
Penguin Books Australia Ltd, Ringwood, Victoria, Australia
Penguin Books Canada Ltd, 2801 John Street, Markham, Ontario, Canada L3R 1B4
Penguin Books (N.Z.) Ltd, 182–190 Wairau Road, Auckland 10, New Zealand

—

First published by Herbert Jenkins 1961
This revised edition first published by Barrie & Jenkins 1976
Published in Penguin Books 1978

—

Made and printed in Great Britain by
C. Nicholls & Company Ltd.
Set in Monotype Garamond

for Monica

... the best writer of English now alive ... the head of my profession.

Hilaire Belloc on P. G. Wodehouse in 1934

CONTENTS

NOTE

The name Wodehouse is properly pronounced Woodhouse. The name Ukridge properly rhymes with Duke-ridge. The name Psmith, its owner claimed, was properly pronounced Smith.

I

...NEEDS NO INTRODUCTION

P. G. WODEHOUSE had double citizenship, British and American. He became Sir Pelham Wodehouse at the age of ninety-three, receiving a knighthood in the 1975 New Year's Honours list. A month and a half later he died, of a heart attack, in a hospital on Long Island, near his home in Remsenburg. He was sitting in a chair, with a three-quarters-finished new Blandings novel in typescript and autograph notes around him. He had gone into hospital for tests to establish a cause, and indicate a cure, for a troublesome skin rash. He had been working right to the end. He had intended to live to his century.

He had loved writing, and he studied his craft with scholarly application. He was a most courteous man, but shy, latterly rather deaf, and serious: never a chuckling Cheeryble. He manufactured humour at his desk and fed it into his typewriter. He wrote nearly a hundred books. He had no message.

I finished the first version of this examination of his works in time for publication on his eightieth birthday, in October 1961. I met him, for the first and only time, with Ethel his wife and Nella, his brother Armine's widow, in their Long Island home shortly before he turned ninety. I have revised the 1961 book, and brought it up to date, having read, as they came out, the twelve new Wodehouse books that were published in his last thirteen years. I have revised some of my 1961 opinions, too. I have cut a good deal. I have

added some late-flowering beauties to the anthology of Wodehouse images with which I cheer this book up between
chapters.

I had intended to add a chapter telling the complete story
of the five talks which Wodehouse, after his release from internment, recorded in Berlin in June 1941, and the German
Foreign Office put on their shortwave radio to still-neutral
America. (The Propaganda Ministry, without asking the
Foreign Office, put the talks out longwave to England later.)
Wodehouse had given me permission, and some facilities, for
gathering the threads of that story, already frayed, for my
1961 book. But he didn't like the result and the chapter never
came to print.

For this edition in 1976 I did a great deal more research, in
England and Germany, and found the story to be much less
simple, much more interesting and much more sad because
Wodehouse suffered so much more obloquy, alarm and des-
pondency than his foolishness had merited. But, as this edition
goes to press, I still see too many loose ends of the story
dangling. It exists, complete, I know, in a Whitehall file: the
report made in 1944 by Colonel Cussen of M.I.5 (later Judge
Cussen of the Old Bailey) for the Home Office when he had
interrogated the Wodehouses in Paris after the Liberation. It
was undoubtedly on the strength of Cussen's report that the
Law Officers in London decided that there was no justification
for bringing Wodehouse back to England for trial. But,
because there was no trial, the report itself became protected
from public scrutiny, and is now locked away under the
Hundred Years rule. Unless it is released earlier, Cussen's
report of the facts will not be publicly available till A.D. 2044.
Wodehouse had told me that I could question his lawyers, his
friends and his enemies – anybody but himself: he was still,
coming up seventy, nauseated by the whole sorry subject. But
Wodehouse's green light to me did not enable the tight-lipped

Cussen to tell me what Wodehouse had told him in Paris and he had told London.

Cussen, inquisitor become friend, strongly advised Wodehouse to write and publish the whole story himself. Many wise friends advised him similarly. But, if Wodehouse wrote it, he never published it.

Some people to whose help I paid acknowledgement in 1961 are now gone, but my debt of gratitude to them remains: William Townend, 'Slacker' Christison of Dulwich and Peter Cazalet, who was married to the Wodehouse daughter, Leonora. My thanks again to Guy and Virginia Bolton, truest and best of Wodehouse's friends, S. C. (Billy) Griffith of the M.C.C., whose two children both had Wodehouse as godfather, Malcolm Muggeridge, who was such a standby and strength to the Wodehouses in Paris in their trouble over the 1941 Berlin broadcasts, the late Harry Flannery, Werner Plack, Aidan Evans (whose meticulous scholarship in the works of W. S. Gilbert and P. G. Wodehouse has enabled me to put a proper value on the debt of the latter to the former), and to Christopher MacLehose, then at Barrie & Jenkins, who visited the Wodehouses frequently on Long Island and encouraged this réchauffé of mine from the start.

Two books by Geoffrey Jaggard, *Wooster's World* (1967) and *Blandings the Blest* (1968), have made it much easier for the addict and the scholar to trace references, people and places in the Wodehouse books set in those two separate worlds. David Jasen's *Bibliography and Reader's Guide to the First Editions of P. G. Wodehouse* (1971) is also very helpful. Two commentaries were published in 1966, both with the title *P. G. Wodehouse*, one by R. B. D. French of Trinity College, Dublin, the other by Richard Voorhees of Purdue University in America. I am grateful to both for ideas and refreshment. It was French's book which pointed out that Wodehouse/

Wooster/Jeeves had wrongly attributed 'tired nature's sweet restorer' to Shakespeare ('The Inferiority Complex of Old Sippy' in *Very Good, Jeeves*, but 'Shakespeare' corrected to 'the poet' in the Omnibus *World of Jeeves*). I now gladly stand corrected, by French, on page 252 here. I have received benefit from Robert Hall jr. of Cornell University and Major N. T. P. Murphy. Hall's *Comic Style of P. G. Wodehouse* applies linguistic scholarship, pure and far from simple, to Wodehouse words and sentences. Murphy's essay in *Blackwood's Magazine* (August 1975) compared the Drones Club and its members' escapades with the old Pelican Club and its ditto: an equation suggesting that Wodehouse had usefully absorbed the writings of Arthur Binstead and such.

Herbert Warren Wind's 'Profile' of Wodehouse in *The New Yorker* in 1971 was a mellifluous appreciation. David Jasen's *P. G. Wodehouse, A Portrait of a Master* covers a lot of theatrical ground and is an essential reference book.

A certain number of people wrote to me when *Wodehouse at Work* was first published and, heatedly or politely, pointed out errors of facts, attribution and date. I have corrected where necessary. I am sincerely grateful for an opportunity at last to correct one hideous misprint, in which I named Joan Farrar as author of *Eric, or Little by Little*.

A shorter version of the Appendix 'The French for P. G. Wodehouse' and a part of the chapter on 'School and School Stories' appeared long ago in *Punch*. I aired the gist of another part of the School chapter in the *Times Educational Supplement*.

Wodehouse was always generous of praise, and he wrote me a charming letter when my book came out. But in an interview with Alistair Cooke he spoke of me as 'a certain learned Usborne' and said 'It's rather a frightening thing, you know. I mean, I'm sure it's very conscientious and impressive to have someone go into one's stuff like that, but it's rather unsettling.

I mean, you turn the stuff out and then public orators begin to declaim and critics analyse it ... well, it's rather unsettling.' One detail ... I know Wodehouse thought I'd paid inordinate attention to his school stories. He reckoned that he had been an amateur when he wrote them and that my praise of them had been uncritical and my criticisms a waste of time.

I myself felt that, throughout the book, I had wandered down too easy paths in building lives and characters (Bertie, Jeeves, Lord Emsworth and so on) from the books and then studying the fictional creatures as living people. It's an old literary game for enthusiastic amateurs. But now that stumps are drawn, let me give you the close-of-play chief individual scores. It is largely a matter of pairings. Not many couples who seem headed for the altar in the happy endings of books are specifically married in a future book. And right to the end Wodehouse would, if he wanted it for his plot, keep a character or couple unmarried whom he seemed, in the last book, to have dismissed to matrimony. So I say 'is marrying', meaning that that's how it was left in the latest news.

Bertie Wooster and Jeeves are still together, and last seen in New York, to which they have escaped, with relief, from aunts (both of them) and fiancées – Bertie's most recent one being Vanessa Cook. Jeeves has been given a Christian name – Reginald. Of Bertie's friends, relations and enemies, Aunt Dahlia is well, in good voice, and she still has Anatole, the chef supreme, to keep Uncle Tom's gastric juices sweet, and to blackmail the greedy Bertie. Tuppy Glossop is marrying her daughter Angela. Aunt Agatha is still at Steeple Bumpleigh as Lady Worplesdon. Florence, Lord W.'s daughter, broke it off with *vers-libre*-writer Gorringe and got engaged to Ginger Winship and broke it off with him in his turn. She then, for a single page, grabbed Bertie again and broke that off too. She is at large again and unmarried.

Chuffy (Marmaduke, Lord Chuffnell) is married to Pauline

Stoker. Sir Roderick Glossop is marrying Myrtle, Lady Chuff-nell. Honoria, his daughter, is marrying Blair Eggleston. Gussie Fink-Nottle eloped with Emerald, sister of Pauline Stoker. The Rev. 'Stinker' Pinker is a country vicar now and playing for the Hockley-cum-Meston rugger side. One presumes that he has dear Stiffy (*née* Byng) as wedded wife, ironing his surplices and urging him to higher office and stipend. Nobby Hopwood and Boko Fittleworth are marrying. Bobby Wickham and Kipper Herrings are marrying. Spode (Lord Sidcup) is marrying Madeline Bassett. Perhaps Sir Watkyn Bassett has by now married Spode's aunt, as planned many books ago. Oofy Prosser is married to the Shoesmith girl, Myrtle, a bit of a tyrant, and serves him right. Corky Pirbright and Esmond Haddock are marrying. Freddie Widgeon is marrying Sally Foster. Monty Bodkin, saved from marrying hockey-international Gertrude Butterwick, is marrying shrimp-sized Sandy Miller, a much better bet. Gertrude is marrying an Old Etonian policeman. Stilton Cheesewright, another Old Etonian policeman, is marrying that fascinating blonde novelist, Daphne Dolores Morehead. Catsmeat Potter-Pirbright has eloped with Gertrude Winkworth.

Lord Emsworth is at Blandings, happy enough when his sisters are away. The last, unfinished, Wodehouse novel provides him with two new sisters, making ten in all, nine of them tyrants and pests. Galahad, his brother, comes and goes. He is a bachelor, a Pelican and a force for good for ever.

Freddy Threepwood is still a dog-biscuit tycoon, and happily married to his Aggie, niece of Angus McAllister, still the Blandings head gardener. George Cyril Wellbeloved is back as pigman at the Castle, and the Empress, having won at Shrewsbury for three years on the trot, has retired from competitive life. The Duke of Dunstable is revealed as having once been engaged to Connie Threepwood, and to have broken the engagement when her father, the Earl, wouldn't give her a big enough dowry. The Duke remains rich, unmarried and disliked by all. Beach is still in his pantry, with his port for visitors and his bullfinch in the cage. Beach's niece, Maudie Stubbs, is marrying Sir Gregory Parsloe-Parsloe over at Matchingham Hall. The Much Matchingham vicar is still, we assume, the Rev. 'Beefy' Bingham. Tipton Plimsoll is marrying Veronica Wedge, dumb, beautiful daughter of one of Lord Emsworth's many sisters. Blandings Castle and its messuages remain as paradisiac as ever. But *A Pelican at Blandings* (1969) put paid to any hopes one might have had of drawing a map of the grounds (the lake, the yew walk, the Empress's sty, etc.) or its interior, floor by floor to the roof. Not since *Something Fresh* (1915) had Wodehouse been so specific about the place. But now questions such as 'Where's the museum with the Gutenberg Bible?' or 'Where's the Portrait Gallery?' or 'Where's Lord Emsworth's bedroom?' are the more dustily answered because Wodehouse in his eighties had half-acquired (only half) the American habit of calling a ground floor 'the first floor' and a first floor 'the second floor'. In the final analysis much depends on how many flights of stairs a man can fall down when taking a single toss.

Bingo Little and his Rosie are still together, their union blessed with issue Algernon Aubrey Little. Sidney McMurdo and Agnes Flack are marrying. Angelica Briscoe, who, though engaged to her cousin, played fast and loose with the loves of those two Dronesmen in the story 'Tried in the Furnace', is still unmarried at Maiden Eggesford in *Aunts Aren't Gentlemen*, the last published novel. Ivor Llewellyn, the Hollywood magnate, head of Superba-Llewellyn, is, after five unwise marriages, happily a bachelor again. He only just escaped Vera Dalrymple in *Bachelors Anonymous*. Chimp Twist is still 'Sheringham Adair', still crooked as a corkscrew, still at daggers drawn with Dolly and Soapy Molloy. After a short stretch in Holloway Gaol, Dolly is as beautiful as ever, and for Soapy she is the only woman, light-fingered though she may be in shops. Ukridge in the last published story about him is still, or again, unmarried, in the soup and out of funds.

Wodehouse was writing humorously for his school magazine and in letters, long before his first paid publication in 1901 at the age of twenty. But though most of his output after that was light, it was not farce. It was only in 1915, when the *Saturday Evening Post* in America bought his largely farcical novel, *Something Fresh*, for serialization that he felt he was on to something solid. Since then, though he still wrote light novels, which were even sentimental in patches, farce became his main product. To the end, in his nineties, butlers were stealing pigs, curates were stealing policemen's helmets, Bertie Wooster and Jeeves were kidnapping Bertie's cousin, young Thos, from prep school, country magistrates were quick to imprison their house guests without trial or appeal, and blackmail, Mickey Finns and impersonations were rife. Wodehouse wrote along the grain of his own sympathies. From beginning to end of his books he backed young against old, nephew against aunt, chorus girl against star, fag against prefect, boy against master, fearless female slush-novelist against willowy writer of prose poems; and anybody and everybody against Percy Pilbeam and Oofy Prosser.

His stories were full of dukes, earls, bishops and millionaires and he treated them rough. He was utterly unsnobbish. He was often out of date: open-topped buses, steam trains, urgent transatlantic hurryings by liners long scrapped, country pubs open at all hours for the sale of potent home-brew ale. He set most of his thirty-plus post Second World War books in England, which he had not visited since 1939, and he gave England perpetual hammock weather and summer-long bathing in lakes, as it might have been in California. He was, of course, dateless, in a never-never-land time vaguely evocative of the 1920s, without wars and largely without the need for jobs: younger sons with valets and Mayfair flats, on allowances from uncles and trying to borrow the wherewithal to square their bookies till the first of the month.

For three-quarters of a century Wodehouse, with better than a book a year, was being funny in print ... to my way of thinking very funny indeed. Among the top dozen books, of his whole output of just short of a hundred, I would include at least four that appeared in the decade after the Second World War, and two more that he wrote in his eighties. If I had to pick one as his happiest, best constructed and most jewel-encrusted, I'd say *Joy in the Morning*, a Bertie Wooster/ Jeeves novel that he published at the age of sixty-six. And don't miss *A Pelican at Blandings*. That was published in 1967, when Wodehouse was eighty-eight.

The purpose of this book is to study Wodehouse's books and characters, and to see what makes them durable across seventy-five years, in spite of their formulas, their repetition and their timeless disregard of changes in social attitudes. I am writing about Wodehouse the professional humorist of the printed word. I have to ignore Wodehouse the playwright, Wodehouse the song-writer and Wodehouse the film-writer. In the years between the wars, Wodehouse, in addition to being a favourite in the magazines and bookshops, had his name in lights in London and New York as a lyric-writer and maker of plays, and he put in two highly paid, if underworked, spells in Hollywood. I cannot add to the information about these activities which he has given in *Performing Flea*, *Bring on the Girls* and, obliquely, in such novels as *A Damsel in Distress*, *Jill the Reckless*, *The Adventures of Sally*, *Laughing Gas* and *Barmy in Wonderland*. The Mulliner stories set in Hollywood may give an accurate summary of what Wodehouse thought about the film capital Dottyville-on-the-Pacific. But he was grateful to Hollywood because the combination of sun, swimming pools, large weekly pay-envelopes and permission from his employers to work at home enabled him, when he had met those employers' demands, never arduous, to steam ahead fruitfully on his own books, stories, plays and lyrics. He found Hollywood a wonderful place to work, and that was the highest accolade Wodehouse could give to a mere place.

Even if I knew much more about Wodehouse's theatre and film work than he has told in print, I could resist writing on the subjects. Theatrical memoirs, except when presented with the sort of dateless boisterousness of *Bring on the Girls*, which Wodehouse wrote with Guy Bolton, have about as powerful an effect on me as ballet on the radio. And printed song-lyrics worry me unless I have the music for them in my head. John (son of Ring) Lardner wrote in *The New Yorker* that Wodehouse's words to Jerome Kern's music were 'the neatest and most functional song-lyrics of the century'. Wodehouse wrote the words of 'Bill' in *Show Boat*. Royalties from this song alone kept him comfortably in stamps, tobacco, martinis and food for his dogs ever after.

My ignorance and ignoring of Wodehouse's theatrical career at least saves me from an otherwise probably necessary essay in equating Wodehouse with W. S. Gilbert. Wodehouse emerged from his schooldays, and into the new century, with a grounding in sixth-form Aristophanes, a facility with light verse in English, a brother who played the piano well, and a determination to make his career as a writer in whatever directions his talent proved fruitful – books, plays, songs, items for *Punch*. He loved the Savoy Operas. Like a million others he could whistle their tunes; but he knew the words, too. It was to Gilbert, rather than to Sullivan, that the young

Wodehouse was listening on the edge of his gallery seat. And Gilbert, most profitably of all loved sources, fed Wodehouse's thesaurus of words, phrases and names. A Wodehouse fan, more expert in Gilbert's texts than I, has positively counted the echoes of Gilbert in Wodehouse's works, and located a hundred and seventy-two of them: thirty-one from *The Mikado*, thirty from *Patience*, twenty-six from *The Bab Ballads*, twenty-three from *The Gondoliers*, seventeen from *Ruddigore* and eleven from *Pinafore* – and so on down. And mere names – Blennerhassett, Rackstraw, Corcoran, the Duke of Dunstable, butler Bowles. They are not thefts or cribs – but *mots justes*, references to, and quotations from, a rich vocabulary better known to his readers, probably, in the first quarter of this century than later. One can trace other loves in Wodehouse – Dickens, Doyle, Anstey, for instance. But Gilbert gave him more than all these put together.

In the theatre Wodehouse was not the Gilbert of his days. There wasn't one. Comic opera, by the time Wodehouse was making his theatrical mark, was sharing its popularity with, and fragmenting its Savoy techniques into, Musical Comedy, Little Revue and Ziegfeld-type Follies. Wodehouse contributed lyrics and dialogue to all these. But there are strands of Gilbertianism in what could be called, just this once, Wodehousianism: the irreverence to Church and State, peers, baronets and magistrates, Shakespeare and policemen. Gilbert's knighthood may have been delayed a decade or so by his unorthodoxy in these departments, but by then he had made such frivolity acceptable and popular. Wodehouse was not breaking new ground here; he was working proved soil. Wodehouse has none of Gilbert's unkindness, none of Gilbert's tendency to preach and very little of Gilbert's sentimentality. Gilbert's faded and unwanted middle-aged females, distressing to Sullivan and to many others, may have seemed useful, in age, sex and authority, to the plot-making

Wodehouse. If so, Wodehouse has gloriously translated them into Aunts.

There is not much personal or biographical material about Wodehouse here. He was an ungregarious man of simple tastes and no pretensions, much admired and envied professionally by his fellow writers, a great worker. He didn't like the periods – days and sometimes weeks – between finishing one book and starting the next. He could never understand how Michael Arlen was able simply to stop writing when he had enough money. Wodehouse made a great deal of money. His copyrights are a blue-chip property in any language.

David Jasen's *P. G. Wodehouse, A Portrait of a Master* (1975) is well informed on personal history, and bibliographically well researched. But *Performing Flea* is by far the best, fullest and safest source of professional material about Wodehouse. And it has the most details about his period of internment by the Germans, and about his wildly misrepresented broadcasts from Berlin in 1941. Sean O'Casey, when the Wodehouse broadcasts started, had become, for him, unusually protective of England's reputation and, in a letter to the Press, had sneered at Wodehouse as being 'English literature's performing flea'. Wodehouse took the phrase gratefully for the title of a collection of letters which he had written between 1920 and 1952 to his school friend, Bill Townend: letters from a writer to a writer.

Here and there in the letters, and more often in Townend's glosses, you get glimpses of Wodehouse with his hands in his pockets, or behind his head. But the main picture is of a busy worker with his hands on the typewriter. This is a book that any headmaster or parent might apply to literary aspirant sprouts, as a combined fertilizer and weed-killer. It is extremely interesting to anybody who wonders how books get written, and it could jerk many readers into realizing that eighty books in sixty years of writing (which was the score then) are a lot of books, and would have kept busy an author who was not also writing plays and lyrics and who never blotted a line. Wodehouse, however, never wrote with ease. It might take him a hundred pages of pencil notes, and long months of trial and error, to establish a six-page typescript scenario before he even started the writing of a novel.

I happened one day to see in the *Times Literary Supplement* an announcement of a sale, at Sotheby's for charity, of autograph manuscripts by famous authors. One was a novel of Wodehouse, *Jeeves in the Offing*, and I went round to inspect it. There was a complete typescript of the book, with a very few final corrections, and some shots at a title. (One he almost used was *Well Really, Jeeves!*) But what a New York dealer eventually bought was not so much the completed story as the seventy quarto pages that went with it – seventy pages of pencilled notes, with each page dated, and their dates covering (in this case) twenty-three months, during which Wodehouse had gouged out of his own mind the plot, and the several sub-plots, before anything went on his typewriter. Twenty-three months was slow going for Wodehouse. In his old age it was his slowness that chiefly worried him.

The notes were Wodehouse talking to himself. The first pencilled words were: 'If this is a Jeeves story . . .' ('If', mark you!) Two or three times on a page the notes start: 'Try this . . .'; 'Try this. Uncle Tom wants a knighthood . . .'; 'Try this. Make hero a curate – cf. B. Pain's *The Refugees* . . .'; 'Try this. Bertie getting married . . .'; 'Try this. Bertie standing for Parliament . . .'; 'Try this. Aunt Dahlia standing for Parliament . . .'; 'Try this. Vet gives Lord E. wrong bottle for Empress – turns her blue. T.P. sees blue pig and it sends him on the wagon.'

Other headings and exhortations from Wodehouse to Wodehouse down the left-hand sides of the pages are; 'Good!'; 'Very Good!'; 'Work on this . . .'; 'Problems to be solved . . .'; 'Mechanism . . .'; 'Okay . . .'; 'Act two . . .' A longer self-communion reads: 'The Story so far. Nov. 15–Jan. 14. ? First high spot. The announcement of B.–B.W. engagement', and then he lists the second high spot, the third high spot and the fourth high-spot. He ends: 'This is all right as far as it goes, but it's only a short story so far. It needs a sub-plot.'

Another series of notes shows that for more than a month he had a character based on a girl in Wolcott Gibbs's *Season in the Sun*, and he used Gibbs's girl's name till he came to the minor chore of inventing another. ' ?Make girl like Deedy Barton in *Season in the Sun*.' 'Deedy has necklace which she wants at dinner.' 'If klep is man engaged to girl, he forgets g's birthday, quickly buys necklace from Deedy.' Another note reads: '*Very good* [underlined]. X. Great idea! Change Mother to a Judge like Barker in Cyril Hare's *Tragedy at Law*.' And others: '. . . Giving up smoking makes chaps irritable'; 'Lover is like Bassington Bassington in *Baa Baa BS*'; 'Call lover X'; and 'Bobbie gets Bertie into trouble . . . e.g. stealing racehorse cat.'

Now do you feel like re-reading *Jeeves in the Offing* to see how much and how little of that note-making led to anything in print?

There is a description by Guy Bolton in *Bring on the Girls* of Wodehouse with a device for feeding long rolls of paper into his typewriter, so that, when he was started on the actual writing of a book, he would not lose pace in the chapter through having to extract and insert sheet after sheet. At the end of the day's work, the story says, Wodehouse would snip the coil of typescript into page lengths and pin each page on the wall. All the pages started by being pinned level and then, when Wodehouse walked round and re-read them, he would unpin, and pin at a lower level, any page in which the story seemed to drop. And where the story seemed to need a twist, he would pin the page up crooked. He then revised, page by page, till he could let all the pages hang level and straight.

A good story, true in essence if not in fact. A number of the many best-selling writers who appear in Wodehouse's novels and stories refer to the inevitable question they get asked by fans and interviewers: 'Do you work regular hours or wait for inspiration?' Wodehouse worked regular and long hours, and his smoothest writing has almost always been the result of his most laborious pruning and polishing. Once he had found his plot and built his scenario, the job of filling it out with narrative and dialogue was another process of frequent trials and errors. And when he was writing farce, his best work and the bulk of his work in the last fifty-five years, he set himself to sustain, inside the intricate framework of what had to happen, a high frequency per page of verbal felicities – gags, laughs, jokes or, as his character Monty Bodkin would say, nifties.

Performing Flea contains a good deal more about Wodehouse's family, friends, houses, dogs, cats, and cheques from editors, publishers and theatre managers than either of his two other semi-autobiographical books, *Bring on the Girls* and *Over Seventy*. But even so it is itself an edited, professionally paced book. And it gives a consistently sunny-side-up picture. In these letters as printed, Wodehouse is kind about friends and fellow authors, modest about his successes and gay about his flops. Was he never catty, frightened, angry, vain or bitter? Was he never selfish or self-centred? Probably not. But if he had shown signs of such human frailties to a friend in the letters of thirty-two years, he would have thought it personally immodest and professionally crazy to have left those parts in letters to be published in his lifetime. At what must have been a haggard period, when he thought he might be going blind (typically, his textbook on the subject was

The Light that Failed), and again when his doctors let him know they thought he had a tumour on the brain, he passed the news on – and off – to Townend almost in parenthesis. It is certainly a refreshing change to find an author less fascinated by his inner self than you are. But you wish that author wasn't Wodehouse.

Wodehouse drove himself hard. But he didn't, in the *Performing Flea* letters (did he in any?), give any clue to how he put on his overdrive. He was grossing £100,000 a year from his typewriter in the fifteen years of his maximum output between the wars. The man was a highly efficient machine. But if you hold, as I do, that his best work, his alpha-double-plus work (and there is a lot of it), is a sort of poetry and that some of his images are pure poetry, you want to know how a machine takes the uncharted step and writes poetry. Wodehouse still had a public-school boy's desire not to be caught 'putting on side' and, although he might have been curious himself about the mechanism of his mind and his art, he felt safer when measuring both in objective terms of cash and commissions. Asked how he invoked his profitable daemon, he once said: 'I sit down at my typewriter and curse a bit.' If you had pressed him for a deeper examination and a more minute explanation, he would probably have drifted into parodying the phrases and rhythms of the stock interviews given by a best-seller to a sedulous reporter for the fans; and it would soon have been making a new piece for *Punch*, or a jovial sentence or two in his next letter to Townend. The possibility of a moment of truth would have faded. The self-consciousness that one had hoped would make him lift the curtain a bit would have become the double self-consciousness of the artist, seeing his own mood as an opportunity to be funny about his mood, or about similar moods in other people.

Wodehouse wrote in *Punch*:

I mean, you take me. I have built up a nice little conservative business over the years and there is no mystery about my beginnings. I started by writing stories about girls who wanted to be loved for themselves alone for *Tit Bits* and *Answers* and similar journals, and from there I proceeded to stories about earls and butlers and young men finding snakes in their beds, and *voilà!*, as our light-hearted neighbours across the Channel would say. You can trace my progress step by step.

On the cover-flap of *Performing Flea* the publishers said:

... there are few modern authors about whom less is known or more is speculated. A gentle, unassuming man, he has side-stepped personal publicity where he could, preferring to retire to quiet backwaters where he could devote himself to his two life interests — reading and writing.

I have done some speculating, and I shall be going to some trouble to suggest origins, influences and affiliations for Wodehouse's stories and characters — the writers whom writer Wodehouse must have read with admiration and fed on to some degree. But if he had tried to imitate any of his elders to one-tenth the extent to which some of his juniors have tried to imitate him, these juniors might have had an easier mark to aim at and an easier pocket to pick. Wodehouse's writing fed joyfully on his reading. The vastly complicated plots of his farce novels reflect his personal pleasure in detective stories. If one could put the same sort of tape-measure to his books as Livingston Lowes put to Coleridge's *Kubla Khan*, it would emphasize in detail the truth of the sentence in *Bring on the Girls* (doubtless written by Bolton) about Wodehouse: 'As Charles Lamb said of Godwin, he read more books not worth reading than any man in England.' Wodehouse had been a devoted reader of trash since his schooldays. He teased it, evoked it, parodied it and played it back in ragtime. And you will be missing much of the best in Wodehouse unless you, too, have drunk deep at the same sort of piffling Pierian springs as he had.

Wodehouse paddled his glass-bottomed canoe serenely over a millpond surface of other writers' clichés. He chose clichés, of words, situations and attitudes, as material with which to make many of his verbal jokes, situation jokes and morality jokes. His popular novelist, Rosie M. Banks, is too sensible to believe that a sane young man in love with a girl would stand beneath her window at night, quietly adoring; but she is also too sensible to omit such a situation from her books. Her readers want to read about such gooey, pre-Raphaelite behaviour. Wodehouse had revelled in such goo since he was a boy, and had adjusted his mind to a three-way stretch. He liked the stuff uncritically in spite of its nonsense. He liked it critically because he knew such nonsense was the stuff to give – if not the troops, at least the Lending Library public. And he liked it professionally because it provided him with a profitable vocabulary for his own humour, and a stock of behaviour patterns to which his nit-witted characters could predictably subscribe in their romantic moments.

Wodehouse laughed at the popular bilge-writers; but, personally and in his books, he preferred them every time to the obscurantists, the highbrows, the 'Great Russians' and all geniuses who seemed to put on side about it. He was steadfastly lowbrow in his attitudes; but he had a scholarly stranglehold on the English language. Among his most addicted readers have been classical professors, headmasters, bishops and highbrow poets. They can spot the scholar behind the comedian's make-up. L. A. G. Strong called Wodehouse a 'lord of language', quoting, as Jeeves would have recognized, from Tennyson on Virgil. It is arguable that only a writer who was himself a scholar and had had his face ground into Latin and Greek (especially Thucydides) as a boy, would dare to embark on such a sentence as:

With the feeling, which was his constant companion nowadays, for the wedding was fixed for the fifth of July and it was already the tenth of June, that if anybody cared to describe him as some wild thing taken in a trap, which sees the trapper coming through the woods, it would be all right with him, he threw a moody banana skin at the loudest of the sparrows, and went back into the room.

Money in the Bank

and would emerge so triumphantly.

But it was not Wodehouse's way to be reverent about anybody or anything in print. He did not use a classical professor as a character in any of his farces; but he made headmasters, bishops and highbrow poets dance to his rag-time tunes. One of his favourite subjects for schoolboy disrespect was Shakespeare. He constantly mocked the Swan of Avon in essays, short stories and novels. In fact Wodehouse was, for his private pleasure, a bit of a Shakespeare-addict, and he said he read the Complete Works every two years or so. He got into the habit during his months of internment. *The Works of William Shakespeare* was the book he picked and packed when the Germans sent him off with a single suitcase from his house in Le Touquet in 1940. He had a donnish knowledge of the Bard thereafter, but in his books he was still making nice fourth-form lowbrow jokes about him, largely through the pen of fourth-former Wooster (B.W.), but with no personal compunction.

He did honour to the Anglican Church by being hilariously irreverent about its ministers, senior and junior, their Trol-lopian wives and fizzy fiancées, their competitive sermons, their orphreys and chasubles, their dangerous village duties, their human hearts seething under spotless surplices. And who says a humorist may not show a clergyman in the grip of strong drink? With a glass or two of Buck-U-Uppo under his apron, the most pompous bishop can be reduced to the golden age of 'a young and rather rowdy fifteen'.

He did honour to the game of golf by taking a steady rabbit's-eye view of its agonies and exultations. In the Wodehouse *Golf Omnibus* his publishers should surely have included, somehow, that little nugget of poignancy which, so far, there has been none (of the commentators that I have read) to praise and very few even to notice. Sixteen-handicap Bertie Wooster, at the beginning of 'Jeeves and the Kid Clementina', goes jauntily down, with Jeeves, to Bingley-on-Sea and takes a suite at the Splendide for the annual Drones Club golf tournament. And then he is outed in the first round. 'And, to increase the mortification of defeat, Jeeves, by a blighter who had not spared himself at the luncheon table and was quite noticeably sozzled.' Wodehouse always insisted that he had no message for humanity. I'd have said that that little, casual throw-away said, about golf, all we know and all we need to know ... that we've got to take the rough with the fairway and, game and popular losers, concede victory to our victors however noticeably sozzled they may be.

Mark Twain wrote: 'If a humorist wants to live for ever, he must be a preacher. And by for ever I mean thirty years.' Nicely put. Not true. But (to drop into teaching jargon) raises an important point.

Mercifully Wodehouse never preached, never tried to teach and was never gnomic. He was never pretentious. And, most laudably when you remember the fashions in humour in the decades in which he has been writing, he was never soppy or sloppy.

In *Pip*, a school story by Ian Hay, there is a nursery scene in an early chapter. Pipette, Pip's sister, tells Pip about their father's examination of her cough in his doctor's consulting-room:

'Did it hurt much?' inquired Pip.

'Not *bewwy* much,' replied Pipette. 'He putted it one end

against his ear and the other against my pinny and said "Hold your breff" and I holded it . . .'

Pip was published in 1907. In *Punch* in September 1909 A. A. Milne was writing, as the opening of a piece called 'The Doll's House':

'Why did you never writed to me on my birfday?' asked Margery.
'Your *what*?' I said in alarm.
'My birfday.'
'I have. I mean I'm going to. It's tomorrow. Thursday.'
'I *fink* it did be on Monday.'
'I know you were born on a Thursday, anyhow,' I argued, beginning to feel anxious.
'My baby dolly,' said Margery, forgetting the point at issue, 'is *always* born on a Fursday.'

This kind of baby-talk, which had strong support from Kipling and others, is nauseating to us today. It is indicative of Wodehouse's discipline and good sense that even in his early days he never did that kind of thing. At the beginning of *Mike* (1909) the youngest Jackson, Gladys Maud Evangeline, aged three, tries to say 'Mike's going to Wrykin' and manages only: 'Mike Wryky. Mike Wryky. Mike Wryke Wryke Wryke Mike Wryke Wryke Mike Wryke Mike Wryke.' And her elder brother Bob makes a remark which probably had Wodehouse's blessing for all time: 'Oh, put a green baize cloth over that kid, somebody!'

To have passed by on the other side all through this 'diddums' period of fashionable nursery humour is itself one of Wodehouse's minor glories. But it is a glory. In fact, of course, far from writing sentimentally about childhood, Wodehouse abuses it and mocks it ruthlessly. Some of his best fiends, villains and thugs are children: ugly and frightening in their cots, shrewd and frightening when they are of an age (say seven or eight) to know the meaning of words such as blackmail, bribery and cosh. It is charming when Lord Emsworth, in 'Lord Emsworth and the Girl Friend', dreamily and courteously gives his slum-child protégée, among the other supplies for her kid brother Ern, a bottle of port. He hopes Ern has no gouty tendencies and assures the girl that her brother will be doing him a favour by giving his opinion of this sample his wine merchant in London has sent down. Cloth-headed old Lord Emsworth, in acting as though Ern is grown up, is of the port-drinking classes, and is a conniosseur, is muddling ages just as delightfully as when he and Beach cut the guy-ropes of the rowdy Church Lads campers in the grounds of the Castle. By making his children behave like adults and his adults like children Wodehouse mined an unending seam of good situations. The formula was as funny in the 1970s as it had been in the 1920s.

Wodehouse seems to have avoided all the pitfalls of fashion in humour, sentiment and gesture. *Wodehouse Revisited*, or a *Tramp through the earliest Romances*, is an enjoyment for its own sake. It is not even necessary to laugh fondly at one's old fondness, as in the play *The Boy Friend*. Wodehouse's books, back to the earliest days, raise no blush of shame in the cheeks of an elderly re-reader today.

There are virtually no dates in Wodehouse's books, and all his recurrent characters remain at the same ages throughout. If you complain that there is not much variety about them as types, at least you are sure that age cannot wither them. Personally I find that custom doesn't stale them, either.

The young men in Wodehouse are a perpetual twenty-five. Their girls are a perpetual twenty. But their behaviour-ages are less. They act like fifteen-year-olds. George Orwell, in his long study of P. G. Wodehouse in *Critical Essays*, says that Wodehouse was fixated in his schooldays. I don't like that head-shrinking word 'fixated'. It suggests, and Orwell meant it to suggest, that Wodehouse was stuck in his school-

days, either unconsciously or against his will. That is nonsense. Wodehouse knew exactly what he was up to, and he
was happy to be up to it. In one of his Mulliner stories a
bishop returned, as an eminent Old Boy, to his public school.
He stayed with the headmaster, who was also an Old Boy,
an exact contemporary. And the Bishop noticed a curious
thing about himself. In the Old School surroundings, forty
years after his schooldays, he began to feel like a schoolboy
again, and his feelings were 'far from unmixedly agreeable'.
The current schoolboy captain of football in all his majesty
'made his gaitered legs wobble like jellies'.

The bishop was puzzled. It was as if some fairy hand brushed
him with her wand, sweeping away the years and making him an
inky-faced boy again. Day by day this illusion grew, the constant
society of the [headmaster the] Rev. Trevor Entwhistle doing much
to foster it. For young Catsmeat Entwhistle had been the bishop's
particular crony at Harchester, and he seemed to have altered his
appearance since those days in no way whatsoever. The bishop had
had a nasty shock when, entering the headmaster's study on the
third morning of his visit, he found him sitting in the headmaster's
chair with the headmaster's cap and gown on. It had seemed to
him that young Catsmeat, in order to indulge his distorted sense of
humour, was taking the most frightful risk. Suppose the Old Man
were to come in and cop him!

Later in the story, after the bishop and headmaster have
helped to unveil the statue of a school benefactor who had
himself been a (distinctly unpopular) contemporary of theirs
at Harchester as a boy, they are feeling depressed and head-
achey, and the headmagisterial '87 port is an inefficient
restorative. They help themselves to a good dose of the Rev.
Augustine Mulliner's tonic, Buck-U-Uppo.

Both were conscious of an extraordinary feeling of good cheer, as
the odd illusion of extreme youth which had been upon the bishop

since his arrival at Harchester was now more pronounced than ever. He felt a youngish and rather rowdy fifteen.

'A youngish and rather rowdy fifteen.' This is the talismanic age in Wodehouse. Bertie and his friends may be actually old enough to drink, drive cars, contemplate or commit matrimony, belong to the Drones and go to prison. But the mental and emotional age of the protagonists in all Wodehouse's books of farce is a young and rather rowdy fifteen.

Take the English fifteen-year-old boy of the social strata of which Wodehouse wrote. In the light novels the hero might have been at Wrykyn. In the farces he was probably at Eton. It doesn't matter. At either establishment the fifteen-year-old has ceased being a fag and is years away from being a prefect. To him, as a fag, everything that was not forbidden had been compulsory. Now he has some free will. He has scope to express himself. But he has no responsibilities. His only way of asserting his superiority to a fag is to despise him (nobody despises the fourteen-year-old at public school so obviously as the fifteen-year-old), jeer at him (as Bertie jeers at Young Thos) and kick him when he's bending (as Bertie kicks Edwin). But the fifteen-year-old is still snootered on all sides by his elders: the prefects, the masters, the Head, the School Sergeant and the House butler. In the holidays he has to be polite to aunts. If his parents live abroad (as Wodehouse's did for most of his schooldays), he is at the mercy of aunts. He tries to keep on good terms with uncles, because they give him tips. At fifteen, he is cunning to escape authority's clutches, but he has learnt enough of the public-school Code to be brave and philosophic when authority catches him and bends him over. He accepts the Code the more strictly because he has not had the time, and is not intelligent enough, to question it.

At fifteen, the public-school boy has a smattering of culture from the reading and repetition which he is forced to do in school hours. He has been driven through Shakespeare to the extent of *Hamlet, Macbeth, Othello* and *As You Like It*, and he may have been forced to act in, or witness, his form's end-of-term production of the quarrel scene from *Julius Caesar*. He strongly suspects that Shakespeare wrote bilge most of the time, and he can raise a laugh with his cronies by repeating, in a parody of his form-master's voice, bits that he has been forced to learn. He can't get 'the poor cat i' th' adage' out of his mind and he doesn't want to: or 'Exit, pursued by a bear'. He knows a certain amount of the Bible, too, through enforced reading in 'Divinity' and listening in chapel. But the bits he remembers best are where What's-His-Name begat Thingummy and where Hivites, Hittites and Jesubites, or Shadrach, Meshach and Abednego made good name-music.

His real reading, though, is (or then was) Henty, Anstey, Conan Doyle, school stories and a great deal of magazine trash. He remembers, half in amusement, half in fascination, a lot of the treacly phrases, and all the treacly social doctrines, of the trash, mostly written by women. He can reproduce the phrases unselectively in his conversation, and, unless he watches out, he will accept the doctrines when he is faced with the problem which is their main burthen, love. At fifteen he thinks, officially, that girls are a nuisance and ought to be suppressed. He can't hit them, but he can affect to ignore them. Unofficially, he is old enough to 'notice' girls and to know the tumults of early love: love chivalrous, love gallant, love jealous, love adoring, love idiotic. But he is too young, and too much afraid of being laughed at, for love passionate or love sexual.

He likes comfort, but he is not a snob. He is greedy, because he is always hungry. He will always help a pal, tiresome though this sometimes is, because the Code tells him he should. The worst things you can say to wound him (at least in print) are that he is an oik, a bargee, a bounder, a tick, that he is a mass of side and that he doesn't wash: that he's fat, uncouth, spotty, and was sick at the House Supper. In *Money in the Bank* the young barrister hero has the 'wet' Lionel Green in the witness-box, and says: 'I put it to you, Mr Green, that when you were at school, we called you "Stinker" and that the school was given a half-holiday when it was proved that you had had a bath.'

This back-to-boyhood age-transference is standard for the young in Wodehouse. Bertie himself can, without forfeiting our credulity or our sympathy, go back to nursery days. He is changed from depression to chirpiness on one occasion at Brinkley by finding a toy duck in his bath. The elders are not immune, either. It needs only an airgun for Lord Emsworth, butler Beach and Aunt Connie herself to sink to the level of schoolchildren and, directed by a force beyond their control, to pot at the Efficient Baxter whenever his back is turned and his trouser-seat invitingly distended ('The Crime Wave at Blandings').

This is all very enjoyable. It appeals to something elemental in most of us. Not least among the pleasures of some young newly marrieds is the shared backward step into childhood, with scuffles about sponges, 'Bags I the broad end of the bath tonight!', jokes about snoring and (Lord Ickenham would insist) a good deal of tickling. So watch the time-machine set for the Wodehouse farces, without dates, with unageing ages and with behaviour patterns for the young pegged back firmly to 'a rather rowdy fifteen'.

Considering his characters' frozen ages, it is remarkable how cleverly Wodehouse avoided most of the annoying difficulties of dating that such a freezing process sets up. Proust's ageing Marcel and Dornford Yates's ageing Berry (to mention only two) were less carefully equated to passing time than the ageless Bertie, who began in pre-Prohibition New York and was last seen returning to New York in the mugging and shooting-up period of the 1970s.

Of all factors which put a story in danger of qualifying for the 'Good Old Days' department, in Wodehouse as in Dickens or anybody else, money values are the most frequent. In *Cocktail Time* (published in 1958 and with a mention in it of flying saucers) an English policeman wins £300 in a football pool, and proposes to buy a pub with it. I wonder when £300 could last buy a country pub in England. But clothes are a danger, too, for someone who writes across seventy odd years:

> They also touched on such topics as the weather, dogs, two-seater cars (their treatment in sickness and in health), the foreign policy of the Government, the chances of Jujube for the Goodwood Cup, and what you would do – this subject arising from Pongo's recent literary studies – if you found a dead body in your bath one morning with nothing on but pince-nez and a pair of spats.
>
> *Uncle Dynamite* (1948)

Any detective who had time to read the classics would know that, even in the year 1948, that corpse must have been a Wodehouse character, and he would have started combing the novels for him. Pince-nez went out of fashion in the 1920s, spats in the 1930s. Since then, in contemporary literature, they appeared only on the noses (in Lord Emsworth's case, down the back) or round the ankles of Wodehouse types. I can't think who would want to murder any Wodehouse male character except Percy Pilbeam. But the identification is incontrovertible. Wodehouse didn't refer much to clothes in the last decades and, when he wanted a top-hat for Lord Ickenham to knock off someone's head with a brazil-nut from a catapult, he shrewdly put his action into the period of the Eton and Harrow match (*Cocktail Time*). Our vague feeling that all Wodehouse's young men are, until proved otherwise, wearing spats, morning coats and toppers is probably encouraged by two things: (*a*) most of them were when we first read Wodehouse; and (*b*) those are the illustrations that we remember, because we haven't seen Wodehouse illustrated for so long. Wodehouse was, to the end, still writing about a world of rich, jobless younger sons, of country house-parties lasting for weeks, of heavyweight butlers, of buttony boots-and-knives boys, of gentlemen's gentlemen, of chefs and tweenies, of men sent to prison having their moustaches shaved off, of white trousers for country-house tea on the lawn, of seedy backwaters in Mayfair and of horse-drawn carts delivering the groceries to the Big House. He knew that this world had gone. But it was the world he liked to write about.

He kept the sexual ethic in his books firmly Victorian. It didn't worry him that other writers were enjoying, even exploiting, new freedoms. New freedoms just weren't his literary cups of tea. He didn't need to change his formula and didn't want to. For his young couples in love it was marriage or nothing, and sometimes it seemed to be marriage *and* nothing. Young men and maidens became engaged or disengaged as the plots demanded. On the last pages the right young couples were kissing and the old, parents and guardians, were writing cheques. The young man had a special licence in his pocket and a two-seater at the door. They drove off the last page to (we hope and assume) wedded bliss.

In a surprising sort of dream-sequence in *Bachelors Anonymous*, published when its author was ninety-two, a young man sketches to his fiancée the joys of love in a garret:

'I'm afraid we shall be very poor, darling, but what of that? What's wrong with being poor if you love one another? It's fun. Everything becomes an adventure. The dreams, the plans, the obstacles that must be surmounted – the rich don't have any of that. They don't know how happy you can be in an attic. With a candle by the bed. When you blow out the candle, you make believe you're in a room in a castle with silk hangings and cupids dancing on the ceiling. Wonderful, wonderful!'

I believe that is the only mention, or suggestion, of a single bed for a married couple in the whole Wodehouse canon of farce.

By and large in the 1960s and 70s some of Wodehouse's nicest males and females, courting, engaged, banns up or married, had seemed positively weird in their unexplained avoidance of what the poet has described as the right true end of love. Soapy and Dolly Molloy, that loving couple of fine American crooks, do, in the last book of their appearance, *Pearls, Girls and Monty Bodkin* (1972), occupy a single bedroom as guests at Mellingham Hall. And I think that's the only time in the books of farce that Wodehouse specifies two people, man and wife, lodged in one bedroom. In the novel published in the year of his eightieth birthday, titled, with an innocent unconcern for its possible third meaning, *Ice in the Bedroom*, Dolly, the better half of that ever criminal pair, emerges from a month's seclusion in Holloway Gaol (shop-lifting) and re-meets her adoring husband, Soapy. On the crest of a wave of prosperity (he has sold dud oil stock far and wide, even to Oofy Prosser), he is, though Dolly doesn't know, staying at Barribault's Hotel, and it is in the lounge of that haunt of maharajahs and Texas millionaires that he has arranged to meet his dearly beloved wife. Soapy suggest lunch in the restaurant. But Dolly thinks the Ivy will be more 'onteem', and that's where they go to celebrate and catch up. At the end of lunch uxorious Soapy says

'What do you feel like doing now?'
'I thought I might look in at Selfridge's' [for some shop-lifting].
'I wouldn't, baby.'
'I need some new stockings awful bad.'
'But not this afternoon. Look, what I suggest is we go to Barribault's and ... well, sort of loll around. We'll think of something to do.'
'Where? In the lobby?'
'In my suite.'

I really do think that Wodehouse meant Soapy's 'sort of loll around' as a suggestion . . . just a hint . . . that they might enjoy an afternoon exercise of their marital rights after Dolly's long single strictness. But, having given his reader ideas, Wodehouse disperses them quickly and we never know whether Soapy's suite at Barribault's had two beds, or one big one: or two bedrooms.

But the major romance in *Ice in the Bedroom* is between Freddie Widgeon and Sally Foster, enabling them to fade out happily towards marriage and coffee-farming in Kenya. Freddie, you remember, had courted more girls than anybody at the Drones. A Bean or a Crumpet said that, if all the girls he had been in love with were placed end to end, they would reach from Piccadilly Circus to Hyde Park Corner. An experienced lover, you would say. But when, in Valley Fields, Sally, the girl he is going to marry, living in the next-door little bungalow over the garden fence, says she's scared of sleeping alone with all these burglars popping about,

Freddie waved a reassuring hand.

'Have no concern whatever, I shall be outside, keeping watch and something. Ward, that's the word I wanted. I'll be in the offing, keeping watch and ward. Don't let burglars prey on your mind. I will be about their bed and about their board, spying out all their ways.'

'No, you mustn't,' said Sally.

'Yes, I must.'

'No. You need your sleep. I shall be all right . . .'

'You don't want me to keep watch and ward?'

'No, you're not to.'

'Right ho,' said Freddie agreeably. Though still a bachelor, he knew better than to argue with a woman. He kissed Sally fondly and left by the front door.

In *Company for Henry* (1967) Wodehouse arranges a happy middle-aged love interest between English Henry Paradene, uncle of the sprightly little heroine, and Kelly, the fizzy American widow, aunt of a grown-up millionaire. At the end of a late-night conference (about ways and means of stealing something) of these twain, in the garden under a summer moon, Kelly says

'... So where do we go from here?'

and the dialogue continues to the end of the chapter thus:

'To bed, I suggest, and sleep on it. We'll probably think of something.'
'Maybe you're right. Kind of hot, though, for going indoors. How would you feel about a swim in the lake?'
'Not tonight, I think. Tomorrow, perhaps.'
'All right, then let's turn in.'

And in they turn, separately, to await another occasion to declare their loves for each other.

Near the end of *A Pelican at Blandings* (1969) Vanessa Polk has been captured (and she says it is for keeps) by the much-previously-married millionaire Wilbur Trout. The time is 2.15 a.m., the place Blandings Castle, where they are both guests. This is the fade-out of the dialogue:

'When I take you for my wedded husband, you'll stay taken. You're going to have me around for an awful long time, Willie.'
'Suits me.'
'You're sure?'
'Sure I'm sure.'
'Then I see no objection to your folding me in your arms again. It felt kind of good the first time. And now we might be going off and seeing if we can't get some sleep. And tomorrow we'll say goodbye to Blandings Castle and drive to London and hunt up a registrar...'

A little kissing and hugging in the darkened shrubbery, and then goodnight till tomorrow's nuptials. Wodehouse was perfectly happy to avoid the bedroom altogether and to keep it all out in the open. Bedrooms were fine as places to search, for the stolen necklace, cow-creamer, policeman's helmet or autograph memoirs. But none, in Wodehouse, do there embrace.

'She showed him the bed and he dived beneath it like a seal after a chunk of halibut' about sums up the sex-ethic of his books: pure as the driven snow, if not purer.

A valid criticism of Wodehouse's books is that they repeat themselves. Of course, at ninety as at forty, Wodehouse could professionally re-work old material if he saw a new book in it. There is an obvious relationship between the excellent *Service with a Smile* (1961) and *A Pelican at Blandings* (1969). And *Ice in the Bedroom* (1961) is in many respects a re-run of *Sam the Sudden* (1925), with several of the same characters, with Valley Fields (that 'fragrant backwater', a mere three miles as the crow flies from London: Dulwich, in fact, where Wodehouse was at school as a boy and very much at home in books afterwards) a frequent setting, and indeed Mr Cornelius singing its praises (to Sam in 1925, to Dolly Molloy in 1961) non-stop-pably in the same sixteen lines of Walter Scott's verse.

Wodehouse could also back-track on a character and change his life-style from one book to another. Ukridge married Milly at the end of the first book and for the rest of his life was a bachelor. Rodney Spelvin, in two stories in *The Heart of a Goof* (1926), is a snaky, bachelor, poet and novelist. His *The Purple Fan*, a disgusting best-seller, is dedicated 'To One Who Will Understand' and he tells each of his girl-friends that this means her. He is a Chelsea type, a good dancer, good on picnics, a hummer of old French love-songs, and a scorner of golf. By the time of *Nothing Serious* (1950) he has become a keen goof golfer. Tutored by Anastatia, sister of William Bates, he eventually marries his tutor. He now writes successful thrillers and is the father of Timothy Bobbin, who must be about ten. Rodney's relapse in 'Rodney Has a Relapse' is into verse, but the verse is now A. A. Milne stuff. I take it that Wodehouse remorselessly changed old Rodney's character here so that he (Wodehouse) could heave a custard pie at Milne, who had heaved a load of bricks at him over the Berlin broadcasts.

In ninety-plus books there are many repetitions of characters (under different names), situations and jokes. Wodehouse chose to till a fairly small field, and he rotated his crops in a fairly tight cycle. In situation comedy, with recurrent characters, there is as much to be said for repetition as against it. Kipling didn't incessantly produce novels about artists who became war correspondents and went blind. Hardy didn't incessantly produce novels about pure farm girls seduced by gentleman rotters. But Kipling and Hardy weren't in the game of situation comedy. Situation comedy in good hands can stand a great deal of repetition and, when you get a good cast of actors together, their sameness from story to story can be half the fun. That was Wodehouse's line of country, and he stuck to it with relish.

IMAGES

Aristotle in his Poetics *said 'I judge genius by the way a man handles his images'. And Shelley said the same, only in English. Metaphors, similes, hyperboles, descriptions of sounds, smells, tastes and moods ... there is so much good imagery in Wodehouse that I propose not to discuss it, but to quote it. Separating the chapters of this book are pages from my own selections from the many hundreds of pleasant images that lace Wodehouse's prose and the dialogue of his best characters. They are in no purposeful order.*

*

Freddie, when buying his beard at Clarkson's, had evidently preferred quantity to quality. The salesman, no doubt, had recommended something in neat Vandykes as worn by the better class of ambassadors, but Freddie was a hunted stag, and when hunted stags buy beards, they want something big and bushy as worn by Victorian novelists. Freddie at this moment could have stepped into the Garrick Club of the sixties, and Wilkie Collins and the rest of the boys would have welcomed him as a brother, supposing him to be Walt Whitman.

*

The magistrate looked like an owl with a dash of weasel blood in him.

*

The medicine had a slightly pungent flavour, rather like old bootsoles beaten up in sherry.

*

'This afternoon he asked me to be his wife, and I turned him down like a bedspread.'

*

Images

As he reached the end of the carpet and was about to turn and pace back again, he stopped abruptly with one foot in the air, looking so like The Soul's Awakening that a seasoned art critic would have been deceived.

*

She looked more like Marilyn Monroe than anything human.

*

Oofy, thinking of the tenner he had given Freddie, writhed like an electric fan.

2

SCHOOL AND
THE SCHOOL STORIES

The Pothunters (1902), *A Prefect's Uncle* (1903), *Tales of St Austin's* (1903), *The Gold Bat* (1904), *The Head of Kay's* (1905), *The White Feather* (1907), *The Luck Stone* (published pseudonymously, as a serial in *Chums*, 1908, but never republished), *Mike* (1909) (this has now been divided into *Mike at Wrykyn* and *Mike and Psmith*), *The Little Nugget* (1913).

WODEHOUSE's father spent his working life in Hong Kong and ended it as a judge and a C.M.G. There were four sons and no daughters. Pelham Grenville was the third boy. He was born in Guildford in 1881 and, at the age of two, went out for a year to Hong Kong, for the first and last time. All his brothers spent their adult lives in the East. Wodehouse (P. G.) was determined to write his way out of the Hong Kong and Shanghai Bank (into the London end of which he went after leaving Dulwich) before they sent him out East, too. He knew that he was going to be a writer, but his father said he must have a steady job until he could prove himself able to live by his typewriter. He had no intention of delaying the proof of that until he found himself in Kobe or Macao.

If the sons of a judge in Hong Kong were going to be educated in England, there had, in the days before aeroplanes, to be long separations from the parents. The Wodehouse boys officially lived with a family named Prince in Croydon, but they were much in the care of aunts and under the jurisdiction of aunts. The Aunt Question is very important in any critical study of the Wodehouse books, and we'd better try to analyse it now.

Boys sent home to school in England by parents who had to stay abroad tended to take an unusual interest both in their schools and in their aunts. Wodehouse spent many more of his school holidays with aunts than with his parents, whose leaves in England were few and far between. The best aunt could not wholly fill the gap left by an absent mother; still less could a plurality of aunts. Wodehouse finally came to know his mother only when he had outgrown his need for her lap and love. He regarded her more as an aunt. He said that his proper aunts were very good to him as a boy, and he wished that, as a boy, he had been nicer to them. His Aunt Mary (Deane) harried and harassed him a good deal, and blossomed later into Bertie's Aunt Agatha. Aunt Mary honestly considered that her harrying and harassing of the young Pelham was for his good; and she may have been right.

Thackeray, Kipling, Saki, Kenneth Grahame and other sensitives, dispossessed too early of their proper complement of parents, looked back in anger and indulged in revenge fantasies against the Olympians whose proxy parentage had chilled their childhoods. Wodehouse blew out the perilous stuff in profitable, plot-fertile mockery. To others their Aunt Gonerils: Wodehouse made his all Aunt Sallies. When he found his feet on solid ground in farce, he adopted aunts and aunthood as good comic business.

The aunt represents authority and interference. The nephew owes her a duty. But there is no absolute necessity for love on either side. A monstrous aunt can be funny. A monstrous mother would be tragic. In Wodehouse's light novels several personable young men, of an age when they should have shed their mothers, retain them, or are retained by them, with sad results. Their girl-friends or fiancées find them weak of will and laggards in love. But give a girl-friend an opportunity to mother a man she is fond of, and all sorts of the right glands start functioning in her. In *A Pelican at Blandings* (1969) it is soon clear that what the stupid, weak, much-divorced American millionaire, Wilbur Trout, needs is a final marriage to sensible, poor, pretty Vanessa Polk, daughter of a long-ago Blandings Castle below-stairs match, a visiting American valet and an English housemaid. In a late-night thieving operation, approved and abetted by Galahad Threepwood, Vanessa, with courage and resource for two, helps Wilbur's courage along with a resourceful flask of strong drink. At the critical moment, when Wilbur should be at his keenest and most alert, Vanessa finds him slumped in a chair, his head lolling: asleep at his post. 'She stood watching him, and was surprised at the wave of maternal tenderness that surged over her ...' There ... Wodehouse has got over that awkward little hump in the scenario – to make the nice girl fall in love ... love for the man, not his money. Vanessa comes over all motherly, with pity and love. Desdemona fell for Othello that way, you recall.

Jeeves, in two or three different stories between the wars, has to help a laggard lover get to grips with his stand-offish girl, and does it by staging an accident to the laggard lover. Seeing a man unconscious and recumbent whom, alert and upright, she had hitherto cold-shouldered, the girl covers his upturned face with kisses so that he wakes and finds himself forgiven, loved, mothered. This, in Wodehouse, is the best use of whatever maternal instinct is going about. Indeed, in the same book, *A Pelican at Blandings*, Wodehouse does it again. Linda Gilpin's love for Johnny Halliday only bursts forth and swamps her anger at him when he falls downstairs and lies stunned at her feet.

Wodehouse in his books has ten aunts to every one mother, and of the many middle-aged females who are both mothers and aunts all are more important as aunts than as mothers. The function of Mrs Spenser Gregson, later Lady Worplesdon, is to be Bertie's Aunt Agatha. It is only incidentally that she is Young Thos's mother. It is Mrs Travers's function to be

Bertie's Aunt Dahlia. It is only incidentally that she is mother of Angela and Bonzo. Wodehouse had to have an older generation as a background to his protagonistic younger set. He chose to make them aunts and uncles rather than mothers and fathers. It gave him much greater scope. It is funny when Bertie slides down drainpipes, or sneaks off to America, to escape his Aunt Agatha's wrath. It would be sad if he were thus frightened by his mother. It is funny when Squire Esmond Haddock, at the end of *The Mating Season*, finally rounds on his oppressive aunts and puts them in their places. It would have been painful had he rounded on his mother and threatened to cut off her pocket money if he had one more yip out of her. When he so threatens his Aunt Myrtle, it is with the rapturous support not only of his charming fiancée, but of the reader.

If you feel that Wodehouse has let his scriptural aunts get away with too much harrying and harassing of nephews in the general run of the books, you should re-read *The Mating Season*. Here the author, in defence of all oppressed nephews, gathered his strength and struck. Esmond Haddock had five aunts living with, and on top of, him at the Hall, and Corky Pirbright said she wouldn't marry him until he had defied them. And so much did Esmond's last-chapter defiance of them impress the onlooking Bertie that Bertie decided to take on his own Aunt Agatha. He refused to countenance Jeeves's routine proposal that he took the water-pipe/milk-train way out. In the last paragraph of all Bertie squared his shoulders and strode to the door, like Childe Roland about to fight the Paynim.

Bertie does not tell us what happened when he strode down to brazen out the just accusation of having kidnapped Aunt Agatha's son from his prep-school. Bertie and Jeeves had made the snatch for the very purpose of giving Aunt Agatha something to do (looking for her only child in Sussex), to prevent her fatally visiting Deverill Hall in Hampshire and breaking up the web of deception and impersonation that Bertie and others were weaving there. Bertie's Aunt Dahlia had several times said she had toyed seriously with the idea of having Bertie certified mad. Aunt Agatha that evening might have toyed seriously with the idea of having Bertie arrested for kidnapping. A case would have lain.

Nepotism, if that is the word I want for the state of being a nephew, is rife in the Blandings, as in the Wooster, books. Lord Ickenham spends all his best time being Uncle Fred; and Bill Oakshott, the hero in *Uncle Dynamite*, is a version of Esmond Haddock in *The Mating Season*. Bill Oakshott returns to his heritage, Ashenden Manor, to find an uncle irremovably self-installed there, bossing the place, occupying the best bedroom and chairs, and perpetually taking the brown egg at breakfast. Bill Oakshott feels like a toad beneath the harrow, and he only lifts the harrow (with Uncle Fred's help) in the last chapter.

By and large all the nice young people in Wodehouse are orphans. No single nice young person of any importance, except Mike Jackson, has both parents alive. Some nice young girls (Bobbie Wickham, Pauline Stoker) have single parents alive and dominant. All the ghastly girls (Madeline, Florence, Honoria) have dominant fathers, but no mothers. Stiffy Byng draws ex-magistrate Bassett as an uncle and guardian. Ukridge is an orphan, dependent on his fierce Aunt Julia. Bingo Little is an orphan, dependent on his Uncle Bittlesham until another uncle dies and he inherits his plenty. Freddie Widgeon is an orphan, dependent on his Uncle Blicester. Jeeves himself is an orphan. Nepotism is cardinal to many of Wodehouse's plots.

Wodehouse has so confidently established by repetition his own picture of the state of aunthood that he can use the word 'aunt' to mean 'a bossy, pernickety woman'. Somewhere he describes a bossy and pernickety young girl as 'growing up to be an aunt', and somewhere else he strains the language even more boldly. He is describing a certain type of garden and house as seen over a fence. He says: 'It was the sort of house of which you could say "Someone's aunt lives here." ' Wodehouse treats the bossy aunt seriously in his one serious book, *The Coming of Bill*. There Aunt Sarah Delane Porter is the villainess of the piece, spoiling her niece's marriage by spoiling her niece's child. There is a satisfactory chapter of aunt-defiance at the end of that book, and the aunt-defiance is a more important resolution of the reader's tensions than the re-establishment of the happiness of the niece with her son and husband.

'In this life it is not aunts that matter, but the courage that one brings to them,' says Bertie philosophically. In his experience aunts create when you try to marry actresses, or go on the stage. Aunts create when you break the vicar's umbrella or are fined in court for pinching a policeman's helmet on Boat Race Night. Aunt writes to aunt about your idleness, excessive income, selfish bachelorhood, spinelessness and uppish manservant. There is no decent reticence about aunts, as there may be with mothers. When you annoy one aunt, she tells all the others. Aunt booms to aunt like mastodons across a primeval swamp. Aunts visit your bachelor flat before you've even had your morning tea. Aunts expect you to board their loathsome schoolboy sons in London and take them to see Shakespeare and Chekhov at the Old Vic; also to the dentist and the school train at the end of the holidays.

In an essaylet at the beginning of a chapter in *Right Ho, Jeeves*, Bertie says:

I remember Jeeves saying on one occasion that hell hath no fury like a woman scorned. And I felt that there was a lot in it. I had never scorned a woman myself, but Pongo Twistleton once scorned an aunt of his, flatly refusing to meet her son Gerald at Paddington and give him lunch and see him off to school at Waterloo, and he never heard the end of it. Letters were written, he tells me, which had to be seen to be believed. And two very strong telegrams and a bitter picture post card with a view of Little Chilbury War Memorial on it.

That is the way aunts behave if you scorn them, and that's the way they behave even if you don't.

If you are as angelic as Bertie, *plein de peur et de reproche*, you accept nepotism and make the best of it. But you still chafe. In *The Code of the Woosters* Bertie says to Jeeves:

'If I had my life to live again, Jeeves, I would start it as an orphan without any aunts. Didn't they put aunts in Turkey in sacks and drop them in the Bosphorus?'

'Odalisques, I understand, sir. Not aunts.'

'Well, why not aunts? Look at the trouble they cause in the world. I tell you, Jeeves – and you may quote me as saying this – behind every poor, innocent, harmless blighter who is going down for the third time in the soup, you will find, if you look carefully enough, the aunt who shoved him into it.'

'There is much in what you say, sir.'

'It is no use telling me that there are bad aunts and good aunts. At the core they are all alike. Sooner or later, out pops the cloven hoof.'

Aunts are nothing new in light literature. Lady Bracknell and even Betsy Trotwood may exist vestigially in Lady Worplesdon and Mrs Tom Travers. But Wodehouse more than any other author has glorified the state of aunthood by chi-iking at it cordially in more than fifty books.

The eldest Wodehouse boy, Peveril, had a weak chest, and was sent to a prep school in Guernsey. Pelham followed (not because he had a weak chest, but because it was a good school), and later went on to another prep school in Dover. The Head of the second school lingers on in the books in the person, and in frequent shuddering mentions, of the Reverend

Aubrey Upjohn, headmaster of Malvern House (sometimes called St Asaph's), Bramley-on-Sea.

Young Wodehouse *tertius* was supposed to be going to Dartmouth and thence to a career in the Navy. But he visited his brother Armine at Dulwich and immediately decided that was the public school for him. He persuaded his father of this, and never changed his mind about Dulwich in the next eighty years. He loved it, then and always. But he followed, as a boy there, in the slipstream of a brother who was a considerable blood. They were friends, but you can notice the cloud of elder-brotherhood, if no bigger than a man's hand, in most of the Wodehouse school stories. In an issue of the *Public School Magazine* of 1901 Wodehouse, discussing brothers together at school, says that this situation sometimes produces internecine strife. 'The elder brother, feeling that his reputation hangs on his brother's conduct, broods over his actions like a policeman. The younger of the two feels himself hampered by this scrutiny.' He suggests that the main use of an elder brother is to get him to do your Latin verses for you.

Armine Wodehouse went to Dulwich as a scholar, was editor of the magazine, and in the cricket side for two years. (P. G. later was all these things, too, but Armine had been there before him. It makes a difference.) And Armine increased his glory after leaving Dulwich and while P. G. was still there. He was a classical scholar at Corpus, Oxford, took Firsts in Mods and Greats and won the Chancellor's Essay Prize. He won the Newdigate Poetry Prize in 1902 with a blank verse entry on the set subject, 'Minos'. He played cricket in the Freshers' Match and was an excellent pianist. He went out to India in educational work and joined up with Mrs Besant and the Theosophists. In 1911 he became president of the Theosophical College in Benares. He may still have been in his young brother's mind when, as Bertie Wooster, he wrote:

Jeeves ... is like one of those weird chappies in India who dissolve themselves into thin air and nip through space in a sort of disembodied way and assemble the parts again just where they want them. I've got a cousin who's what they call a Theosophist, and he says he's often nearly worked the thing himself, but couldn't quite bring it off, probably owing to having fed in his boyhood on the flesh of animals slain in anger and pie.

Armine was two years older than Pelham Grenville. Pelham Grenville (hereinafter called Wodehouse) was a boarder at Dulwich when his parents were abroad, a day-boy when they were home on leave. His father was never anything of a scholar or athlete, though his brother's son, Norman Wodehouse, (later Vice-Admiral and killed on convoy duty in the Second World War, was Captain of England at rugger one season before the First World War. Wodehouse's father was a great walker and he was enthusiastic about any athletic triumphs that his Dulwich sons achieved. He offered a regular tariff of tips: five shillings for six wickets; ten shillings for making fifty; and so on.

Dulwich College comprised sixty-five acres of green fields, chestnut avenues and Victorian red-brick buildings. There were six hundred boys in Wodehouse's time, mostly day-boys. Dulwich was a rugger school. The fives they played was also the Rugby game, which provides the best sort of court for school fights, having no buttresses, steps or other hazards. Sheen has a fight in a fives court in *The White Feather*. Wodehouse remembered no fights at all during the six years he was at Dulwich. His contemporaries say there were one or two fairly serious ones, but that it was typical of Wodehouse to have forgotten them. What he did not forget were cricket and football matches.

I was in the Dulwich cricket team in 1899 and 1900, and I am always proud to think that in 1900 I used to go on to bowl before N. A. Knox (I admit he was a child of about ten then). If only I could have got Scotty Gibbon, the greatest captain of football ever seen at Dulwich, to see eye to eye with me, I should have been in the football fifteen as early as 1897, but it was not till 1899 that I got my colours. We had a great team that year, not losing a school match, but the season was spoiled by the scratching of both Bedford matches, the first because of fog, the second because of frost. We had played a scoreless draw with Haileybury, who had a tremendous side that year, and as Haileybury had beaten Bedford 9–nil, we were expecting to beat Bedford. I was a forward, weight 12.6. Boxing: I was to have boxed at Aldershot in the heavyweights but illness prevented. Fortunately, I realise now, as I should have been murdered. I was never really much good.

This is from a letter Wodehouse wrote at the age of seventy-five. The contemporary 'characters' and statistics from the school teams' lists in the Dulwich College magazine, the *Alleynian*, were:

P. G. Wodehouse

First XV (1899–1900) 12 st. 6 lb. A heavy forward. Has improved greatly, but is still inclined to slack in the scrum. Always up to take a pass. Good with his feet. Still too much inclined to tackle high.

First XI (1899) Bowled well against Tonbridge, but did nothing else. Does not use his head at all. A poor bat and very slack field.
(1900) A fast right-hand bowler with a good swing, though he does not use his head enough. As a bat he has very much improved, and he gets extraordinarily well to the pitch of the ball. Has wonderfully improved in the field, though rather hampered by his sight.

Averages: 1899. 10 inns. 26 runs. Av. 6.14 (always went in last wicket).
1900. 10 inns. 48 runs. Av. 6.8.

It would seem a poor reward for sweating for your colours to get pilloried in print as Wodehouse was at the end of his first cricket season; but boys are tough creatures.

Wodehouse was a school prefect and two years in the Sixth. Boys below him in form got scholarships at Oxford and Cambridge, and Wodehouse would probably have done so, too. But, as he explained in *Over Seventy*, his father's pension was in rupees, and rupees fluctuated, so Wodehouse could not go to Oxford in the wake of his elder brother. Whether, had he done so, he might have won the Newdigate in his turn is a matter of interesting conjecture, if you note the attitude that Wodehouse took in all his books to serious poetry and (more gleefully) serious poets. As a sixth-former at Dulwich, Wodehouse's best and favourite subject was Latin and Greek Verse compositions. He wrote Verses (in public-school Sixths in those days Verses automatically meant verse in Greek or Latin; many English scholars have written and published limpid Latin and Greek verse all their lives without trying their hands seriously at verse in their mother tongue) with facility and pleasure, and did in fact contribute some light verse in English in the W. S. Gilbert manner to the school magazine. There is some anonymous serious verse in the numbers of the *Alleynian* of which Wodehouse was joint editor, and it is strongly suspected by carpers and cavillers that Wodehouse wrote them and was proud of them. But the weight of evidence was not enough to bring a case against him. He was not pleased when, in the 1950s, editors in America dug up rotten detective stories which he had written for the pulps in 1912 and 1913, and reprinted them, with the author's name big, in Romance/Suspense magazines. But for us to tie the albatross of serious poetry in the school magazine round Wodehouse's neck would be monstrously unkind. Wodehouse unkindly tied this albatross round the neck of Ukridge's friend and constant money-lender, George Tupper.

There has always been a good turnover of Wodehouse's books in the school library. He gave them a complete new set in 1953, and was thanked for it in a letter by the then headmaster, Gilkes, son of the headmaster who terrorized and amused Wodehouse there as a boy. Wodehouse had had a schoolboy habit of decorating or, as masters would say, defacing his form textbooks with tiny matchstick human figures, page after page. In the Sixth one day Headmaster Gilkes, six foot four and with a long white beard, asked Wodehouse to lend him his Euripides. Gilkes handed the book back, saying with a shudder: 'No thank you. This book has got a man in it!' This, William Townend told me, made Wodehouse laugh for about a year.

Dulwich, situated near to London and having good late-night and early-morning trains, has, as a dormitory suburb, attracted the stage and press. The school has probably produced a higher proportion of writers and actors than any other great English public school. It was, by all accounts, a happy place. Wodehouse was certainly very happy there. He said that his schooldays went like a breeze. He realized that it was all wrong for a sensitive and spiritual writer to have enjoyed public school. He insisted, too, against all the wishful prying of snoopers hoping to get their hooks on some psychological trauma in the early years, that his father had been 'as normal as rice pudding'. The stubborn psychologist, daunted by finding no trauma at home, and that the great writer Wodehouse wasn't a mouse or a misfit at school, ought possibly to study him as, in that respect, abnormal. Look how unhappy their schooldays were for Shelley, Paul Nash and George Orwell! But Wodehouse came through Dulwich smiling, and the Dulwich area is often affectionately remembered for casual addresses, or as Valley Fields in his stories.

Wodehouse between the wars went and watched Dulwich cricket and rugger matches as often as he could, and sometimes wrote them up, knowledgeably and seriously, for the *Alley-nian*. He wrote of Trevor Bailey on one occasion: 'Bailey awoke from an apparent coma to strike a four', which slightly annoyed Bailey at the time of publication, but has amused him since. Bailey remembers that, in his first year in the Dulwich cricket side (1938), they won all their school matches, and Old Boy Wodehouse treated the team to a dinner in the West End, followed by the London Palladium. Bailey, then fourteen, was much impressed.

'Billy' Griffith, who captained the Dulwich rugger side through a season without defeat, told me that he had a letter from Wodehouse (whom he had not met) after the last desperate school match. Wodehouse, writing from the Dorchester, said he had tried to see the match through from the touchline, but couldn't bear the tension and had had to go and walk round the outside of the school grounds, waiting for the whistle and the final cheer to make sure that Dulwich had held their slight lead to the end. When he deduced the good news, he walked home to his hotel and found he remembered absolutely nothing of the seven-mile footslog through the streets, as he was thinking only about the match.

After his death, Lady Wodehouse sent the school some manuscripts and complete typescripts of books, many pages of pencilled notes for books and short stories, his working desk and chair, his typewriter, a half-leather-bound set of the Autograph edition of his books, a number of other authors' books, some of them signed gift copies, two spectacle cases, half a dozen pipes in a pipe rack, two tobacco pouches and a pencil tray full of pens and pencils. By now there is probably some P. G. Wodehouse Corner in a public room at the school in memory of a very eminent Old Boy, and exhibiting the tools of his trade.

A boys' magazine called the *Captain*, then a year old, published in April 1900 the beginning of a public-school serial called *Acton's Feud*, The first sentence was:

Shannon, the old Blue, had brought down a rattling eleven – two internationals among them – to give the school the first of its annual socker matches ...

The eighteen-year-old Wodehouse thought that opening sentence the best of any he had come across in school literature. Victorian public school fiction, favouring the second, rather than the first, half of *Tom Brown*, had kept to a frowsty formula of Chapel and Sanatorium. This was something new in school stories. Wodehouse decided that he was going to write like this himself, if he could. He anonymously reviewed *Acton's Feud*, when it appeared as a book, in the *Public School Magazine*. He called it a classic, and quoted that opening sentence.

When he left Dulwich and went to work in the bank, he wrote in the evenings and on Sundays. He was writing not so much for all time as for money. But the question was, what to write? He saw there was no market in the magazines for preparatory-school stories, even though a large proportion of the readers of the *Captain* and the *Public School Magazine* were of preparatory-school age. So he gave the reading world no sustained worm's-eye view of any St Custard's of the late 1880s and early 1890s. He did put the action of one of his early novels (*The Little Nugget*) in the setting of a prep school. Very good the action is, and very well the prep school is described. But it is described from the assistant master's point of view, and Wodehouse's confidence in the subject came to him, not from his own schooldays, but from periods when he used to go and stay and write at his friend Baldwin King-Hall's prep school at Emsworth, on the border of Sussex and Hampshire. *The Little Nugget* is a light thriller, and the school is Sanstead House, Hampshire, where, for fairly nefarious reasons, Peter Burns, the first-person-singular hero, has signed on as assistant master under Mr Abney, the snobbish Head. The pupils number twenty-four, sons of the nobility and gentry. To this strength is added thirteen-year-old Ogden Ford, bulgy, rude, chainsmoking son of an American million-aire – the kidnappers' prize and joy.

As a not too dedicated prep-school master, Peter Burns has some good observations to make about prep schools, their smells, their boys and their masters. Of the two other masters:

> ... headmasters of private schools are divided into two classes: the workers and the runners-up-to-London. Mr Abney belonged to the latter class.

and:

> Mr Glossop was a man with a manner suggestive of a funeral mute suffering from suppressed jaundice.

Although at one moment an American gunman holds up Peter Burns and his enraptured class with a revolver, you will not, if you have been at a prep school as a boy, find Sanstead House a travesty of your memories. Prep-school masters insist that *The Little Nugget* shows that Wodehouse cared for them, too, knew their job, and added a small gem to the literature of their calling.

But only a highly sophisticated boy of prep school age, and one who needed his head smacked, could properly appreciate *The Little Nugget*. His easier, and preferred, reading would be Wodehouse's seven or eight public school books. Your best chance today of finding those Wodehouses together, including the one-volume *Mike*, is to look through the locked cupboard of the bookshelves of a prep school (not public school) Mr Chips. He keeps them in the locked cupboard because they are books that cannot easily be replaced, and so must be lent, with care and circumspection, only to favoured boys with fingers guaranteed jam-free.

If old bound volumes of the *Captain* occupy the bottom shelf of the school library, you can even more enjoyably trace the same stories (except *The Pothunters*) serialized and illustrated there. But while you're looking, and before we discuss the stories that later became books, see if there are any bound volumes of *Chums* on the same shelf. If so, and if the volume starting September 1908 is among them, extract it. The *Captains* can wait for a moment, and the bound books, too. In that volume of *Chums* is a serial school story called *The Luck Stone*, by 'Basil Windham', who was P. G. Wodehouse with an assist from W. Townend. *Chums* commissioned the story. Wodehouse paid Townend a tenner for his help. You're fortunate to have discovered *The Luck Stone*. Read it.

It is an off-beat Wodehouse. His other school stories, expertly tailored for the *Captain*, were still of the stuff of his own schooldays. *The Luck Stone* was fiction born of fiction, professionally written and produced from wide and purposeful reading of *Chums*. It is the only story that Wodehouse ever had in *Chums*. *Chums* wanted a blood-and-thunder school story, and Wodehouse gave it to them. He was twenty-seven then, and had been a successful London freelance journalist for six years. For his official correspondence he had a letter-head printed with his name in red, half an inch deep, at the top, and four lists going just short of half-way down the quarto page: '*Author of*: –; *Part Author of* : –; *Contributor to* : –; *Some Recent Song Successes*: –'. He gave his permanent address as the *Globe* newspaper. He had been to America and was due to go again the next year. Doubtless Wodehouse enjoyed writing *The Luck Stone*. Doubtless he found it pretty easy going, too. He had shown, in breezy asides throughout his school novels, and in breezy essays in the *Public School Magazine*, *Punch* and elsewhere, that he had read acres of catch-penny fiction, had enjoyed it all and knew all the tricks of it. *The Luck Stone* shows that he could imitate it, too, at the rustle of a cheque. Wodehouse wrote it within months of finishing *Mike*, which is not bilge at all. Never under-estimate the power of a professional.

Chums in 1908 was a twenty or twenty-four-page illustrated weekly for boys: about the size of the *Daily Mirror* of today, but with thicker paper. Its front cover generally gave most of its space to a lurid line-illustration of a lurid episode from one of the lurid stories inside. Its back cover had advertisements for Gamages, offering all sorts of things from bicycles to joke goods, cricket bats to violin outfits ('Violin, extra set of strings, resin and Tutor, lined case: 12/6 complete, carriage 9d. Beginner's full size violin: 5/11'). Inside were a number of illustrated editorial features, mostly instructive ('This is the right way to carry a boa-constrictor. This is the wrong way'), elevating and anti-'frowst'. But the main guts of the magazine were the five or six fiction stories, of which two or three were serials. Captain Frank Shaw's *The Vengeance of the Motherland* had London invaded by the Russians. '*Suppose your home were shelled.* Have you ever considered what you would do? Get next week's *Chums.*'

The illustrations were cheap and bad. Although photography had by then enabled two of their artists in particular, Caton Woodville and Stanley Wood, to draw splendidly animated horses, charging the reader head-on ('The Russian brigade thundered over the bridge, firing at their pursuers'), other artists were less felicitous with Restoration sword duels, express trains bearing down on a prison warder tied to the rails (a 'trusty' risking his life to get the man untied), a boy astride the back of a tiger which has got its forefeet across a little girl ('its teeth began to close on the slim white neck') in an English school playing-field, and Colonel Sir Henry Babcock, Bart., firing pointblank into the mouth of a charging lion.

In *The Luck Stone* ('A Story of fun and adventure at School') the schoolboy hero's father, Colonel Stewart, D.S.O., Indian

Army (Rtd), had been political agent to the Maharajah of Estapore, and now he is guardian to the Maharajah's heir, of Eton and Cambridge and a century-maker in the Varsity cricket match. When the story opens, Colonel Stewart has been away from England for nine months, big-game shooting in Africa. It means that Jimmy Stewart has to deal with his problems alone at first.

Jimmy ought to be back at Marleigh College for the Christmas term, but he has just had mumps, and must stay at home. Then a mysterious sunburnt stranger from India turns up at the Stewart house. Nice chap (he addresses Jimmy as 'Well, matey . . .'), if a bit dazed. Jimmy questions him politely: 'The man opened his mouth to reply, when suddenly something hummed past Jimmy's ear like an angry wasp. The man from India reeled, staggered back, groping blindly with his hands, and fell in a heap.'

'*To be continued next week*' gives only a seven days' interval, and then Jimmy is looking round at the window and seeing a face 'with piercing, cruel eyes, the lower half covered by a beard'. (What had laid out the man from India was a silenced air-gun. He was bringing from India, for Colonel Stewart to give to his ward, the heir, a talisman stone belonging to the Maharajahs of Estapore.) And, when Jimmy gets back to Marleigh, he thinks there is something fishy about the new master, Mr Spinder . . . the same piercing, cruel eyes . . .

The Luck Stone story did not come from anywhere deep in the recesses of its author's personality. He had read Wilkie Collins's *The Moonstone*. He had read Doyle's *The Sign of Four*. The sympathetic and comic-talking schoolboy from Calcutta, Ram, shows that he had also read Kipling's *Kim* and Anstey's *Baboo Jabberjee*. He had read *Chums* for years, and knew its needs. It was open-cast mining for him to slice out the story off the top of his brain.

Wodehouse's other public-school stories (republished) are

also highly professional jobs, but done for magazines whose demands were less lurid, though no less strict, than those of *Chums*. The first, *The Pothunters*, appeared serially in the *Public School Magazine*. The rest appeared in the *Captain*. The *Captain* was very much about, and supposedly for, public-school boys. The great athlete C. B. Fry was Athletics Editor. After the death of C. B. Fry in 1956, a correspondent wrote to *The Times* referring to Fry's 'editorship' of the *Captain*. This correspondent was put in his place by another correspondent, who gave the correct fact (as above), ending his letter with: '*Inter alia*, the *Captain* printed the earliest work of P. G. Wodehouse, school stories of unmistakable quality, in which there appeared for the first time the immortal Psmith.' As a correction to this it should be pointed out that P. G. Wodehouse's earliest work was printed in the *Alleynian*, *Tit Bits*, *Fun*, *Sandow's Magazine*, the *Weekly Telegraph*, the *Universal and Ludgate Magazine*, *Answers*, the *Globe*, *To-day* and (regularly and extensively) the *Public School Magazine* before he sold so much as a short story to the *Captain*.

In the era of Wodehouse's contributions to the *Captain*, the editor was R. S. Warren Bell, and, under the title 'The Old Fag', he did an 'Answers to Correspondents' column that is, to the later researcher, one of the most strange, delightful and time-wasting columns in literature. Fry had done a similar column in the first years of the paper's life, and Fry had established the forthright style:

C. S. (Radley)	Fish and cutlet for breakfast, cold beef for lunch and whatever you jolly well please for dinner.
H. C. Lott	I expect you have outgrown your strength. Try leaving off the cold bath.
'Weakling'	You are the first man I've met who measures his chest in feet. You are all right. Time will adjust your ins and outs.

Then came 'The Old Fag', who for years advised, teased, lectured, hectored and snapped at his pen-pals, male and female, without fear or favour.

J. Y. Miller	I do not know of any way of curing knock-knees. I may mention that bicycling will make you more knock-kneed than you are now. There are hundreds of thousands of people who would not be knock-kneed if there were any remedy for it.
A.L.F.	Abandon once and for all any idea of going on the Stage. I wonder at any fellow of nineteen hesitating between the Army and the Stage. Be a soldier, my friend.
One of My Readers	Of course you can take Holy Orders without going to Oxford or Cambridge.
G.N.E.	Just at present I don't want any photographs of Quebec.
'Dejected'	I should think that if you tried hard and practised constantly, you could soon learn to pronounce your 'r's' properly. I have no particular advice to give you concerning it. But if any other Captainite has conquered this difficulty perhaps he will write to me, as then I will forward his advice on to you.
The Baby	I think a girl might adopt a more profitable recreation than shooting. It is not exactly a pastime that fosters womanliness.
Nellie	The French for iodide of potassium is *iode de potassium*. *Iode* is pronounced ee-ode.
D.M.F.	Yes, you write abominably. Let me see how you have improved in three months' time.
B.S.	If the Boy Scouts in your neighbourhood are as riotous as you say, they are certainly no credit to that craft, but you must always re-

member that in a widespread movement there are bound to be some less considerate of their self-respect than others. As a whole, I think the Boy Scouts behave themselves most commendably.

F.R.   Something is wrong either with your friend's digestion or his teeth. A dentist would recommend him a wholesome mouthwash, which would do much to alleviate the unpleasantness you speak of.

Med Student   If you would say what 'monomania' you suffer from, I might be able to give you some advice. Probably your complaint is 'nerves', for which exercise and fresh air are the best cures.

Julius Caesar Why bother about your ears, Mr C.? I believe elastic bands can be obtained from chemists and surgical appliance manufacturers, but I cannot help repeating ... Why bother about them?

It is proper that we should know the splendidly unevasive manner of the editor, so that, when he speaks about the stories in his own magazine, we may know he speaks the truth.

'Anxious enquirer',   not being a boy, has serious doubts about the *Captain* school stories. 'Are they true to life,' she asks, 'or are they only piffle?' and she waits in trepidation for my reply. How glad I am to be able to assure her that they are the real thing and are written by men who know. 'Anxious enquirer' need be anxious no longer.

From privileged reading of the files of Wodehouse's letters to Townend from which *Performing Flea* was hewn, I deduce that, for a period in 1908/9, Wodehouse himself was doing a clandestine temp. fill-in job as editor of this 'Old Fag' column. I commend that as a field of exploration for some literary dowser with a more sensitive divining rod than mine.

Somerset Maugham tells of rereading the first book of short stories he ever had published, *Orientations*:

It sent so many cold shudders down my spine that I thought I must be going to have another attack of malaria. As a measure of precaution I dosed myself with quinine and arsenic ... [The stories] had passages so preposterously unreal that I could hardly believe it possible that I had written them.

If Wodehouse reread his public-school books, he did so, I am sure, without needing to run to the medicine cupboard. He would not have agreed with the editor of the *Captain* that they were either true to life or the real thing, but he would not have thought them piffle. They never had, nor were intended to have, any high moral tone: which puts them right out of the class of *Tom Brown*, *Eric* and *The Hill*, to name but three.

In the *Public School Magazine* in 1901 there is an anonymous essay on 'School Stories'. I had noted Wodehouse's style in this even before finding him, in a later piece on 'Fictional Improbabilities' under his by-line, referring back to what he had written in 'School Stories'. In these two contributions he says:

The worst of school life, from the point of view of a writer, is that nothing happens. ... Of course, if you are brazen enough to make your hero fall in love with the Doctor's daughter ... A time may come when a writer shall arise bold enough and independent enough to retail the speech of school as it really is, but that time is not yet. The cold grey eye of the public-which-holds-the-purse is upon us, and we are dumb. Rudyard Kipling went near it ... a gallant pioneer of the Ideal; but even the conversation of *Stalky & Co.* leaves something unsaid: not much, it is true, but still something.

Wodehouse referred to a school story called *Gerald Eversley's Friendship*, published in 1895. The book had already drawn the disapproval, in print, of E. F. Benson on the grounds, among others, that its hero 'spends most of his leisure time forming theories of life, and wrestling with spiritual doubts ... all this at the age of thirteen ...' Young Wodehouse adds:

Gerald intends to commit suicide, but finally Nature provides him with a galloping consumption and with his death the story ends, as all school stories should, happily ... Sudden death is always good ... but to make your hero die on a sunset evening, in a bathchair, placed under a big cedar tree, looking o'er the shining waters of the lake, and quoting extracts from obscure Greek poets, is, I aver, a mistake ... No, the worst thing that ought to happen to your hero is the loss of the form-prize or his being run out against the M.C.C. There should be a rule that no one under the age of twenty-one be permitted to die, unless he can get the whole thing finished in a space of time not exceeding two minutes ...

Improbabilities about villains are the worst. The villain always has too much pocket money, and he *will* spend it on gin, billiards and cigars. The man who drinks without getting drunk is unknown ... He comes to roll-call with the regulation reel and hiccough which we know so well from Dean Farrar's books ...

One cannot but agree with every word of young Wodehouse's sentiments above. But for the first few lines he must have had a book other than *Gerald Eversley's Friendship* in mind. *Gerald Eversley's Friendship* had a different plot, though it is still an excruciatingly wet novel. The author was J. E. C. Welldon, who was (often called 'a great') Headmaster of Harrow when this, his only novel, was published. It might well be taken as the ultimate in evangelical public-school fiction of a type that got its start in *Tom Brown's Schooldays*, and was by no means dead until Alec Waugh's *The Loom of Youth* gave it its last clout in 1919.

Wodehouse's school stories are good yarns, full of games, ragging and study teas, with occasional sixth-form words ('stichomythics', 'intempestive') and references to the humming watchman in *The Agamemnon* and Nicias's speechmaking in Thucydides – not wholly out of place in serials for a public-school magazine. There is not much reason why anybody should want to read these stories for the first time now, except as interesting Wodehouse *juvenilia*, showing the Santeuil that later became a Swann. But, although schoolboy literature as a rule dates very quickly in sentiment, and tends to look, even in short retrospect, soppy or pompous or both, Wodehouse's books carry their years lightly. The slang inevitably dates a little. One of the stories in *Tales of St Austin's* is entitled 'How Payne Bucked Up'. We no longer use the phrase 'to buck up' quite so absolutely today. You can find it in Poet Laureat Alfred Austin's *The Human Tragedy*:

When with staid mother's milk and sunshine warmed
The pasture's frisky innocents bucked up . . .

There is a nice period flavour, too, about 'brekker', 'rotting' and 'bar' meaning 'dislike' ('the governor bars Uncle John awfully'). Boys wear nightshirts; a school suit costs 42/-; the Head drives in a carriage and pair; the school doctor prescribes 'leeches and hot fomentations' for practically everything; and cigarettes are $2\frac{1}{4}$d. for twenty.

When, in 1953, Herbert Jenkins reissued the long, single-volume *Mike* (1909) as two books, *Mike at Wrykyn* and *Mike and Psmith*, they did a little modernization on the text. Cricketers Fry, Hayward and Knox became Sheppard, May and Trueman, the indoor game diabolo became yo-yo, 'bunking' (a match) became 'cutting', and 'jingling, clinking sovereigns' became 'crisp, crackling quids'. (But the Gazeka still wore pince-nez, and Adair still went for the doctor on his bicycle.)

These were not big changes to ask after forty-four years, and they are already mostly out-dated now. The stories themselves are absolutely valid as public-school fiction today. The Code is broadly right. The games blood is more glamorous than the Balliol scholar. In fact, the swot is a figure of mild derision. Ragging and rule-breaking are good things, and a skill in these is the next best thing to eminence at games. But even if you play cricket for your county in the summer holidays, you must not put on side.

Wodehouse refers to 'the public-school boy's terror of seeming to pose or do anything theatrical'. One of the least likely snatches of chatter ever recorded in a public-school novel comes in the first chapter of Horace Annesley Vachell's *The Hill* (1905). The school is unashamedly Harrow.

By this time the boys were arriving. Groups were forming. Snatches of chatter reached John's ears. 'Yes, I shot a stag, a nine-pointer. My governor is going to have it set up for me ... What? Walked up your grouse with dogs! We drive ours ... I had some ripping cricket, made a century in one match.'

Mike, a first-chapter new boy at Wrykyn, is told: 'Nothing gets a chap so barred here as side.' Mike faces the problem in a fairly acute form when he becomes a cricket blood while still a new boy: and in an upside-down of that when, going on to Sedleigh at the age of eighteen, he becomes a new boy while a considerable blood.

Wodehouse sold school stories (but no serials) to the *Public School Magazine*, the *Royal*, *Pearson's* and the *Grand*. But the *Captain* was his best market. Its editor never commissioned anything from Wodehouse, but he never rejected anything from him. Wodehouse gave the *Captain*'s readers an extra in humour, much of it at the expense of school stories such as *The Luck Stone*. Almost the first remark that Psmith, in fact an Old Etonian but also technically a new boy, makes to Mike Jackson when they meet at Sedleigh is: 'Are you the Bully, the Pride of the School, or the Boy who is Led Astray and takes to Drink in Chapter Sixteen?' There is a distinct streak of parody already in Wodehouse, and he pulls the leg of the *Chums* type of story for the *Captain* just as easily as he imitates it for *Chums*.

When a boy is accused of frequenting a public house, the head magisterial mind leaps naturally to Stale Fumes and the Drunken Stagger.

In stories, as Mr Anstey has pointed out, the hero is never long without his chance of retrieving his reputation. A mad bull comes into the school grounds, and he alone (the hero, not the bull) is calm. Or there is a fire, and whose is that pale and gesticulating form at the upper window? The bully's, of course. And who is that climbing nimbly up the Virginia creeper? Why, the hero. Who else? Three hearty cheers for the plucky hero!

In *Tales of St Austin's* Wodehouse included an essay, which first appeared in the *Public School Magazine*, about and against *Tom Brown's Schooldays*. He doesn't mind the first half of *Tom Brown*, but suggests that the second half of the book was compiled, not by Hughes, but by the S.S.F.P.W.L.W.T.R.O. E.B.A.S.T.H.G.I. (Secret Society For Putting Wholesome Literature Within The Reach Of Every Boy And Seeing That He Gets It). Wodehouse wrote for boys, not for their parents or their schoolmasters. Hughes's *Tom Brown*, Dean Farrar's *Eric or Little by Little* and *St Winifred's or the World of School*, and an unfair amount of other school fiction, were written with strong moral purpose or overtones. It was *Eric* and *St Winifred's* that Stalky's aunt gave 'To dearest Artie', and for which Stalky could only get ninepence the pair from the Bideford bookseller. Such books have done well as gifts, but can very seldom have been willingly bought, out of his own cash, by a boy intending to read them. Wodehouse wrote, refreshingly, for guineas, sometimes even for half-guineas, but never to do good. In Wodehouse's books there is no piety, no purity, no pathos. There are virtually no parents, either. In the *Public School Magazine* for March 1901 the nineteen-year-old Wodehouse had an anonymous contribution, an Essay 'Concerning Relations'. It starts with the pithy sentence: 'The part played by relations in school life is small but sufficient.'

In none of Wodehouse's school fiction is a boy shown writing home to his mother. To his father, yes, asking for money; but never to his mother. In *The Luck Stone* the school-boy hero, Jimmy Stewart, has a fine soldier father, but no mother. The absence of a mother isn't even remarked on.

No Wodehouse schoolboy dies, even in the Sanatorium. Ever since Dickens's *The Old Curiosity Shop*, schoolboy mortality seems to have fascinated school-fiction writers, if not their readers; the white angel-face on the pillow, the thin pale hands plucking at the coverlet in fever (Jeeves would have known the technical name for this: carphology), or resting, in near-posthumous blessing, on the head of some kneeling and weeping chum. I think that there is only one death, and one near-death, of boys in *Tom Brown*. But boys in Dean Farrar's books fall off cliff-tops, spend fatal nights on wave-whipped rocks, or just decline and perish. And you may (happily) have forgotten the *Stalky* story in which the great headmaster rested from his canings and saved a boy's life by 'sucking the diphtheria stuff' out of his throat through a tube. That rescue was at least successful.

The death-wish is strong in many subsequent authors of public-school novels, even after Wodehouse had publicly jeered at the propensity. If death in the Sanatorium is avoided, the hero is apt to die young, fair and pure, as though too good for life, in war or warlike adventure. Harry Desmond of *The Hill* is shot through the heart in a hail of Boer bullets in

South Africa. The Head preaches about him in Harrow Chapel. Mark Lovell, C. B. Fry's hero in *A Mother's Son* (1907), after many chapters of schools and Oxford, riding the winner of the Grand National, and off his own batting and bowling, almost winning a Test Match against the Australians at Lord's, marries and then finds that he has heart trouble. It is somehow in keeping with the rules of the Code that Mark should not tell his wife or his doting mother about this, but should enlist, take his heart out to South Africa and get shot through it, leading a cavalry charge. In Wodehouse's books nobody, boy or Old Boy, gets anything worse than a case of mumps.

His boys' main interests are in the school. They like their school and they hope it will win the matches. Their conversation is mostly about games, ragging, other people's rows, who's funking his tackles and, generally, who's bucking up and who's not. There is no bullying, though boys occasionally have fist-fights in bad blood. Their favourite reading is the *Sporter* (otherwise the *Sportsman*), Haggard, Anstey, Doyle, Hornung, Gilbert and Dickens. If a boy is in the Classical Sixth, he writes two Greek and two Latin compositions a week, can 'do' Virgil and Livy unseen, but has to battle, with labour and lexicon, with the apparently maniac speeches in Thucydides. He writes an essay for the headmaster in his spare time. He will get a scholarship of sorts to Oxford or Cambridge. But all this is not considered swotting. Swots are the boys who read their Thucydides and *Paradise Lost* beyond Books 2, translate the choruses of the *Agamemnon* into verse for the Mag., and read Herodotus in the original (little Geordie did this in *Tom Brown*, too) with their feet on the mantelpiece. All of which is rather regrettable and frowsty. It will probably end up in a Balliol scholarship or a breakdown.

Mike is Wodehouse's most mature, and by far his best schoolbook. Mike Jackson is a cricketing genius. The name of Foster was certainly in Wodehouse's mind when he wrote the book. Seven Foster brothers of Malvern played cricket for Worcestershire, and in one county match two of them made a century in each innings. Mike Jackson, whose four elder brothers were fine cricketers, for school, county and England, had gone to Wrykyn at the age of fifteen. He had made seven centuries for his prep school. He was headed to being the best cricketer of all the Jacksons, and among his difficulties at Wrykyn were how to be decent about competing with elder brother Bob for the last place in the XI, and how to combine a school life devoted to games with enough work to satisfy his father. Both were valid problems, and neither of them a cliché in school-fiction. Mike succeeded in his first difficulty, failed in his second. Just when he was due to be Captain of Cricket at Wrykyn in his last term, his father removed him and sent him to Sedleigh, a smaller public school, more obscure, but with a reputation for teaching boys to work.

There is some sense in comparing *Mike* with Ian Hay's school story *Pip*. *Pip* was published in 1907, *Jackson Junior* (as the first half of *Mike* was called in serialization) first appeared in the *Captain* in 1908. Wodehouse had read *Pip* when he was writing *Mike*. He admired Ian Hay as a writer always. But *Pip* is written from a master's-eye point of view. *Mike* is written from a boy's-eye point of view. *Pip* dates. *Mike* dates very little.

In *Pip* there is romance. In *Mike* there is none. In *Pip* the schoolmaster plays the father-figure to the cricketing hero. In *Mike* there is no father-figure. The difference between the books on this is a very wide one. Mike is on his own, he has to consume his own emotional smoke and to pick up his wisdom, in matters of public-school life, from his fellow schoolboys. He has no pigtailed girl friend to dream of, no cosy clergyman in whose book-lined, tobacco-scented study he can browse on books and blub in bewilderment. But you can read of Mike's triumphs in the cricket field without feeling that they are very surprising. Wodehouse has made you identify yourself with the character and the skill; it is you that he is taking through the fears and perils of the Ripton match. If you have played cricket at all, it is you out there playing Mike's innings with him. But you are not bowling with Pip; you are sitting with Ham, smoking a pipe, watching someone, perhaps your own son, do an extraordinary headline feat of bowling.

It is really very unlikely that a father would remove his son from one public school and send him to another for a single term. But that's what Father Jackson and Father Smith both did, to the great advantage of public-school literature. Mike Jackson and Psmith turned up at Sedleigh together. The two eighteen-year-old new boys teamed up, proposing to devote their attention exclusively to ragging, and thus perhaps to salve the indignity that their fathers had inflicted on them. (As a serialized sequence to *Jackson Junior* in the *Captain*, the second, Sedleigh, part of the story was titled *The Lost Lambs*.) They wouldn't play games, and they joined the archaeological group so that they could disappear and hunt rabbits.

There had been a foretaste of this mood in a long story in the 1903 *Tales of St Austin's* book. Charteris had gone bolshy because the headmaster had called him a buffoon (a thing no humorist can stand). He determined to devote the rest of his time at St Austin's to ragging and rule-breaking. And, in what seems to be the only hint of a boy–girl romance in Wodehouse's school stories, he got put back on the rails by the headmaster's twelve-year-old niece, Dorothy. Mike did not have Charteris's luck. It needed a fist-fight between him and the school captain, Adair, to resolve his not very attractive sulks about playing cricket. Adair was the devoted and dedicated Sedleighan:

He had that passionate fondness for his school which every boy is popularly supposed to have, but which really is implanted in about one in every thousand. The average public-school boy *likes* his school. He hopes it will lick Bedford at rugger and Malvern at cricket, but he rather bets it won't. He is sorry to leave, and he likes going back at the end of the holidays, but as for any passionate, deep-seated love of the place, he would think it rather bad form than otherwise. If anybody came up to him, slapped him on the back, and cried, 'Come along, Jenkins, my boy! Play up for the old school, Jenkins! The dear old school! The old place you love so!' he would feel seriously ill.

Adair was ready to lick the boy who refused to be keen. Mike knocked Adair out in fair fight and this drained the bad blood out of Mike; he agreed to be keen, to go on fielding-practices before breakfast, and to play against the M.C.C. And he even managed to fix a match between Sedleigh and Wrykyn. Sedleigh won. So Sedleigh was able to get better fixtures in the future, Adair was rewarded for his devotion to the school, and everybody was happy. Psmith who, if truth were told, would have got his place in the Eton team for Lord's that year had he survived, also played against Wrykyn and bowled well.

The last-term new boys left school with honour, and with every intention of having a good time at Cambridge for two or three years to come.

'Behave yourself. Don't make a frightful row in the House. Don't cheek your elders and betters. Wash.' Those were the words of advice that the Gazeka had given the new boy Mike at Wrykyn. Doctrinally you won't find Wodehouse burrowing much deeper into the mystique of the English public school than that.

Counting that as a generalized First Commandment, you might construct the rest of the Decalogue as:

2. Thou shalt not put on side.
3. Thou shalt not sneak on other boys.
4. Thou shalt not lie except to get other boys out of trouble.

5. Thou shalt think thine own school the best in England, and thine own House the best in the school.
6. Thou shalt sponge thyself with cold water after a long soak in a hot bath.
7. Thou shalt not smoke: it is bad for fitness. If thou dost smoke, let it be a pipe and not cigarettes.
8. Thou shalt consider games more important than work.
9. Thou shalt not talk about thy parents except in jest.
10. Thou shalt not smarm thy hair with pungent unguents.

And the Eleventh Commandment is for all healthy public-school rule-breakers:

Thou shalt not be found out. Otherwise thou mayest get sacked and have to go into a Bank.

Tom Brown was enough of a classic for Wodehouse to have been able to laugh at it as such, and as it deserves. But *Stalky* had appeared while Wodehouse was at school and was still among the best-sellers. To a young writer of school stories, not sure which way to turn, *Stalky* must have been a great temptation. It had clearly influenced Ian Hay when he was writing *Pip*. Ham in *Pip* is the Reverend John in *Stalky*: both wise padres, both good with boys. Mr Bradshaw in *Pip* is King in *Stalky*: both Balliol scholars, both fools in their treatment of boys.

You can find evocations of *Stalky* in Wodehouse's school-books, too, and an interesting scholarship question might be: 'If Beetle is the stripling Kipling, and Charteris/Mike the stripling Wodehouse, how do they compare in actions and character?' (Notes: Beetle and Charteris both edited a maga-zine: both were called 'buffoon' by masters. Beetle went off to a job at £100 a year in India: Mike went into a £54 a year job in a bank which would eventually have sent him out East.) One can suggest that there is parallelism between the turning off of the gas-main (*Stalky*) and the ringing of the fire-bell

(*Mike*); Sergeant Foxy in *Stalky* and the school sergeant in *Mike* who was 'feeflee good at spottin''; the masters, King and Downing; the angry squire fussing about his pheasants in *Stalky* and the ditto in *The Pothunters*. Perhaps the Wrykyn Head who beat the boys so liberally after the great Wyatt Walk-Out is a memory of 'Prooshian' Bates of Westward Ho!, who never stopped beating boys, even when he was being cheered by them for his heroism on behalf of the boy with diphtheria. (Wodehouse checked his admiration for head-masters at a sensible point and in his later books teased them quite a lot.)

There is a whiff of *Stalky* in Mike's atonement to games-playing at Sedleigh: Stalky himself, largely to please the Head, had played football in that Old Boys' Match. There are parallels in the ganging-up, three to a study, three to a dormitory (Stalky, Beetle, M'Turk ... Mike, Psmith, Jellicoe), the bug-hunters and the archaeologists, using these pursuits as excuses for far-ranging and ragging. There are comparisons to be made between Stalky and Psmith as characters. But the Kipling/Wodehouse analogy breaks up on attitude and view-point. Wodehouse always felt that Kipling's schoolboys were not boys, they were at least twenty-five years old. Wodehouse (to repeat) was writing for boys, Kipling for masters, parents and Old Boys. Wodehouse was not trying to teach anybody anything, Kipling was teaching, in a sense, all the time. He was saying: 'What a great school, what a great headmaster, what clever and interesting boys! That's the way other schools, headmasters and boys ought to be.'

Obviously *Stalky* would have been too difficult, allusive, gnomic, sophisticated and painful for the *Captain* (one won-ders whether 'The Moral Reformers', the story of bullying and counter-bullying in *Stalky*, read as revoltingly in 1898 as it does today). Perhaps there is a small, symbolic summing-up in M'Turk's remark, 'The Head never expels except for beastliness and stealing.' 'Beastliness' is a purely pi-jaw word, and M'Turk would never have used it, even evasively, to Stalky and Beetle. *Stalky* was written, not for 'boy, just boy', but for grown-ups and for a certain Calvinistic relish of the author's own. The *Captain* offered stories for boys. There is no 'beastliness' in them, mentioned or inferable. It was left to 'The Old Fag' to deal with that in that 'Answers to Correspondents' column of his. Boys (and, at least once, a mother) apparently wrote to him fairly regularly about beastliness; and he castigated it frequently and with enthusiastic commination.

What about girls? If the *Captain* had an official editorial attitude on what a sister wanted her brother to be, it might be deduced from this nerve-racking poem, by Grace Mabel Hudson, printed, with all italics, double-quotes and exclamation marks, in the *Captain* in October 1910, titled 'My "ideal" brother'.

He is straight as a pine, and as broad as an oak,
And his jokes unto laughter a cat would provoke!
He's not handsome, oh no, but his kind, honest face
Tells you plainly *he*'ll never his people disgrace!

He's a 'dab' both at cricket and 'footer', and yet
When it's tennis I'm wanting he'll put up the net,
And when off for a spin he will pump up my tyres
And help me up hills if occasion requires!

He calls hard work at school 'quite the silliest rot',
But he's head of his class, so he knows how to 'swot'.
Though when *I'm* playing scales he will burst in and shout
'Where's the tune? I say, stop it, kid; let us go out!'

He's a critic of blouses, and really quite wise
In the matter of neckbands and colour of ties,
And I *know* I look nice when *he* says I'm 'all right',
As I know that I *don't* when he says I'm a fright!

He's not *perfect* – his chums call him just 'a good sort' –
And he does not do always the things that he ought,
But he's *sterling good stuff*, and that is to my mind
Quite the nicest ideal for a brother you'll find!

What and when did the Wodehouse schoolboys think about girls? Not much and not often is the answer. There are very few girls about, and I remember only Marjorie Merevale, the housemaster's sporting little daughter; twelve-year-old Dorothy who reformed Charteris; and Mike's own sister Marjory, a great admirer of his cricket, but hopeless at keeping a secret. It was Marjory Jackson who coolly revealed, in a letter to brother Bob, that Mike, in order not to keep Bob out of the last place in the Wrykyn side, had pretended he had hurt his wrist. Mike, thoroughly embarrassed by being shown up for a martyr by the young squirt, decided that no girl ought to be taught to write until she came of age. Female kids! Pshaw! A rather older menace appears in a story in a *Tales of St Austin's*, a Miss Beezley who marries Dacre, the housemaster. Miss Beezley reads Browning and is a blue-stocking forerunner of Florence Craye, Honoria Glossop, Heloise Pringle and other over-educated girls who put Bertie Wooster through the mangle in the later years.

In *The White Feather* Wodehouse studied with some interest and seriousness the situation of a boy, of prefect level, shunned by his fellows. He says somewhere in that book that to experience exclusion and loneliness in its deepest sense breaks one of the unwritten laws at a public school. Sheen, in *The White Feather*, had funked a fight with a townee. Everywhere else in his school-books, Wodehouse excellently conveys the sense of inclusion, of moving in coveys and thinking in teams. He also gives the other sense of the word 'inclusion', instantly recognizable to anyone who has been at one of the older, and older-fashioned, public schools: the sense of being behind bars and perpetually challenged to climb out.

'Climbing out' is a rag or a crime, at a public school, in a virtually intransitive sense, without need of any explanation of whence or why you are climbing out. (I still use the present tense, because this was truth in my between-the-wars public-school days as in Wodehouse's.) It is assumed that all windows are barred, as in a prison or a nursery. It is never clear what the outside dangers are from which one is being so scrupulously locked in. It is simply that from the clanging of one bell to the clanging of another all doors to the outer world are locked. The house is an effective fire-trap. If you take the bars away from windows of public-school houses, you may save a few boys from being burnt to death in each decade, when the fire-alarm for once turns out to be genuine. But you also rob schooldays, or rather nights, of one of their immemorial excitements, climbing out.

The boy – what, otherwise, will he become? Old Wrykynians and Old Austinians in the Wodehouse school-books seem not to have aged farther than being at the Varsity, and wearing 'push' (smart) waistcoats; so we are not clear whether the tendency was, later, to go into the Army, the I.C.S., the Church, Politics, or the Arts (two playwrights, brief, sympathetic characters, appear in the Wodehouse school-books, and one nice character-actor; his name is Higgs, and his model was Wodehouse's friend Seymour Hicks).

The brightest hope, especially of the athlete, is to be given an open-air job as an agent on someone's large estate. You play in the M.C.C. match in your last term. A lordly Old Boy sees you hit up a good century, and asks someone: 'Who's that chap?' He is told, and then he says to you: 'I saw your century, my boy. Now, I hear you're not going to the Varsity. Bank, eh? Hm. Look. I shall need a land agent, and a land agent who can play cricket and strengthen my team, at my place in Scotland in a few years. If your pater'll change his mind and send you to Oxford for three years, I'll pay, and give you the land agent job at the end of it.' And the pater does. The hero is saved from a life of frowst, and he can go on playing cricket like a gentleman. This happens to Venables in one of the *Tales of St Austin's*. C. B. Fry's Mark Lovell in *A Mother's Son* becomes a land agent, too, though there the old landed lord is in love with Mark's mother, and that makes it easier.

Mike and Psmith were due to go to Cambridge after Sedleigh. But then Mike's father lost a 'very large' sum of money, and Mike had to go into a Bank – the durance vile that was waiting for even the starriest school athlete if he got sacked, the sticky end of freedom for even the best classical scholar if his father 'failed' before he was through at the Varsity.

Now it is a Bank for Mike. The New Asiatic in the City will give Mike £4 10s. a month, and his father will add £5 a month to that. Mike finds digs out in Acacia Road, Dulwich: for cheapness and because being near a public school, with chances of cricket and fives, will be a little week-end comfort to balance the dull drudgery of sticking on stamps from Monday to Saturday near the Mansion House.

But relief is at hand, light relief, the right relief … Psmith. (We are well into *Psmith in the City* now.) Psmith comes to work at the Bank. Psmith removes Mike from Dulwich and makes him share his flat with him in the Strand. Psmith supplies suppers at the Savoy and cabs. Psmith harries Mr Bickersdyke, the pompous manager of the New Asiatic. Psmith takes Mike along to 'rag' at a Socialist meeting on Clapham Common. And when Mike, suddenly asked, on the telephone at the Bank, to come and play for his county at Lord's, walks out and does so, Psmith and Psmith's father provide the cushion for Mike's downfall. Mike makes 148 for his county, but it'll be the sack at the Bank. Mr Smith says he wants Mike to be the agent on his estates … which means three years at Cambridge, training, and then a good open-air job for life.

Wodehouse wrote what the *Captain* asked for and wrote it better than anyone else in the magazine at the time. He peddled their dreams back to its readers. He accepted the magazine's formulas and was perhaps saved a lot of bother and thinking by the restrictions that the formulas imposed. George Orwell called *Mike* 'perhaps the best light school story in the English language'. And Rupert Hart-Davis records in his biography *Hugh Walpole* that in 1908 Walpole, then a schoolmaster, started to write a school novel which he planned to be like P. G. Wodehouse's.

IMAGES

There would have been serious trouble between David and Jonathan if either had persisted in dropping catches off the other's bowling.

*

It was one of those bulging babies. It looked a little like Boris Karloff and a little like Winston Churchill.

*

You get about as much chance to talk in this house as a parrot living with Tallulah Bankhead.

*

The stationmaster's whiskers are of a Victorian bushiness and give the impression of having been grown under glass.

*

A young man with dark circles under his eyes was propping himself up against a penny-in-the-slot machine. An undertaker, passing at that moment, would have looked at this young man sharply, scenting business. So would a buzzard.

*

She was feeling like a mother who, in addition to having to notify him that there is no candy, has been compelled to strike a loved child on the base of the skull with a stocking full of sand.

*

Reggie looked like a member of the Black Hand trying to plot assassinations while hampered by a painful gumboil. His manner was dark, furtive and agitated.

*

A sort of writhing movement behind his moustache showed that Sir Aylmer was smiling ... Then Sir Aylmer's eye fell on the remains of the what-not and the smile vanished from his face like breath off a razor-blade, to be replaced by a scowl of such malignity that Pongo had the illusion that his interior organs were being scooped out with a spade or trowel.

*

She was standing scrutinising the safe, and heaving gently like a Welsh rarebit about to come to the height of its fever.

3

PSMITH

Enter Psmith (1935) and *Mike and Psmith* (1953), both virtually
the same book, made from the second half of *Mike* (1909), *Psmith
in the City* (1910), *Psmith Journalist* (1915), *Leave it to Psmith* (1923),
The World of Psmith omnibus (1974).

PSMITH is Wodehouse's first adult hero. At Sedleigh he is
already the Old Etonian, the grown-up among boys, the
sophisticated among the callow. His eyelids are a little weary,
and he wears a monocle. In a schoolboy world, where nobody
else has done much but play cricket and see the latest Seymour
Hicks show at the theatre, Psmith talks and behaves like
someone who has swept together ten thousand experiences,
and is never going to be surprised at anything again. In his
first book he patronizes his headmaster, in his last he patronizes Lord Emsworth.

Psmith is like a breath of good, stale night-club air coming
through the healthily open, if precautiously barred, windows
of common room, study and dormitory. To readers of Wodehouse, he is the link between Awkward Adolescence and the
Great After Life. He leads us to the new world of the City,
America, gangsters, crooks, clubs, Psocialism and Blandings
Castle. Those of us who are unable to dissociate Wodehouse's
school-books from our own schooldays (a test of their
excellence for the market for which they were written) have
been, for seven books, moving in the smell of cooked cabbage
and old plimsolls, in the sound of bells and whistles and clanging clocks. We have been sitting, if at all, on lockers and
benches, with chilblains and spots, red wrists, rude health,

huge hungers and bull-calf enthusiasms. Psmith is a lazy man who likes his comforts. He is strongly opposed to missing his sleep, and he quotes a learned German doctor's theory that early rising leads to insanity. Psmith offers us late breakfasts, deep armchairs, the smell of cigar-smoke, the folding of the hands in repose after good lunches in clubland, and a lifetime truce to 'training'. Psmith wafts us painlessly from the School Close to Piccadilly.

Psmith does not despise his schooldays. But he is unsentimental about them. He is finished with them. His father hoped that his one term at Sedleigh might 'get him a Balliol'; but Psmith avoids anything so swottish. He looks back to his Eton days without regret and without rancour. At Cambridge he is objective enough to decide that his happiest memory of the school whose Old Boy blazer he wears with his sky-blue pyjamas is of a certain hot bath after 'one of the foulest cross-country runs that ever occurred outside Dante's Inferno'. He would have played for Eton at Lord's in his last half; but in the matter of cricket he is more likely to remember that, in a village match, he had been caught at point by a man wearing braces. 'It would have been madness to risk another such shock to my system.'

The first adult, Psmith is also the first man of means in Wodehouse. There was 'a tolerable supply of simoleons' and doubloons in the Psmith family old oak chest: much more, one feels, than in the Jackson chest. Psmith's father, though eccentric, was County, landed and a man of capital. In the Sedleigh period, Psmith's money is immanent, but unimportant to the story. In *Psmith in the City* the Psmith simoleons are useful in softening the asperities of London clericalism, both for Psmith and for Mike. And in *Psmith Journalist*, Psmith's money is cardinal to the plot. In fact, Psmith returns to Cambridge after that book, the owner of a successful New York weekly paper, *Cosy Moments*. Then his father dies, the money disappears, and Psmith goes into, and out of, his uncle's fish business. Hence the 'Leave it to Psmith! Psmith will help you. Psmith is Ready for Anything,' etc., advertisement on the front page of the *Morning Globe*. A member of four London clubs, and due to be a member of two more, Psmith is without means of support. He needs that secretary's job at Blandings when Baxter is driven forth.

But the job is, in fact, an afterthought. Psmith has been working for Freddie Threepwood at Blandings, not for personal profit, but to get, by a concatenation of events that would follow if he stole the necklace, the £3,000 that Mike Jackson needs to buy the farm in Lincolnshire. When that is accomplished, Psmith takes the job with Lord Emsworth.

Psmith is not afraid of poverty. But he is afraid of being bored. He prefers danger to being bored. And, though this compulsion has produced heroes as innocuous as Water Rat in *The Wind in the Willows* and as nocuous as Bulldog Drummond, it needs a little study in the Psmith and Wodehouse context.

Psmith might have developed into a Raffles after *Psmith Journalist*, with gun-play and detection providing breezy excitements. His exploits in *Leave it to Psmith* were mildly in the Raffles vein, and there was gun-play in the last chapters. But Wodehouse veered to farce and away from heroics, and the derring-do in his books veered away from revolver-shooting to pig-stealing and policeman's helmet-pinching. The Psmith-type Wodehouse hero does not have to duck the bullets again after the early 1920s. He does, however, seek to avoid boredom still, and (as Psmith did) he uses his tongue as a weapon in that cause. This is the essence of the 'buzzer' in Wodehouse. He buzzes in the hope that his talk will 'start something'. Buzzing cheers him up and makes him feel better himself. But there is always the possibility that it may also cause someone else to do something exciting that will relieve the monotony.

Although Wodehouse didn't coin the word till *Money in the Bank* in 1946, Psmith is the first integrated 'buzzer' in the books. He emits radiations of sound. What he says may, or may not, be true. It may have much meaning, or none. But it may be reckoned to lift dull reality a notch or two into the air and, if it starts nothing more than a train of thought to play with, it has done a job. 'Comrade Jackson's name is a byword in our literary salons', 'Comrade Jackson is possibly the best known of our English cat-fanciers.' Both these claims are made by Psmith, in New York, in *Psmith Journalist*, to a prominent New York gangster. Neither is true. But this kind of typical buzzer's remark induces two kinds of danger, plays with two kinds of fire. There is the danger that the gangster will realize that Psmith is engaged in persiflage, and take steps. And there is the danger that Mike, hearing himself thus described, will switch from surprise to giggles. In that case, too, the gangster may take steps. By inducing this kind of danger the buzzer staves off boredom from himself. Buzzing is a conversational excitement-inciter. It is a Wodehouse proprietary patent medicine, and Psmith is its first dispenser.

Wodehouse had been playing with the ingredients of buzzing in his first book, *The Pothunters*. Charteris is 'seldom silent'. Dallas describes his housemaster airily as 'a man of the vilest antecedents' (an echo of Conan Doyle). In later school stories you get Marriott and Jimmy Silver putting their feet up and simply persiflating. These, to change from the chemist's shop to the music-room, are Wodehouse's five-finger exercises which will break into the chords of Psmith, just as soon as that local habitation and name occur. Who is talking now?

... there are stories about me which only my brother knows. Did I want them spread about the school? No, laddie, I did not. Hence, we see my brother, two terms ago, packing up his little box, and tooling off to Rugby. And here am I at Wrykyn, with an unstained reputation, loved by all who know me, revered by all who don't;

courted by boys, fawned on by masters. People's faces brighten when I throw them a nod. If I frown ...

That's Clowes, in the first half of *Mike*, three years, as the fictional calendar goes, before Psmith appears at all: a mere twenty chapters, as the pages of *Mike* turn. Psmithery is there, in the keys of Wodehouse's typewriter, waiting to come out. Wodehouse said he got the character of Psmith handed to him on a plate when a Wykehamist cousin told him about a school-mate, Rupert, son of the Savoy Opera's D'Oyly Carte. He called his fellow Wykehamists 'Comrade', wore a monocle and was orotund of speech. In the orotundity of speech that Wodehouse gave Psmith I think one can hear, also, Sherlock Holmes, Baboo Jabberjee, Beetle imitating King, Stalky, Dick Swiveller, Mr Micawber and, perhaps, Raffles.

But just because Psmith has emerged, and is going to recur, why should the faithless Wodehouse not go on using some of his ingredients for pleasant characters in the books between? In 1915, midway between Psmith's appearance at Sedleigh and his reappearance, in 1923, in *Leave it to Psmith*, Ashe Marson, hero of *Something Fresh*, goes to Blandings, disguised as Mr Peters's valet, to steal a scarab, much as Psmith later, disguised as the Canadian poet, goes to Blandings to steal Connie Keeble's necklace for her husband. And this is Ashe addressing his employer, the testy millionaire:

'I've come to read to you,' said Ashe.

'You fool, do you know that I have just managed to get to sleep?'

'And now you're awake again,' said Ashe soothingly. 'Such is life. A little rest, a little folding of the hands in sleep, and then, bing, off we go again.'

Here is Ashe again, describing to Joan Valentine, who is pretending to be a lady's maid, his success in the Servants' Hall:

'Let us look on the bright side ... the commissariat department is a revelation to me. I had no idea that servants did themselves so well. As for the social side, I love it ... Did you observe my manner towards the kitchen maid who waited on us at dinner last night? A touch of the old *noblesse* about it, I fancy? Dignified, but not unkind, I think? ...'

And who's speaking now?

'The advice I give to every young man starting life is "Never confuse the unusual with the impossible!" Take the present case, for instance. If you had only realised the possibility of somebody some day busting you on the jaw when you tried to get into a cab, you might have thought out a dozen crafty schemes for dealing with the matter. As it is, you are unprepared. The thing comes on you as a surprise. The whisper flies around the clubs: "Poor old What's-his-name has been taken unawares. He cannot cope with the situation." '

No, that's George Bevan, who marries the lady named in *The Damsel in Distress* (1919). Bevan is a playwright, and supposed to be an American, too. Perhaps he met Psmith in New York in the *Psmith Journalist* period, and decided to model his own conversational style on Psmith's.

This business of 'starting something' is recurrent through-out Wodehouse, and in his later years he has made it the mainspring of one of his best girl characters. Bobbie Wickham periodically feels the urge to 'start something' just for the heck of it. Bobbie, a human ticking-bomb, is, in that sense, the female of the species Psmith. In the post-school books the Wodehouse male ragger, whoever he may be, from Psmith to Lord Ickenham, has to have a good cause, such as helping a friend, as an excuse for anything more than verbal ragging. The female can start something for the purpose of doing down an enemy (Stiffy Byng *v*. the village policeman) or (Bobbie Wickham) merely through boredom. Lord Ickenham insists that all the best girls are apple-pie-bed-makers, preferably of bishops' beds. In fact, prime movers of misrule.

Psmith's buzzing, and the buzzing of all successors to Psmith in Wodehouse, is a one-man verbal rag. Psmith buzzes, not to call attention to himself. That happens, and must be tolerated. He buzzes in order to attract causes for amusement, to make amusement occur, so that he may be amused.

Psmith, in appearance and, very broadly, manner, is the Knut. The Knut was not a Wodehouse invention. He was a fashion-eddy of late Edwardianism, though his line goes back to the dandy and the fop of earlier centuries. Captain Good, R.N., in Rider Haggard's *King Solomon's Mines*, wore a gutta-percha collar, a monocle, matching hat and jacket and impeccable other kit in the African bush, to the amusement of his companions and Rider Haggard's readers, but not to the lessening of his own dignity. *Punch* was making jokes about the Knut at the same time as Wodehouse was using him as part of Psmith.

The Knut was an amiable person. You could laugh at him kindly. He cultivated a 'blah' manner and vocabulary. Some of Psmith's vocabulary was from early Knut sources. 'Oojah-cum-spiff' and 'Rannygazoo', both Knut locutions, were used by Psmith first, and later by Bertie Wooster. When Bertie Wooster used 'Oojah-cum-spiff' and 'Rannygazoo' in the 1920s, they sounded, to the reader too young to have known the Knut language, like personal Wodehouse/Wooster fabrications. In the Wodehouse play *Good Morning, Bill* of which the novel *Dr Sally* is virtually a transcript, Lord Tidmouth, a Knut, says good-bye in six different ways: 'Bung-ho', 'Teuf-teuf', 'Tinkerty-tonk', 'Toodle-oo', 'Poo-boop-a-doop' and 'Honk-honk'.

Knut language, like any other generic slang, substituted for the sake of substitution. It was the manner of the Knut to call a man a 'cove' or a 'stout sportsman'. In *The Lighter Side of*

School Life Ian Hay, discussing Dean Farrar's *Eric*, says 'No schoolboy ever called lighted candles "superfluous abundance of nocturnal illumination".' Psmith could have. Psmith, instead of 'tea' says 'a cup of the steaming'. Psmith, first in Wodehouse, plays variations on the already several-times-removed-from-reality imagist phrase 'in the soup'. Psmith refers to '*consommé* splashing about the ankles' and someone being 'knee-deep in the *bouillon*'. He always prefers the oro-tund to the curt. Instead of 'shoot a goal' he says 'push the bulb into the meshes beyond the uprights'. 'Archaeology will brook no divided allegiance from her devotees', and 'the dream of my youth and aspirations of my riper years' – these are pleasant enough suggestions of pulpit pomp. In the crowded school study they would certainly be given in a parody voice, adding a specific victim to the general parody. The headmaster or the padre would be the local wax figure for the group to stick their verbal pins into.

Even if Psmith had not first appeared in a school story, one might shrewdly assess that his language and manner had been born and bred in a school society. It is at that impressionable age, and in that sort of confined study-fug, that speech-forms and humour-forms sprout most proliferously and, by applause and fierce criticism, are shaped and tailored for a wider public.

At English schools in my boyhood, humorists were divided into two classes, both unpopular. If you merely talked amusingly, you were a 'silly ass'. ('You *are* a silly ass!' was the formula.) If your conversation took a mordant and satirical turn, you were a 'funny swine'. And whichever you were, you were scorned and despised and lucky not to get kicked. It is to this early discouragement that I attribute the fact that no Englishman, grown to man's estate, ever says anything brighter than 'Eh, what?' and 'Most extraordinary'.

This is Wodehouse in *Over Seventy* (1957). 'Silly ass!' and 'funny swine!' may well have been appellations of oppro-brium addressed to Psmith at Eton. In that term at Sedleigh covered by *Mike and Psmith*, Jellicoe once says to him 'You *are* a lad!', and once, 'You *are* a chap!' Perhaps Psmith was too old and formidable for anyone to call him 'silly ass' or 'funny swine' with impunity at that stage; but he was an amusing talker, and he started something in the Wodehouse books. Take a line through Psmith and fifty young heroes and heroines of stories and novels, and you fetch up at the biggest of all the irrepressible buzzers, Lord Ickenham. His talk is like the flail of a tank going through a minefield.

'Don't *talk* so much! I never met a fellow like you for talking!' complained Freddie Threepwood to Psmith in *Leave it to Psmith*. Mike Jackson in *Psmith Journalist* simply fell asleep to Psmith's conversation. It is stated of Psmith that 'conversation always acted on him as a mental stimulus', and he was the more attracted to Eve in the last book because she 'let him talk oftener and longer than any girl he had ever known'. The pleasant Psmith buzz, a rich mixture of glancing parodies, quotations, word-muddles and false concords, contained as ingredients three main, separable styles. Wodehouse soon thriftily and successfully isolated them for the individual use of others. The first he developed for the subsequent buzzers, the conscious maestros of racy conversation, invective and persiflage: Galahad and Uncle Fred, and all those chirpy young heroes of whom testy tycoons say in opening chapters that they are 'a darn sight too fresh'. These are clever men, who talk that way because it amuses them. A second ingredient of Psmith's talk has gone, in later books, to those unconscious humorists at the lower I.Q. level, of whom Bertie Wooster is the finest flower. Bertie jumbles his words, phrases and concords through innocence and stupidity; he stumbles on his images; he seems only just to be listening to what he himself is saying; and at occasional pinheaded moments he can stop to be intrigued by something he has just heard coming out of his own mouth, like a kitten intrigued by the flicking of its own tail. Such innocents are vulnerable and lovable. But they are burblers, not buzzers.

The third form in which the Psmith manner was bred out is the Jeeves style. In essence that style is the Ciceronian/Johnsonian. It is the parliamentary or Civil Service style, level, pompous, circumlocutory, didactic. It is the language of leaders, school sermons, toastmasters and treaties. It is funny when used out of place – as by Mr Micawber – and consistently by such as would seem to have no need of it: butlers and gentlemen's gentlemen.

In Psmith this super-fatted style becomes dominant only when he talks to people who would be most dazed by it. In New York, with a six-inch bullet-hole in his hat after a skirmish with gangsters, Psmith addresses three cops with a battery of yard-long sentences, polysyllables and subjunctives:

'I am loath to interrupt this very impressive brain-barbecue, but, trivial as it may seem to you, to me there is a certain interest in this other matter of my ruined hat. I know that it may strike you as hypersensitive of us to protest ...'

Apart from the blah Knut manner, the two strongest influences in the rhythms and locutions of the Psmith language are, first, Conan Doyle's Sherlock Holmes stories, and, second, 'babu'. Wodehouse recalled to Townend (in *Performing Flea*) the excitement of waiting for new issues of the *Strand Magazine* on Dulwich Station. Schoolboys and paulo-post-schoolboys of Wodehouse's own vintage, and of Psmith's a decade later, were not only steeped in the Sherlock Holmes stories, but they knew that they could recognizably bandy the language of them with anyone else of their age and class. Stalky and his friends dropped into Brer Rabbit language almost as a code. Wodehouse's first major conversational parodist, Psmith, is constantly echoing Sherlock Holmes (indeed, the Holmes *Valley of Fear* influence probably to some extent suggested the plot of *Psmith Journalist*). Psmith has verbal 'lifts' from Sherlock Holmes, with direct quotations of words, and copying of manner. 'You had best put the case in my hands . . . I will think over the matter.' 'Do not disturb me. These are deep waters.' ' . . . Omitting no detail, however slight' – these are the parts of the iceberg that appear above the water. In *Psmith Journalist* a snatch of Psmith dialogue is:

'It is possible that Comrade Windsor may possess the qualifications necessary for the post. But here he comes. Let us forgather with him, and observe him in private life before arriving at any premature decision.'

There, only 'But here he comes' is a direct lift from Holmes. But we could not be sure of that unless the surrounding rhythms were making us alert for identifications of exact phrases.

The element of Psmith's language that was hived off later for the use of the burblers such as Bertie Wooster is babu-English, and I'd like to take a few minutes here to have a look at F. Anstey's 1897 book, compiled from pieces in *Punch* in 1896, called *Baboo Jabberjee*. (I shall spell it 'babu' from now on.) Wodehouse read all Anstey's stuff as a boy, including, as is obvious from his school stories, *Vice Versa*. But *Baboo Jabberjee* (which is quoted by name in *Love Among the Chickens*) was powerfully seminal to Psmith and the quintessential Wodehouse style of false concords.

Anstey's Hurry Bungsho Jabberjee, B.A., is a Bombay law-student in England. He uses the appellation 'Hon'ble' more or less as we say 'Mister' and the *Uncle Remus* characters say 'Brer'. Psmith's appellation 'Comrade' chimes well with Jabberjee. Jabberjee has learnt his English from books. He uses absurdly inflated phrases, and he makes unintentional false concords. He writes, for instance:

'The late respectable Dr Ben Johnson, gifted author of Boswell's Biography, once rather humorously remarked, on witnessing a nautch performed by canine quadrupeds, that, although their choreographical abilities were of but a moderate nature, the wonderment was that they should be capable at all to execute such a hind-legged feat and *tour de force*.'

Some of Jabberjee's false concords are repeated verbatim by Bertie Wooster. Some of his inflated phraseology goes into Jeeves's vocabulary. Isn't that last quotation, apart from its howlers, rather reminiscent of Jeeves when he muffles the furious Pop Stoker with a chloroform mask of verbiage in *Right Ho, Jeeves*? Jabberjee writes: 'As poet Burns remarks with great truthfulness, "Rank is but a penny stamp, and a Man is a man and all that." ' This is a pleasant skid on the banana skin of education. Bertie and Jeeves, you remember, get tangled up in this same quotation at a moment of great crisis.

Rem acu tetigisti, non possumus, surgit amari aliquid, ultra vires, mens sana in corpore sano, amende honorable – these are gobbets of education that Jabberjee uses and Jeeves takes over. And (this is sad) we find that it was Jabberjee, and not Bertie, who first made that excellent Shakespeare emendation, only conceivable through the ears, only translatable through the eyes. Jabberjee writes: ' Jessamina inherits, in Hamlet's immortal phraseology, "an eye like Ma's to threaten and command".' There are other trace elements of Jabberjee in the wider Wodehouse. Jabberjee, describing an evening of professional boxing matches in a London hall, mentions the NO SMOKING notice, and says that everybody goes on smoking just the same. This point is made by Corky when describing an East End boxing evening in a Ukridge story. Jabberjee's 'I became once more *sotto voce* and the silent tomb' is a phrase Bertie evokes once or twice, if perhaps with faint quotation marks in his voice. Jabberjee's mystification at Stratford, on finding that all the portraits of Hon'ble Shakespeare are unalike, and that none bears any resemblance to the bust, is a point which Wodehouse sharpens in an essay. Jabberjee who, like Bertie Wooster *passim*, is plagued by being engaged to a girl he wishes he were not engaged to, speaks of a 'manly, straightforward stratagem' for oiling out of the commitment. Wodehouse gets variations on this happy phrase into the mouths of Ukridge, Bingo Little, Tuppy Glossop and Bertie on separate occasions. Jabberjee, like Dick Swiveller, sucks the knob of his cane. So does Bertie. So does Freddie Threepwood. So does Motty, Lord Pershore, in the early Jeeves story.

Jabberjee introduces himself to 'Hon'ble Punch' as 'one saturated to the skin of his teeth in best English masterpieces of immaculate and moderately good prose extracts and dramatic passages'. Take your line through Ram, an actual babu schoolboy who appeared in *The Luck Stone*, into Psmith the buzzer, Bertie the burbler and Jeeves the orotund, and you may feel inclined, as I do, to pay a passing tribute to F. Anstey for planting a seed in the rich soil of young Wodehouse's burgeoning mind. Or, if you prefer the image, for putting a piece of grit into the Wodehouse oyster shell, so that Wodehouse built it into a pearl, richer than all his tribe of humorous writers.

Psmith is not the first fictional schoolboy whose main characteristic is clever talk, nor is he the last of the schoolboy Knuts. Anthony Pembury at St Dominic's, in Talbot Baines Reed's novel, is the son of the editor of *Great Britain* weekly review, the inheritor of his father's sharp tongue. He is a cripple, so he cannot play games or 'pursue'. But 'he can talk and he can ridicule, as his victims all the school over know.' The Knut with the eye-glass and faultless clothes has become more or less a stock character in Frank Richards and post-Frank Richards schoolboy fiction. Perhaps Psmith is the only example of the Knut with clever talk. The tradition of the Knut in *Magnet* and *Gem* is that he should be a Lord, pro-

nounce his 'r's' as 'w's', and say 'you wotter!!!' with at least
that number of exclamation marks. The smallness of his vocabulary fits the smallness of his intelligence, and his vocabulary
is further limited by the need to find words for him which
have 'r's' to mispwonounce.

Psmith has a large vocabulary and wide range of imagery.
Many of his quotations, verbal images and conceits pass into
the Wodehouse language, free for all later pleasant characters
to use: restoring the tissues; *solvitur ambulando*; making us
more spiritual; of all sad words of tongue or pen; Patience on
a monument; couldn't find a bass drum in a telephone booth;
this tendency . . . fight against it; it would be paltering with the
truth; not so but far otherwise; I have my spies everywhere;
the man who discovered that alcohol was a food long before
the doctors did.

Psmith is the first runner in the Wodehouse Non-Stop
Quotation Stakes: the recitation, printed as prose, of gobbets
from the better-known poets. At one moment he feels like
some watcher of the skies, and keeps the feeling going ac-
curately for three and a half lines of Keats. This stands as the
record distance, until he beats it himself with four lines of
uninterrupted Omar. Wodehouse appropriated this trick, I
suspect, consciously or unconsciously, from Dick Swiveller
in *The Old Curiosity Shop*:

'An excellent woman, that mother of yours, Christopher,' said
Mr Swiveller. 'Who ran to catch me when I fell, and kissed the place
to make it well? My mother. A charming woman . . .'

This is one of Psmith's own quotations, and Jeeves's and
Bertie's. And that typographical manner of quoting poetry as
prose became a pleasant habit of Wodehouse's. (Mr Cornelius
of Valley Fields holds the record with sixteen lines of Scott.)
There are a few rather surprising moments when Psmith
positively becomes a conscious wag, almost a buffoon. In

Psmith Journalist, he has a throwaway line: 'We will now recite that pathetic song, "Baby's Sock is now a Blue-Bag ..."' In *Leave it to Psmith* he makes one suspect three or four times that he has been dipping into the works of Dornford Yates and admiring Berry: when he has to go forth in the night, and puts a white rose into the lapel of his pyjamas and a Homburg hat on his head; and when he describes an aspect of Blandings:

'We are now in the southern pleasaunce or the west home-park or something. Note the refined way the deer are cropping the grass. All the ground on which we are now standing is of historic interest. Oliver Cromwell went through here in 1550. The record has since been lowered ...'

And when Eve tells him he is terribly conceited, he says: 'No, no, success has not spoiled me.'

Psmith had been 'resting' for eight years after *Psmith Journalist*. In those eight years Wodehouse had written the first of the Blandings saga, the book and the play of *Piccadilly Jim*, *Jill the Reckless*, his first book of golf stories, and two books of Jeeves. For a Wodehouse who had turned so many corners and advanced so far as a writer, it must have been a little difficult to keep the revived Psmith exactly in register with his previous self. Wodehouse said that he had had trouble with the last half of *Leave it to Psmith*, and, indeed, had to rewrite it after the first edition. It is not the most successful Psmith book or the most successful Blandings book. Its main interest to us in these days is for its attempt, even if not too happy, to develop Psmith as a Raffles and at the same time make him fall in love.

Was Psmith's a happy marriage? 'Marry someone eccentric,' her friend Cynthia had said to Eve. Psmith was certainly eccentric. How long did he last as Lord Emsworth's secretary? That is one of the expendable jobs in the Blandings saga, and we see several other incumbents in later books: Hugo Carmody, Monty Bodkin, Jerry Vail and even Baxter himself again. Also not a few girls. Presumably Psmith and Eve married soon after the end of *Leave it to Psmith*. Eve was quite a character in her own right, 'straight and slim' with a 'cheerful smile', 'boyish suppleness of body', a 'valiant gaiety', a 'golden sunniness'. She was 'joyously impecunious'. She got £150 a year from a deceased uncle and couldn't touch the capital; but she spent dangerously on buying hats and betting on horses. Did Mr and Mrs Psmith 'live in' at Blandings after she had finished cataloguing the library? That might have been a bit unkind to Freddie Threepwood, who had thought himself so deeply in love with Eve, and who was from time to time incarcerated at Blandings by his infuriated father.

My theory had been that that fish-magnate uncle of Psmith's died and left him a new pile of money, and that Psmith went off somewhere in Shropshire (perhaps buying back his childhood home, Corfby Hall in Lower Benfield) and became a gentleman of easy leisure, like The Infant at the end of the first *Stalky* book. Psmith and Eve would have the Mike Jacksons to stay when Mike could get away from his farm and the claims of Lincolnshire on his cricket. Psmith would grow grey, but not fat. He would perhaps look more like the Peruvian llama in middle age than he had even in youth, but he would keep his figure and his eyeglass and his smart clothes. Eve would make him resign from five of his London clubs and remain a member of the Drones only. Psmith wouldn't come up to London very often. He would remind you a good deal of the Earl of Ickenham.

In the Preface that Wodehouse wrote for the 1974 omnibus *World of Psmith*, the four novels in one book, he said:

A married Psmith would not be quite the same. But obviously a man of his calibre is not going to be content to spend his life as Lord Emsworth's secretary. In what direction he branched out I cannot say. My guess is that he studied law, became a barrister, was a great success and wound up by taking silk. If so, I see him as a genial judge like A. P. Herbert's Mr Justice Codd, whose last case, in the book entitled *Codd's Last Case*, is possibly the funniest thing that great humorist ever wrote.

IMAGES

Unseen, in the background, Fate was quietly slipping the lead into the boxing-glove.

*

The hell-hound of the Law gave a sort of yelp rather like a wolf that sees its Russian peasant getting away.

*

There came into his eyes a sudden wild gleam of hope, such as might have come into the eyes of some wretched man on the scaffold, who, just as the executioner is spitting on his hands with a cheery 'Heave ho!', observes a messenger galloping up on a foaming horse, waving a parchment.

*

For, like so many substantial Americans, he had married young and kept on marrying, springing from blonde to blonde like the chamois of the Alps leaping from crag to crag.

*

She was quite pretty in a rather austere kind of way. She looked like a vicar's daughter who plays hockey and ticks off the villagers when they want to marry their deceased wives' sisters.

*

They had then withdrawn, laughing heartily, like a couple of intoxicated ambassadors who have delivered their credentials to a reigning monarch and are off to get a few more quick ones before the bars close.

*

Many a man may look respectable, and yet be able to hide at will behind a spiral staircase.

*

His manner was now meek and conciliatory, like that of a black-beetle which sees the cook reaching for the insect powder and does its best to show her that it fully realises that it had brought this on itself.

*

'Certainly not, sir,' he said with cold rebuke, staring at me like an archdeacon who has found a choir-boy sucking acid drops during divine service.

4

UKRIDGE

Love Among the Chickens (1906 and, somewhat rewritten, 1921), ten short stories in *Ukridge* (1924), three short stories in *Lord Emsworth and Others* (1937), three short stories in *Eggs, Beans and Crumpets* (1940), one short story in *Nothing Serious* (1950), one short story in *A Few Quick Ones* (1959) and one short story in *Plum Pie* (1966).

UKRIDGE is the only arrant rogue among all Wodehouse's public-school immoralists. (Oofy Prosser is an unpleasant immoralist.) Ukridge spans sixty publishing years, starts as a married man, and then goes backwards in time into previous bachelorhood. He is a handier property when he can be single-mindedly selfish, and when the reader's relish of his knavery is not edged with pity for his wife, the adoring little Millie.

In one's memory Ukridge seems to be dressed in one of three garbs or outfits: pyjamas and filthy mackintosh (hurriedly kicked out by Aunt Julia at midnight); filthy grey bags and filthy mackintosh (in pubs, on Battling Billson business); or top-hat, morning coat and all the fixings (temporarily sunning in the gilded Wimbledon cage of Aunt Julia's approval). His socks and shirts are almost always purloined from his friend Corky. His collar is often detached from its back-stud. And he is always wearing his pince-nez attached to his flapping ears with ginger-beer wire. Modern readers will scarcely have heard of pince-nez. Since they have never seen stone ginger-beer bottles with corks held in with wire, the phrase 'ginger-beer wire' will have them guessing. The idea of a young man wearing a top-hat and morning coat in Wimbledon for anything but a wedding or a funeral will seem absurd. But Ukridge himself can be confidently recommended in print to anybody who remembers Tony Hancock, a not dissimilar fantasist, on radio and television. *The Times* wrote this of Hancock in 1958:

> Mr Hancock is a comedian governed by the basic humours of vanity and greed. The odds are heavily weighted against his satisfying either, but all disasters are effaced from his memory by invincible egoism. Action springs either from his delusions of orientally voluptuous grandeur or from his taste for ludicrously elaborate conspiracy. There is constant alternation between fantasy and realism.
>
> Defeat, indignity, physical cowardice, and moral turpitude are constantly recurring, but they are saved from embarrassment by the aggressiveness of the comedy. Mr Hancock is not a clown to be trampled on: he is a belligerent grotesque who engulfs all surrounding characters, who never descends to pathos, and who speaks an idiom all his own that is a compound of vehement slang, satirised cliché, and extreme literacy.

It would be a fairly faithful description of Ukridge.

His friend Bill Townend gave Wodehouse, in a letter, the background material – the desperate chicken-farm and its bellowing owner – for *Love Among the Chickens* in 1906. Townend knew the real chicken-farmer, who had been a master at a prep school where Townend had boarded after leaving Dulwich. Wodehouse never met Ukridge's real-life prototype, then or later, and he built up Ukridge's character from several other sources: one school friend in particular, a clothes-borrower, whom he mentions in *Over Seventy*. My guess is that yet another model was James Cullingworth, the amiable villain in Conan Doyle's *Stark Monro Letters*. Cullingworth has a little, timid wife, Hetty, who adores him, and whom Monro (largely Conan Doyle) feels he wants to pick up and kiss. Hetty is not unlike Ukridge's Millie, who has something

of the same effect on James Corcoran (largely Wodehouse).
Cullingworth calls Monro 'laddie'. Cullingworth is always, he
thinks, on the edge of riches, and always, in fact, on the edge
of bankruptcy, with duns and county court summonses
threatening. Monro's last words on Cullingworth, who was
finally planning to make a vast fortune as an eye-surgeon in
South America, were:

'He is a man whom nothing could hold down. I wish him luck,
and have a kindly feeling towards him, and yet I distrust him from
the bottom of my heart, and shall be pleased to know that the
Atlantic rolls between us.'

Ukridge appeared in print before Mike Jackson. *Love Among
the Chickens* in its first version was on the bookstalls three years
before the book *Mike*. In fact, although *The White Feather*
came out as a serial in the *Captain* in 1905 (the £60 cheque for
it went into Wodehouse's bank in October that year), *Love
Among the Chickens* appeared before the book of *The White
Feather*. *Love Among the Chickens* came out as a book, without
advance serialization, in August 1906, and had netted £31 5s.
8d. in royalties for its author by January of next year. *The
White Feather* was on the bookstalls in October 1907 (advance royalties £17 10s.). The book, *Mike*, didn't appear till
1909.

It is as well to be a bit bibliographical about this, to establish that Wodehouse wrote a novel about adults and love
before he had written his last school book. Put it the other
way round: *Mike*, which is his longest and best school novel,
was a return to schooldays, written by Wodehouse the novelist.
It is as well, also, that, continuing to be bibliographically
technical, we should compare the 1906 version of *Love Among
the Chickens* with its 1921 successor.

In the dedication at the beginning of the 1921 version,
Wodehouse says:

... I have practically rewritten the book. There was some pretty bad work in it, and it had 'dated'. As an instance of the way in which the march of modern civilisation had left the 1906 edition behind, I may mention that, on page twenty-one, I was able to make Ukridge speak of selling eggs at five for sixpence.

There wasn't really much original bad work, or much rewriting: only some tidying. And Ukridge himself comes through from 1906 and 1921 with hardly a word altered. He is not the main character in the book, anyway. It is Jeremy Garnet's love, among Ukridge's chickens. In the Blampied drawing on the dust jacket of the second *Love Among the Chickens*, it is Jeremy Garnet in plus-fours chasing the fowls. Of the four charming black-and-white illustrations by H. M. Brock in the 1906 book, only one showed Ukridge. He was leaning on a gate, between his wife and Garnet, looking at chickens. Ukridge is a much bigger person there than Garnet. But in that book and in those days Ukridge was not specifically a clothes-borrower. In the later stories, when Garnet ('Garny, old horse!') became changed to Corcoran ('Corky, old horse!'), Ukridge and his narrator were about the same size sartorially – which Ukridge made the most of, and Corky regretted.

The revised version of *Love Among the Chickens* gave Ukridge more prominence only by playing down Garnet. The epilogue of the 1906 book showed the wedding of Garnet and his Phyllis in playlet form. Ukridge was best man, but Garnet and Phyllis were the couple in the fade-out. Wodehouse cut this epilogue out of the 1921 version. The new fade-out shows Ukridge and his Millie doing a moonlight flit from Combe Regis, their debts unpaid, their chickens a flop, and Ukridge already thinking big about his next venture, a duck-farm. This gives Ukridge the fat at the end, though it leaves the story of Jeremy and Phyllis a little undecided.

In 1906 the first five chapters were in third-person-singular narrative. After that Jeremy Garnet took over in the first person. In the 1921 *Love Among the Chickens* Jeremy Garnet tells the whole story, starting at Chapter I. All the chapter titles, and the order of the chapters, are the same in both versions. Wodehouse changed the price of eggs to suit the march of modern civilization. And Combe Regis was itself a change from the earlier, franker Lyme Regis. In 1906 the flower was the lubin, and in 1921 the lupin. Mr John Redmond became Sir Edward Carson, and the sentence 'If Maxim Gorky were invited to lunch with the Czar . . .' became 'if Maxim Gorky were invited to lunch with Trotsky . . .' Those that say that Wodehouse always lived in a timeless and fantastic world, hampered only by the price of eggs, should take note how stern reality, and the passing of fifteen years of history, affected this story.

But in style we can catch the maturer Wodehouse putting some recognizable new spin on the old ball. In 1906 Chapter VII ended:

'Charawk,' said the hen satirically from her basket.

In 1921 this read:

'Charawk!' chuckled Aunt Elizabeth from her basket, in the beastly, cynical, satirical way which has made her so disliked by all right-thinking people.

The name 'Aunt Elizabeth' had been given to this unpleasant hen by Ukridge, 'on the strength of an alleged similarity of profile to his wife's nearest relative'. Somewhere between 1906 and 1921 Wodehouse had discovered the comedy value of aunts. On the other hand he was still, in 1921, attracted by sixth-form words. In *Jill the Reckless*, published that year, he used 'vagrom' and 'equivoque', and he did not disturb the 1906 use, in *Love Among the Chickens*, of the word 'logomachy' when it came to revising for 1921. These three words would never have appeared in the books of Wodehouse's Indian summer, except perhaps in the mouth of Jeeves.

In any depth-analysis of the development of the Wodehouse style, a detailed textual comparison between the two versions of *Love Among the Chickens* should be revealing, not only for what the maturer Wodehouse cut out, but for what he left in. But remember that Wodehouse had four books published in 1921, and he was also knee-deep in theatre-work in London and New York. It would be straining probability to suggest that he would have taken much time that year to go creatively broody on *Love Among the Chickens* a second time. He would have pruned and tidied expertly and fast, but left things alone where they would get by. Today, knowing how acute was Wodehouse's ear for clichés, you may think it surprising that in 1921 his hero should still have to talk to a dog in order to reveal his thoughts and plans to the reader. Shakespeare did this, but so many people were following Shakespeare's lead in the use of man–dog unilateral dialogue at the beginning of this century that Wodehouse might have become sick of it by 1921. The homily on pipe-smoking seems to have a fusty air in a 1921 Wodehouse. A man with a pipe in his mouth and a frown of concentration was, by the rules of fiction, more manly and heroic than someone without either. Wodehouse in his *floruit* decades used pipes and pipe-smoking as comic plot-makers: pipes are things for authors to be photographed with, and for other characters to give up in agony. But in *Love Among the Chickens* there is the same crooning and philosophizing over pipe-smoking as one finds in John Buchan's 1900 novel, *The Half-Hearted*:

These are the pipes to which a man looks back in after years with a feeling of wistful reverence, pipes smoked in perfect tranquillity, mind and body alike at rest ...
Love Among the Chickens, by P. G. Wodehouse.

It was as if the essence of all the pipes he had ever smoked was concentrated into this last one. The smoke blew back, and as he sniffed its old homely fragrance, he seemed to feel the smell of peat and heather, of drenched homespun ...

The Half-Hearted, by John Buchan.

You find the same pipe-dream in Charles Kingsley, in Barrie's books and plays *passim*, in Milne's early *Punch* pieces and indeed in *Punch* pieces by many other hands into the middle 1930s.

In *Love Among the Chickens* the seven pages of 'Man Versus His Conscience' describe a mental tussle in terms of a boxing match, round by round. Should Garnet cause Phyllis's father to be tipped out of a boat in Combe Regis harbour, so that Garnet can then rescue him and thus endear himself to someone who, he hopes, will become his father-in-law? This may be the first time in all Wodehouse that we get the bones of this plot, deliberately pinched by Jeremy Garnet from books. But it interrupts the flow of the *Love Among the Chickens* story. Chapter XVII, 'Of a Sentimental Nature', and the first half of the following chapter are fifteen pages of polite poodle-faking in the fashion of Anthony Hope's 1899 *Dolly Dialogues*. By 1921 Dornford Yates would, one might have thought, have killed it as a technique for Wodehouse. Tom Chase, R.N., the dashing young lieutenant who is Garnet's apparent rival for Phyllis's love, may in 1906 have been a pleasantly fresh type; but in 1921, through no fault of Wodehouse's, he must have been sounding a bit like Berry and Boy Pleydell or any of Milne's Playmates.

'Hullo, so you're back,' I said.
'You've discovered my secret,' he admitted; 'will you have a cigar or a coconut?'

and

'I never make mistakes,' Mr Chase replied. 'I am called Archibald the All-Right ...'

are from *Love Among the Chickens*, not *Berry and Co.*

Tom Chase, by the way, must be the first and last officer of any Service whom Wodehouse introduces, as such, except for farcical purposes. He is given quite a long speech describing naval goings-on at Malta, and his conversation has a peppering of naval images in it. He talks of Phyllis's father 'going off like a four-point-seven'. Also in *Love Among the Chickens* is the handyman-housekeeper, Beale, retired from the ranks of the Army. Wodehouse has one or two knowing and mildly Kiplingesque things to say about Beale: Beale's 'passion for truth had made him unpopular in three regiments'; Beale 'had supported life for a number of years on incessant Army beef'. Archie Moffam in *The Indiscretions of Archie* (1921) has a good deal to say about front-line fighting in the recent war. In *Jill the Reckless*, published the same fertile year, the heroine's Uncle Chris, a retired Major and a sympathetic mixture of Mr Micawber and Ukridge, thinks back to scenes of Army action, more in the Kipling manner. Faced with the imminent horror of proposing marriage to a wealthy American widow,

he felt as he had felt when a raw lieutenant in India, during his first hill campaign, when the etiquette of the service had compelled him to rise and walk up and down in front of his men under a desultory shower of jezail-bullets. He seemed to hear the damned things *whop-whopping* now ...

Garnet, in *Love Among the Chickens*, hearing Chase call Phyllis by her Christian name, assumed they were practically engaged. Was that still valid plot-making in 1921? It probably was. But as late as 1964, in *Frozen Assets*, it was surely an anachronism. The starchy English diplomat Henry Blake-Somerset questions Jerry Shoesmith about his acquaintance with Kay Christopher:

'So you and Miss Christopher were just shipboard acquaintances?'

'Yes.'

'The boat trip took how long?'

'Five days.'

'And she calls you by your first name! ...'

'Well, she calls *you* by your first name.'

'That,' said Henry rising, 'is no doubt because we are engaged to
be married ...'

These are small points, collected haphazard. It is conceivable that Wodehouse in 1921 was more knowledgeable of
what was old and new in 1921 than we can be more than half
a century later, but *Love Among the Chickens* remains a fairly
juvenile compilation of episodes – the funny tennis match, the
funny golf match, the funny dinner party, the funny boat-
upsetting. The book is important only because it introduces
us to Ukridge.

The main difference between the 1906–21 Ukridge and the
Ukridge of the later short stories is that Ukridge is married in
the first book, and unmarried ever afterwards. He meets
Millie and wins her love, and her aunt's agreement to their
marriage, in the last of the ten stories in *Ukridge* (1924). The
seven stories that have appeared since then have put Ukridge
in the pre-Millie state again. In one of the stories in *Ukridge*,
'No Wedding Bells for Him', Ukridge is trying to oil out
of his engagement to fat, giggly Mabel Price, of Balbriggan,
Peabody Road, Clapham Common. He says to Corky:

'I was just thinking that, if you were to write them an anonymous letter, accusing me of all sorts of things ... Might say I was
married already.'

'Not a bit of good.'

'Perhaps you're right,' said Ukridge gloomily ...

But we are used, by 1924, to the blithe clutch-slippings and
backfires of Wodehouse's time-machinery. The name of

Aunt Julia's butler changes from Oakshott to Barter to Baxter and back to Oakshott again. The Beale of *Love Among the Chickens* turns up again as Bowles, the man who keeps the digs where Corky lives and where Ukridge is given the freedom of the house (by Bowles). But Bowles, in the maturer Wodehouse manner, is now an ex-butler, not an ex-soldier.

Having used Ukridge as a supporting character the first time, Wodehouse found that he was full of 'capabilities'. He gave him star treatment, put his name in lights (the literary equivalent being the titles of the short stories in which he appeared), and built a company round him.

Jeremy Garnet, the narrator of *Love Among the Chickens*, had met Ukridge when they were both masters at the same prep school. But the Ukridge of the later stories was an Old Wrykynian, and Corky, Tupper and Looney Coote had all been at school with him. When Ukridge becomes, or is revealed as, an Old Wrykynian, you realize that he has put down a tap-root. Admittedly he had been sacked from Wrykyn. He broke bounds and rules one night to go to a Fair. He disguised himself in false beard and whiskers, but left his school cap on top of the whole mess, and was easily apprehended. But it is the old-school fellowship that makes Ukridge's limpet-rock, predator-prey relationship with Corky and Tuppy understandable and acceptable; and Corky is able to describe his old school friend with the ruthlessness that (outside a family) only an old school friendship really warrants. Shared incarceration at a boarding school produces some embarrassing and incompatible acquaintanceships; but, whatever the candour they encourage in the exchange of personalities, they trail inescapable loyalties. None saw this more clearly than Wodehouse, and no author has used and exaggerated the fact more deliberately, joyously and successfully than Wodehouse. But, whereas Bertie Wooster and his

Aubrey-Upjohn's-and-Eton friends play the Old School Loyalty gambit for farce (albeit as a convenient hinge in the plot), Wrykyn is a shade more serious. Mike Jackson, Sam Shotter, Ukridge, Tuppy, Looney and Corky are a little closer to Wodehouse's heart and further from his funny-bone. Subliminally, Wrykyn is Wodehouse's own school, Dulwich. When he puts Ukridge at Wrykyn, Ukridge is part of the inner family, and in the long run he will be rescued from his worst idiocies. This gives the reader a rewarding sense of security. He feels able to laugh the louder when Ukridge falls, because he knows Ukridge must be put on his feet again and all will be well, not only with Ukridge (temporarily maybe) but with his own old school conscience. So one's hope for a financially set-fair fade-out for Ukridge is valid. A pity Wodehouse never got round to it.

Ukridge is a thief, a blackmailer, a liar and a sponge. He alternates self-glorification with self-pity, and sometimes has a bout of both in the same paragraph. He is as full of precepts as a preacher in the pulpit and, like a preacher, he swoops from the particular to the general, scattering moral judgements. Ukridge himself is a total immoralist, and he dulls the moral sense in others. He is totally selfish. The most that can be said in his favour is that he has knocked round the world on tramp steamers from Naples to San Francisco, he is good with dogs, Bowles admires him and fawns on him, he is not a snob, and girls sometimes, and for short stretches, like him.

Corky at one point calls Ukridge the 'sternest of bachelors', but his success with girls is curiously believable. Certainly, after the first mendacious build-up, the girls tend to get caught and crushed, with Ukridge, in the machinery of truth and justice. But Ukridge never lets a girl down as he lets Corky and Tuppy and his other male friends down – at the drop, Tuppy might complain, of a top-hat. Ukridge never fascinates in order to speculate. When he gets engaged to

Myrtle Bayliss, daughter of the Sussex jute-king, it is through love and not for her money. When he tries to beat the Bart to the favours of Mabel of Onslow Square, it is for love, and not for money or security. Even when he finds himself talked, by her family, into an engagement with Mabel of Clapham Common, he cannot just walk out of the embarrassing involvement, as any strong-minded, sensible rogue would. He is hobbled by the Code. To quote *Jill the Reckless* again: when Sir Derek Underhill breaks his engagement to Jill, Wally Mason, the Anglo-American hero, says to Freddie Rooke:

'I can't understand you, Freddie. If ever there was a fellow that might have been expected to take the only possible view of Underhill's behaviour in this business, I should have said it was you. You're a public-school man. You've mixed all the time with decent people ... Yet it seems to have made absolutely no difference in your opinion of this man Underhill that he behaved like an utter cad ...'

This suggests that Ukridge's attempts to save Mabel Price's fat face, and to get their engagement broken *by her*, may be a last enchantment, a last fleck of a cloud of glory, that Ukridge trails from Wrykyn days.

If the 'bewilderingly pretty' Millie (with whom Ukridge fell in love on an Underground train, at first sight and without knowing her South Kensington and knightly background) ever reads the stories of Stanley's previous involvements with the two Mabels, 'poor little Dora', and Myrtle Bayliss, she will undoubtedly believe every lying word of Stanley's protestations that he has been traduced by his snake-in-the-grass friend Corky; that these are foul aspersions made by a struggling penny-a-liner just to sell to a magazine; that one of these days he, Stanley, will sue the magazine for slander and everything else available and that this is his big chance of achieving the capital which will lead to a stupendous fortune. We get the cosy impression that Millie Ukridge still, after about fifty years of misty marriage, probably thinks Stanley a king among men, and believes he had come to her in that Underground train clean and unsullied by any previous romances.

It is a great tribute to Corky/Wodehouse that he can make such an anti-social menace as Ukridge appealing. There is not a word of sentimentality in the Ukridge stories, but they have a positive charm. They are, in technique of construction and writing, Wodehouse short stories at their springtime best. They are vintage stuff. They are extremely funny, and yet you feel that Corky, the narrator, is not a humorist. He is a dry commentator, incisive and objective. It is his subject, Ukridge, and Ukridge's story, that make the laughs. You are scarcely conscious that Ukridge is being brilliantly presented and his story brilliantly told: you are so taken with the man in front of the floodlights that you forget the man behind them.

But keep half an eye on Corky. He is really a very interesting background character. He is modest and amusing about his go-anywhere-write-anything trade of Pleasing Editors, but perfectly sure that this is the work he wants to be in. He is fallible and flatterable (he goes and helps Ukridge and Boko at their electioneering largely because he wants to hear the crowds singing the noble election jingle which he has composed for Boko; he falls completely for Ukridge's Millie and her 'Stanley has been telling me what friends you and he are. He is devoted to you'). But he is able to get tough when annoyed. His description of the Pen and Ink Club dance in 'Ukridge Sees Her Through' has, below its alert descriptions of sound, smells, gilt chairs and potted palms, a cold anger. Here for the first time Wodehouse rolls his sleeves up against the Phonies of the Pen. Charlton Prout, the sleek, stout secretary of the Club, whose main relish is pushing his own books and excluding from membership authors who lack 'vision', gets Corky's dagger between the ribs. He gets Miss Julia Ukridge's own wrath later, as a blunt instrument on the side of the head. Corky, having stage-managed Miss Ukridge's attack on Prout, tiptoes away, his heart bleeding delightedly.

Ukridge is to some extent a walking parody of careers-thinking by the young, careers-talk *to* the young by headmasters, uncles and self-made business tycoons interviewed by the magazines, and careers-fantasies encouraged by the fiction in the other pages of the same magazines. 'Vision, and the big, broad, flexible outlook' comes from headmasters, uncles and tycoons in print. The rich uncle from Australia, the rich aunt in Wimbledon, the lonely millionaire who needs a secretary, the bright business idea that leads to fortune – these are from the fiction pages. The only young man with a steady profession in the Ukridge stories – George Tupper of the Foreign Office – is treated as a bit of a bore. He had written sentimental poetry in the School Magazine, and was always starting subscription lists and getting up memorials and presentations. He had 'an earnest, pulpy heart'. Ukridge could get fivers out of him with a sure touch.

Orwell in his Essay on Wodehouse has pointed out that the first object of the Wodehouse hero is to find a soft spot for sitting pretty on financially; anything that brings the security of three meals a day is good enough for him. Ukridge seeks quick opulence, to finance eternal leisure for himself. His friends certainly hope he will find it, so that he will keep his hands out of their pockets. Even George Tupper thinks he has found an answer when he suggests him as secretary to his friend Bulstrode. It never seems to occur to anybody that Ukridge might become a common or garden daily-breader. Did nobody get at him when he was sacked from Wrykyn and try to put him in a Bank? Did Aunt Julia's inheritance loom always, preventing him from learning a trade because he saw the promise of getting her money in the end? If so, why was he so keen, while waiting for her money, to make a fortune for himself?

There are still people who say, sometimes in print, that Wodehouse wrote only about the rich and was, by inference, a snob. It is an absurd criticism, and the answer to it is either short and rude or long and boring. One of the pleasantest things about Ukridge is his complete un-class-consciousness. He is genuinely happy in the company of Battling Billson and the boxing fraternity. He is genuinely knowledgeable about the barmaids in Kennington:

> It appears that Billson has fallen in love with one of the barmaids at the Crown in Kennington. 'Not,' said Ukridge, so that all mis-apprehension should be avoided, 'the one with the squint. The other one. Flossie. The girl with yellow hair.'

Ukridge can go into criminal partnership with all the servants in his aunt's house while she's away, and treat them as equals. Yet he enjoys from Bowles, the ex-butler, fawning treatment that, by the rules of his guild, a butler only gives to one of the true gentry. Bowles doesn't treat Corky like that. He wouldn't treat Tupper like that. But Ukridge might be the fourth son of an earl as far as Bowles is concerned.

Love Among the Chickens is not the rounded Ukridge or the rounded Wodehouse. The short stories are the thing, and one wonders why Corky, who could write those stories, was still a struggling contributor to *Interesting Bits* at thirty bob a time. There is some beautiful translation of ideas into words in the 1924 collection *Ukridge*. Corky, thrown on to his ear from the pub in the Ratcliff Highway of the East End, is picked up by Billson and, in the process, 'gets a sort of general impression of bigness and blue serge'. And the barman, later ejected by the avenging Billson, 'did a sort of backward foxtrot across the pavement'. Corky, stranded with Flossie the barmaid's ghastly mother with the terrible hat, suggests that they go to Westminster Abbey: 'I had a fleeting notion, which a moment's reflection exploded before it could bring me much comfort, that women removed their hats in Westminster Abbey.' Corky's reaction to the caricature of Boko Lawlor, put up by his enemies in the Redbridge election, is: 'You could see at a glance that here was one who, if elected, would do his underhand best to cut down the Navy, tax the poor man's food, and strike a series of blows at the very root of the home . . .' Boko himself, towards the end of the electioneering, is speaking 'with a husky confidence' in his success. Finally, in that same story, there is Corky's description of the smell coming up on to the platform at the monster meeting at the Associated Mechanics' Hall – 'a mixed scent of dust, clothes, orange-peel, chalk, wood, plaster, pomade and Associated Mechanics'.

In the seven Ukridge short stories that have appeared since *Ukridge*, Corky only narrates one in its entirety. That's 'Buttercup Day'. For the other six, after a page or two of introduction by Corky in the manner of The Oldest Member or Mr Mulliner, Ukridge takes over in double quotes. Ukridge's language and manner of narration are racy and wonderful, but the note of farce is more strongly stressed than in the earlier stories where Corky is the 'I' character. Ukridge has an ebullient style, of forceful parody, injured self-pity, strongly emotional prejudices and cool justification of egregious immorality. Ukridge, that 'human blot'; that 'foe of the human race'; that 'hell-hound'; that giver of false names 'as an ordinary business precaution'; that man with one pair of trousers who spent the night in jail on a plank bed and was – an indignity even for him – forcibly washed by the authorities; that visionary, that manic-depressive, that moralizing immoralist ('. . . I don't know, Corky, if you have ever done the fine dignified thing, refusing to accept money because it was tainted and there wasn't enough of it, but I have always noticed on these occasions ...') – Ukridge is one of the great Wodehouse creations.

IMAGES

Whenever I meet Ukridge's Aunt Julia I have the same curious illusion of having just committed some particularly unsavoury crime and – what is more – of having done it with swollen hands, enlarged feet, and trousers bagging at the knee on a morning when I had omitted to shave.

*

Too often, when you introduce a ringer into a gaggle of Pekes, there ensues a scrap like New Year's Eve in Madrid; but tonight, after a certain amount of tentative sniffing, the home team issued their O.K., and he left them all curled up in their baskets like so many members of The Athenaeum.

*

He resembled a minor prophet who had been hit behind the ear with a stuffed eel-skin.

*

The Duke's moustache was rising and falling like seaweed on an ebb-tide.

*

'I'm not speaking to you. I wouldn't speak to you if your shirt were on fire.'

*

He gazed at the girl like an ostrich goggling at a brass door-knob.

*

He felt like a man who, chasing rainbows, has had one of them suddenly turn and bite him in the leg.

*

Well, you know what the Fulham Road's like. If your top-hat blows off into it, it has about as much chance as a rabbit at a dog-show.

*

There is something about a Welsh voice when raised in song that no other voice seems to possess ... a creepy, heart-searching quality that gets right into a man's inner consciousness and stirs it up with a pole.

5

LORD EMSWORTH AND BLANDINGS

Something Fresh (1915), *A Damsel in Distress* (1919), so nearly a Blandings novel that it should be read in the Blandings sequence, *Leave it to Psmith* (1923), *Summer Lightning* (1929), *Heavy Weather* (1933), *Uncle Fred in the Springtime* (1939), *Full Moon* (1947), *Pigs Have Wings* (1952), *Service With a Smile* (1962), *Galahad at Blandings* (1965) and *A Pelican at Blandings* (1969). Those are the novels. Six short stories set at Blandings occur in *Blandings Castle* (1935), one in *Lord Emsworth and Others* (1937), one in *Nothing Serious* (1950) and one in *Plum Pie* (1966).

THE LONG ENTRY on Homer in my edition of the *Encyclopaedia Britannica* is by the late Professor Gilbert Murray. In 1957 Murray said: 'When I became ninety, many telegrams came to congratulate or perhaps condole with me. The first was from the Prime Minister of Australia. The second from the Prime Minister of England. The third from P. G. Wodehouse. I have a great admiration for Wodehouse and the sequence gratified me.'

Murray did not bring any references to Wodehouse into his Encyclopaedia article on Homer, but I have heard Oxford dons elaborate a theory that, quite apart from Murray's admiration for both, there is a mystical communion between the two authors so widely separated by the centuries. These Senior Common Room scholiasts (the *Oxford English Dictionary* defines a scholiast as an ancient commentator upon a classical writer, so I have the *mot juste*) say that Homer and Wodehouse write, with deliberate artistic purpose, about comparable societies, lordly or near-lordly, past, almost timeless, and yet in certain respects engagingly anachronistic; that each author writes a private language, rich in imagery, allusions, repetitions, formulaic expressions and suppressed quotations; that if the sub-title of *The Iliad* was *The Wrath of Achilles*, the sub-title of any *Omnibus* of Bertie Wooster's writings could well be *The Wrath of Aunt Agatha*. And so on.

Personally I would add to the dons' spot passages a quotation from T. E. (Lawrence of Arabia) Shaw's Introduction to his translation of *The Odyssey*. Shaw was writing of the sort of man he deduced, from internal evidence, the author to have been. The italics are mine. The parallels are remarkable:

... a bookworm, no longer young, living from home, a mainlander, city-bred, domestic ... a dog-lover ... fond of poetry, a great, if uncritical, reader ... with limited sensuous range, but an exact eyesight which gave him all his pictures ... tender charity of heart and head for serving-men ... the associate of menials, making himself their friend and defender by understanding ... loved the rural scene. No farmer, he has learnt the points of a good olive tree [*for Wodehouse read 'pig' or 'pumpkin' for 'olive tree'*] ... He has sailed upon and watched the sea ... seafaring not being his trade [*Wodehouse had been destined for the Navy as a boy*]. Neither landlubber nor stay-at-home nor ninny ... He makes a hotch-potch of periods ... pages steeped in a queer naïvety ... sprinkled tags of epic across his pages ... very bookish, this house-bred man ... verbal felicity ... recurring epithets ... the tale was the thing ...

It is at Blandings Castle that Wodehouse seems to offer his Homeric parallels most noticeably, particularly in the matters of trophies and counters of exchange.

There is no money in Homer, of course. And of course many of Wodehouse's characters have it in plenty, But, especially at Blandings, cash and coin are immanent rather than actual. The counters of exchange at Blandings are generally of the order of the Homeric *keimelia* (the possessions that represented 'prestige-wealth', that changed hands but were never 'cashed': the armour and the trophies; iron, gold, cauldrons and tripods). The plot-making *keimelia* at Blandings are less often amounts of cash than items of prestige-wealth such as pigs, pumpkins, vicarages, manuscripts of Memoirs, jobs as secretary, air-guns and scarabs. Most Wodehouse plots are variations of Hunt the Slipper. But there is something about aristocratic Blandings that makes one feel that here is the Lord's or Wimbledon of the game. Freddie Threepwood's sackful of rats was a case in point.

'I have here, Aunt Georgiana,' said Freddie Threepwood, holding up a sack in the amber drawing-room at the after-dinner coffee hour, 'a few simple rats.' This, though Beach removed the sack unopened, was enough to put an end to Gertrude's infatuation with Orlo, the side-whiskered tenor, and make her beefy clergyman fiancé appear in his true lights as a dog-fight-stopper and a king among men. For devious but sufficient reasons, it got 'Beefy' Bingham a vicarage at Much Matchingham too, and thus the ability to marry Gertrude. It got Freddie well placed to land the dog-biscuit contract from Gertrude's mother. It got the plot unravelled and the happy endings. The sack of rats was 'the goods', a typical item of Blandings prestige-wealth.

In shape and size and messuages Wodehouse's Blandings Castle owes a good deal to his boyhood memory of Corsham, the stately home of the Methuens near Bath. The young Pelham, spending school holidays with a clergyman uncle nearby, was taken to Corsham to skate on the lake, and the image of the great house remained on the retina of his inward eye. And when, in his early thirties, a resident alien in New York, writing away for dear life and for any American editor who would buy anything, Wodehouse decided to try farce about the English aristocracy, he called his stately home Blandings, his chatelain Lord Emsworth and his story *Something New* (*Something Fresh* in England, 1915).

If Wodehouse studied Corsham only in the skating months, he has been seasonally unfaithful to his memories in the books. Admittedly the weather was cold when Ashe Marson arrived at Blandings in *Something Fresh*. But thereafter, book after book, it seems always to be high summer weather, with tea under the cedars on the lawn, hammocks and deck-chairs, the rose garden a glory and the lake calling the ninth earl down for a bathe. Admittedly Wodehouse is not such a knowledgeable gardener as Lord Emsworth, and tulip-time, rhododendron-time, rose-time, hollyhock-time and pumpkin-time are all much the same to him. Admittedly the house-party in *Something Fresh* is timed weirdly as 'falling between the hunting and the shooting seasons'. The point is that, apart from hot thunderstorms, Blandings basks and, when Lord Emsworth potters out to commune with his pig, he puts on a hat but never an overcoat.

Emsworth is, in fact, a town on the border of Sussex and Hampshire, in a district rich in place-names that have acquired glory in song or legend. Hilaire Belloc's Ha'naker and Duncton Hill are near-by, and Wodehouse has taken from the villages of Bosham and Warblington names for Lord Emsworth's heir (Lord Bosham) and one of his many sisters (Lady Ann Warblington). Blandings Castle in fiction is in Shropshire. Obviously Belpher Castle in Hampshire, the setting for *A Damsel in Distress* (1919), is, in the literary fourth dimension, somewhere on the Emsworth–Corsham–Blandings road. To all intents and purposes *A Damsel in Distress* is a Blandings novel. Lord Marshmoreton in it is an echo of Lord Emsworth, Lord Belpher of Lord Bosham, Lady Caroline Byng of Lady Constance Keeble, Reggie Byng of Freddie Threepwood, Keggs the butler of Beach the butler, and Macpherson the gardener of McAllister the gardener. In fact, Lord Marshmoreton's family name appears to be Bosham. His second son, Freddie Bosham, marries a Phyllis Jackson of 'the Jackson jam-making family'. In the second Blandings novel, *Leave it to Psmith*, you have Mike Jackson married to Phyllis, step-daughter of Lady Constance Keeble.

When an author in a hurry digs down for some names for characters, he will occasionally draw a duplicate. Wodehouse would get his types together before he knew their names, and churn them up into a plot before he knew where the events would happen. He drew his names out of a hat, but in the case of *A Damsel in Distress* forgot that some of these were old ones that had got put back after the last draw. He had not, at the stage of *A Damsel in Distress*, seen saga possibilities in the Blandings set-up of *Something Fresh*. All he knew was that he was happy and at home in an English castle, with a widower earl in the garden, his tough sister as chatelaine, his fat butler in the pantry sipping port, and assorted secretaries, chorus girls and impostors making a plot.

When Blandings assumed saga proportions, the castle became simply a roof under which any member of the Emsworth family could stay and invite friends to stay, where errant sons and nieces were incarcerated (the incarcerated sometimes referred to Blandings as a Bastille, sometimes as a Devil's Island) to make them cool off from love affairs, where detectives were summoned to watch pigs or jewels, brain-specialists were summoned to watch defective dukes, and librarians, valets and secretaries were hired and fired. Blandings is a place where things happen, with lots of time on everybody's hands for things to happen in, lots of bedrooms to put up unlimited *dramatis personae*, lots of corridors, shrubberies, terraces, gardens, pig-sties, water-meadows and parkland for exits and entrances; and the hamlet of Market Blandings two miles away, with plenty of pubs and inns (The Emsworth Arms, The Wheatsheaf, The Waggoners' Rest, The Beetle and Wedge, The Stitch in Time, The Blue Cow, The Blue Boar, The Blue Dragon and The Jolly Cricketers) from which outlying plotters can plan their approaches to the Castle stage.

Rather too close is the village of Much Matchingham, home of the dreaded Sir Gregory Parsloe-Parsloe, so often unworthily suspected by Lord Emsworth and his brother Galahad of trying to do harm to Blandings pig or pumpkin that, in the printed synopsis at the beginning of *Pigs Have Wings*, Herbert Jenkins said '. . . on previous occasions the unscrupulous baronet has made determined attempts to nobble Lord Emsworth's favourite pig.' Not true. Sir Gregory was always innocent of the strategies which the Blandings brothers imputed to him, and Herbert Jenkins ought to have remembered it. Poor Sir Gregory. His only sins (other than overeating) were that, in his hot pre-title youth, he had, or Galahad thought he had, nobbled Galahad's dog Towser before a rat-killing contest and, as a bloated baronet, he had taken on as his pig-man, at higher wages, George Cyril Wellbeloved, who had been guardian, chef and caterer to Lord Emsworth's zeppelin-shaped Black Berkshire sow, the bemedalled Empress of Blandings.

Galahad Threepwood has spoken frankly and sharply to Sir Gregory of his past known, and present suspected, skulduggeries. Lord Emsworth has never yet accused the baronet to his face. But the living of Much Matchingham is in Lord Emsworth's gift, and it was with cunning pleasure that Lord Emsworth gave the Rev. 'Beefy' Bingham the vicarage there, trusting that this ham-handed man of God would be as sharp a thorn in Sir Gregory's flesh as he had been in Lord Emsworth's when he had been infesting the Castle and courting Lord Emsworth's niece, Gertrude.

Lord Emsworth, euphoric, amiable, but bone-headed ninth Earl, has changed little in the sixty publishing years between *Something Fresh* and the last unfinished novel. He no longer seems to collect things, and his Museum, much in evidence in the first book, is no longer a show-room of the Castle. He is no longer a patron of Christie's in London. His younger son, Freddie, formerly a pain in the neck to his father, no longer gets into debt or writes poetry to chorus girls. Marriage to the daughter of an American millionaire (Aggie, *née* Donaldson, was, incidentally, a relative of the Blandings head gardener, McAllister) has made a man of Freddie. In *Full Moon* (1947) Freddie shows his new-found manhood by turning and rending a roomful of tough aunts, uncles and millionaires who are trying to treat him like the worm he had been. It is a great defiance. Freddie is a hard-working and keen Vice-President of his father-in-law's dog-biscuit business now. In fact, Lord Emsworth, who had long despised his son as a drone and a wastrel, in a recent short story ('Birth of a Salesman') was nettled to find his son was now despising *him* for much the same reasons. Lord Emsworth was able to take steps and show himself a salesman and go-getter in America and on American lines.

Lady Constance Keeble is still a threat to her brother's peace. She is the sister (there is a host of them) who most frequently rules the Blandings roost, imports too many literary young men to stay, insists on choosing her brother Clarence's secretaries for him and wants to retire Beach the butler. She is Rupert Baxter's champion. She sees nothing but worth in that gimlet-eyed, lantern-jawed efficiency expert and, if she can't ring him in again as Lord Emsworth's secretary, she rings him in as tutor to Lord Emsworth's schoolboy grandson. Lord Emsworth who, in the first book, was not wholly anti-Baxter, has always since been sure he was potty, a judgement which Baxter reciprocates on Lord Emsworth. Baxter has suffered much indignity at Blandings – the cold tongue, raided from the larder, against the cheek in the dark, and thought to be a corpse; the hail of air-gun pellets against the trousers; the egg, hurled into outer darkness by the Duke of

Dunstable, which hit Baxter in the face; the flower-pot episode and the yellow pyjamas; the pig parked in his caravan; the perjured persiflage of Lord Ickenham. But Baxter feels, deep in his lonely soul, I think, that the Castle is a shambles and Lord Emsworth needs him as managing director.

Lord Emsworth is stated to have been at Eton in the 1860s. The statement was made at a time when Wodehouse had not learnt to avoid dates. Lord Emsworth comes of a long-lived family. His father, revealed in *A Pelican at Blandings* to have been irascible and domineering, was killed hunting at seventy-seven. His uncle Robert had lived to nearly ninety, his cousin Claude to eighty-four, when he broke his neck trying to jump a five-barred gate (presumably on a horse). Lord Emsworth's age for Wodehouse's purposes is pegged at just short of sixty – not too old for Galahad to be able, for his private ends, to impute to him an infatuation with a young girl; old enough to be psychosomatically deaf and forgetful, so that his sister Connie and other characters can shout the plot and the plotters to him in a way most comforting to the unalert reader. But Lord Emsworth is too old ever to be moulded by Baxter, or made to enjoy his stiff collars, speech-makings, visits to London and other ghastly duties that his sister imposes on him. Give him his flowers to sniff, and his pig loading in her calories; give him Whiffle to read in the evenings, and a glass of port; keep his multitudinous sisters and all other relatives (with the exception of Galahad) away from him. That's all he asks. And that's what he gets, happily, at the end of the last published novel. Lord Emsworth is one of the very nicest lords in literature.

If you come to suspect from the insistence of the Duke of Dunstable and the exasperations of sister Connie that Lord Emsworth is pottier than the normal run of the Wodehouse aristocracy of England, you might reflect on how many members of his family have made him trustee for their sons and daughters. Possibly the Blandings Estate looks after all the family, from Galahad downwards, and Lord Emsworth has, simply by primogeniture, not by merit of brain, to be the final arbiter of who gets what inheritance and when. Potty or not himself, Lord Emsworth had married a wife with insanity in her own family. She herself appears to have had delusions of poverty. Her only recorded words are 'Oh dear, oh dear, oh dear', spoken when she had given birth to her second son, and occasioned by her fear that his education would be a great expense. An uncle of hers had thought he was a loaf of bread, and had first announced the fact (or fancy) at Blandings. Lord Bosham, heir to Blandings and the Emsworth title, is pretty potty in his turn. He has had a breach of promise case in his day, he has bought a gold brick, he has lent Lord Ickenham his wallet, and he talks almost total drivel. With Lord Emsworth, Lord Bosham, the Duke of Dunstable and Lord Ickenham all together at Blandings (*Uncle Fred in the Springtime*), the castle becomes an inferno of potty peers. But Wodehouse holds by the cheerful view that there is pottiness in all the most aristocratic English families, and he is frank and fearless about mentioning its incidences among the forebears of his favourites. (He also indicates that pottiness occurs in the best American families, too: the millionaire Baileys in *The Coming of Bill* and the millionaire Stokers in *Thank You, Jeeves*.)

The potty Threepwood genes have gone more to the males of the young generation than to the females. Except for Veronica Wedge, that lovely dumb blonde who might have come out of an Evelyn Waugh novel, all the Emsworth nieces are girls of mettle, and they tend to marry the nice young men of their own choice, rather than the vapid peers of their Aunt Connie's. Ronnie Fish may have, in his Uncle Galahad's words, looked like a minor jockey with scarlatina, but he married Sue Brown, the charming chorus-girl daughter of Dolly Henderson, who had charmed Galahad and Lord Emsworth when she had been singing at the Tivoli in pink tights. Sue is one of the best in the longish line of nice Wodehouse chorus girls, and Ronnie is lucky to have won her, and to have kept her against all the slings and arrows operated by his disapproving mother. I forget now what typically Wodehouse future Ronnie and Sue face together. Ronnie is going to be a bookmaker, or run a roadhouse or a night club, or keep an onion-soup-bar, or start a gymnasium, or breed dogs, or farm. He has got his girl. He has got his capital out of Uncle Clarence. He has got his eye on a job somewhat more life-enhancing than working for Lord Tilbury. He has driven off in the two-seater towards the happiness-for-two reserved for most of the young, however blah, in the last pages of a Wodehouse novel.

At any stately home the size of Blandings there is an interesting life teeming behind the green baize doors. You should re-read *Something Fresh* to see this described from a servant's-eye view. Ashe Marson (a detective story-writer) and Joan Valentine (a journalist) represent the main young-love interest. They are both visiting Blandings, for shady reasons, as servants. Ashe is valet to Mr Peters, a dyspeptic American millionaire, and Joan is taken on as lady's maid to Aline Peters, the millionaire's daughter. It is through Ashe's eyes that we get our first close-up view of Sebastian Beach, the Blandings butler, with his appearance of imminent apoplexy, his dignified inertia, his fat hands, his fruity voice 'like tawny port made audible', his fear of Socialism, his corns, his ingrowing toenails, his swollen joints, his nervous headaches, his blurred vision and weak stomach. Most of these complaints are forgotten in subsequent books, possibly because Beach never again has the opportunity to talk about them to another servant. In *Something Fresh* we first meet Mrs Twemlow, the housekeeper, and we count the heads of Merridew, the under-butler, James and Alfred the footmen, a flock of male guests' gentlemen and lady guests' ladies. We hear of the chef, the groom of the chambers, Thorne the head gardener (McAllister doesn't come on till a later book), the chauffeur, the boot-boy, and a whole host of laundry maids, housemaids, parlourmaids, scullerymaids, kitchenmaids and between-maids. And the ordering of their lives is described with as much detail and ten times as much humour as in Victoria Sackville-West's *Edwardians*, George Moore's *Esther Waters* or anywhere in Dornford Yates. In later books we shall take the servants' hall for granted, and go only to Beach's pantry for port. In *Something Fresh* is a survey of the Servants' Hall which shows us that Wodehouse knew his stuff about below-stairs grandeur, loved the grandees and sympathized with the whole company, from butler to buttons.

Blandings footmen come and go in later books; the office of attendant to the Empress, pig-man or pig-girl, is apt to change hands dramatically; Beach rounds out into being a force for good in every plot, even if he does have to put a green baize cloth over his bullfinch's cage when young lovers talk, or bribe, him into stealing his master's pig. Beach possesses the finest library of thrillers in Shropshire, having inherited Freddie Threepwood's collection when Freddie went West. Beach is no innocent. In really critical moments (such as when Lord Emsworth decides to grow a beard) Beach will regretfully decide to resign his long-held post. Sometimes, tried just short of resignation, he will drink brandy in his pantry instead of port.

His physical ailments forgotten in the later books, Beach remains a rock, a stately procession of one, a sportsman and a sentimentalist. For the people he likes he will do anything. For Lord Emsworth and his niece Angela, Beach chants 'Pig-hoo-o-o-o-ey!' to the Empress. He brings Galahad a whisky and soda all the way to the Empress's sty. He gets kissed by Sue Brown for all the help he has given her and her Ronnie in their troubled wooing. It's a pity that the autograph manuscript of Galahad's memoirs was consumed by the Empress, because there were mentions of Beach in its chapters. Beach, and Beach's mother in Bournemouth (or was it Eastbourne?), would have been pleased to see the family name honoured in print. It was good, though, that Beach had time to read in the manuscript the story of Gregory Parsloe and the prawns. It is possibly the only time in Wodehouse that we see a butler really laugh. 'HA ... HOR ... HOO!' he roared, admittedly believing himself alone and unobserved. (Wodehouse died without telling *us* the story of those prawns, or of Lord Ickenham and Pongo at the Dog Races.)

Is the Gutenberg Bible still in the Blandings Library? A copy, described as probably the last in private hands, was, in 1974, being offered by a dealer at a sum of Swiss francs equivalent to £1 million sterling. Does Galahad still wind clocks when time hangs heavy? Is Blandings now frequently open to the public? There are bedrooms in it so magnificent that they have never been slept in since the first Queen Elizabeth's day. Is Jno. Banks still the Market Blandings hairdresser? At the Emsworth Arms (G. Ovens, Propr.) is the 'large, pale, spotted waiter' still waiting, and is there still the smell of 'cold beef, beer, pickles, cabbage, gravy soup, boiled potatoes and very old cheese' in the coffee-room? Does the boiled turbot still come up as a 'rather obscene-looking mixture of bones and eyeballs and black mackintosh'? And does the inkpot still contain that 'curious sediment that looked like black honey'? Does Blandings still run the old Hispano-Suiza car? And what are the trains to and from Paddington these days? Wodehouse was constantly changing their times, and it is a constant astonishment to me that so many impostors managed to catch them and arrive safely to get down to their plottings at the Castle.

Wodehouse was more than half-way through a new Blandings

novel when he died. Sixteen chapters are fairly complete in typescript, and Wodehouse's autograph notes take it, in scenario, to the end – a total of twenty-two chapters. He had not given it a title.

A walk round the deserted workshop shows the tools bright and sharp, even if the product itself is taking a recognizably old (see *Service with a Smile*, published in 1962) shape. Galahad Threepwood and Frederick Lord Ickenham have long been nearly interchangeable. Both can 'tell the tale' or 'deviate from the truth' with fluency and the full approval of the author and his readers. Lord Ickenham was rampant at Blandings in *Service with a Smile*. Here it is Galahad slogging it out, across Lord Emsworth's limp body, with their sister Florence ... a new sister, which, with the other new one, Diana, in this book, gives them ten sisters in all, and all menaces except Diana. Diana's first husband, a big game hunter, far too handsome and a bit of a rotter (as most handsome men are in Wodehouse), has been eaten by a lion. Now she is going to marry an old adorer who has, since abandoning the chase of Diana to the lion-hunter, become Chancellor of the Exchequer. As usual, the job of being secretary to Lord Emsworth is open, and, as usual, that leaves the door open to an impostor, whom Galahad is instantly ready to usher in through it. The Empress's portrait is to be painted for the Gallery. (Who will paint her? That's another door open for an impostor.) Hammocks, deck chairs and their required weather are all there, all the time. Blandings now has, or it is now revealed that Blandings has, a croquet lawn, and Galahad refers to it in the same sort of erotic terms as the rose-garden ... a strong attraction for young lovers.

So far, so good: sixteen out of twenty-two chapters. In his notes Wodehouse communed with himself on work done and work to be done. When a chapter seemed to him ripe and ready, he marked it 'Aziz', i.e. to remain as is. Most of the first sixteen chapters are marked 'Aziz'. In his notes for the remaining six it looks as though he had a stolen necklace as a strong plot-twister in an earlier scenario. But he hadn't needed the necklace up to the end of Chapter 16, and we can assume that it had been counted out. There is a suggestion, marked with a query in Wodehouse's scribbled notes, that Beach the butler might be made the uncle of nice Jeff Bennison, who captures the love of nice young Vicky Underwood, the step-daughter of this new Threepwood sister, Florence. Florence is now a widow, but she had married Vicky's father, an American newspaper millionaire.

Jno. Robinson's station taxi is still chugging along. Beach's bullfinch is still in his cage in the pantry, and Beach still dispenses port there to his friends. At the pub near the station Ovens's homebrew is still a mocker for the thirsty after the long train journey from Paddington. There is a Bentley in the Castle garage. Galahad is ever the old Pelican. Lord Emsworth's son Freddie is rather the old silly ass of *Something Fresh* days than the go-getting dog-biscuit tycoon of the more recent novels and short stories.

The last chapter of *A Pelican at Blandings* (1969) had been a very happy requiem. The Empress in her bijou residence had turned in for the night. Voules the chauffeur was playing his harmonica somewhere. Beach brought Lord Emsworth and Galahad their dinner (leg of lamb, boiled potatoes and spinach, followed by well-jammed roly-poly pudding) in the Library. Lord Emsworth was wearing his old shooting coat with the holes in the elbows, and his feet were sensuously comfortable in bedroom slippers. Through the open window came the scent of stocks and tobacco flower. Constance, the Duke of Dunstable, assorted god-sons, impostors and pretty girls had all paired off and gone away. It seems a pity that Wodehouse should, five years later, get them all stirred up again in a further book. But perhaps Chapter 22 of the unfinished, unnamed novel would have been an even better ending to the Blandings revels and provided an even fonder last look at its cloud-capp'd towers. Evelyn Waugh in his tribute to Wodehouse on his eightieth birthday wrote 'For Wodehouse there has been no fall of Man: no "aboriginal calamity" ... the gardens of Blandings Castle are the original gardens from which we are all exiled.' Well, yes.

IMAGES

To Lord Emsworth the park and gardens of Blandings were the nearest earthly approach to Paradise. Freddie, chafing at captivity, mooned about them with an air of crushed gloom which would have caused comment in Siberia.

*

He was a vintage butler of obviously a very good year.

*

She spoke with the mildness of a cushat dove addressing another cushat dove from whom it is hoping to borrow money.

*

Bad moments of your life, the remembrance of which, as you are dropping off to sleep, banish that drowsy feeling and cause you to leap on the pillow like a gaffed salmon.

*

Imagine how some Master Criminal would feel, on coming down to do a murder at the Old Grange, if he found that not only was Sherlock Holmes putting in the weekend there, but Hercule Poirot as well.

*

Unlike the male codfish, which, suddenly finding itself the parent of three million five hundred thousand little codfish, cheerfully resolves to love them all, the British aristocracy is apt to look with a somewhat jaundiced eye on its younger sons.

*

John was in the grip of the peculiar numbed sensation, so like that caused by repeated blows on the head from a blunt instrument, which came to all but the strongest who met Lady Constance for the first time when she was feeling frosty. It was as though he had been for an extended period shut up in a frigidaire with the first Queen Elizabeth.

*

A small fair-haired girl who looked like a well dressed wood nymph.

*

Years before, when a boy, and romantic as most boys are, his lordship had sometimes regretted that the Emsworths, though an ancient clan, did not possess a Family Curse. How little he had suspected that he was shortly to become the father of it.

6

UNCLE FRED

The story 'Uncle Fred Flits By' in *Young Men in Spats* (1936), *Uncle Fred in the Springtime* (1939), *Uncle Dynamite* (1948), *Cocktail Time* (1958), *Service with a Smile* (1962).

LORD ICKENHAM leads the dance in four novels and a short story. He is an excellent invention, and worth a short, sharp look.

Wodehouse in *Performing Flea* refers to this sprightly old earl as 'a sort of elderly Psmith'. 'Don't *talk* so much!' said Freddie Threepwood to Psmith in *Leave it to Psmith*. 'Don't *talk* so much, Uncle Fred!' said Myra Schoonmaker in *Service with a Smile*. Lord Ickenham referred to himself in *Uncle Dynamite* as 'one of the hottest earls that ever donned a coronet'. He emerged, a rounded character, fully fledged and fully armed to deceive, in a short story, and it shows Wodehouse's pleasure in him that, though his next appearance was in a Blandings novel, he had his name in the title. He is a whirring dynamo of misrule. As a boy he was known as 'Barmy' and now, in what should be the autumn of his days, he plays the giddy goat with an irrepressible springtime frivolity. He is extremely kind at heart and, for his own amusement as much as anybody's, very funny. He is a sort of performing flea himself, and something of an analogue of Wodehouse the writer.

Frederick Altamont Cornwallis, fifth Earl of Ickenham, is in his middle-sixties, with iron-grey hair, a slim, youthful figure, an American wife (always off-stage) who tries to keep him under control ('American girls try to boss you. It's part

of their charm '), and a stately home, with far too many nude
statues in it, at Bishop's Ickenham in Hampshire. Luckily for
Barrie & Jenkins, Lady Ickenham occasionally let the fifth
earl go to London, for reputable reasons like the Eton and
Harrow match, though threatening to skin him with a blunt
knife if he didn't return on the dot. And occasionally she
herself departed for the South of France or the West Indies
to tend an ailing mother; which gave Lord Ickenham his
freedom to go A.W.O.L.

It is Lord Ickenham's nephew and heir, Pongo Twistleton-
Twistleton, who suffers most acutely from his Uncle Fred's
enlargements. Lord Ickenham claims that London brings out
all the best in him and is the only place where his soul can
expand like a blossoming flower and his generous nature find
full expression. Pongo has rooms in Albany – or had until
Uncle Fred saw to it that he married Sally Painter. Uncle
Fred descends on Pongo and, sooner or later, the trouble starts.
The first time, often referred to, but never reported in detail,
Uncle Fred had lugged Pongo to the Dog Races, and they
had been in the hands of the constabulary in ten minutes.
Lord Ickenham complained that they were letting a rather
neurotic type of man into the Force these days, and that on
this occasion a better stamp of magistrate would have been
content with a mere reprimand. But, as he had given his
name in court as George Robinson, of 14 Nasturtium Road,
East Dulwich (the first recorded of his many impersonations),
Lady Ickenham presumably never heard about it.

That his dear wife should hear about him is about the only
thing Lord Ickenham fears in this world. One must suppose
that the fine he had to pay in court, for himself and Pongo,
was not big enough to require a cheque. Lady Ickenham
believes in a strong centralized government and handles the
Ickenham finances. She gives her husband enough for golf-
balls, tobacco and self-respect. No more. Pongo, loyally

or spinelessly, doesn't sneak on his Uncle Fred to his Aunt Jane; but Pongo's sister Valerie, a girl of spirit, is quite prepared to threaten these reprisals when she finds her Uncle Fred interfering in her love-life. Uncle Fred is a keen match-maker, and, in bringing A and B together, he generally has to bust up their existing unsuitable engagement to C and D respectively. 'Help is a thing I am always glad to be of,' says this splendid old nuisance: his mother had been frightened by a Boy Scout.

Lord Ickenham is an intrepid impersonator. As a dis-simulator he has, when young, like all good Wodehouse elders, worn false moustaches and whiskers to baffle creditors. (Lord Ickenham says the Archbishop of Canterbury probably had to do the same when he was a young man.) But today he prefers simulation, or at least simply passing himself off as somebody else. He says, in fact, that he never feels comfortable going to stay at houses under his own name. It doesn't seem sporting. Played under the Wodehouse rules, this game isn't so foolhardily sporting as it sounds. An important Wodehouse subsumption is that the popular press, gossip columns and their photographers can be disregarded as a factor, or regarded as in baulk. Which means that, for the purposes of these stories, nobody who hasn't actually met Lord Ickenham needs know what he looks like. In *Uncle Fred in the Springtime* the old buster goes down to Blandings Castle, for a protracted stay, as Sir Roderick Glossop; and the reader accepts that Lord Bosham, the Duke of Dunstable, Aunt Connie and, more dangerously, Rupert Baxter will not know, from previous acquaintance, or from press photographs, either the fifth earl or the eminent loony doctor, and will thus take t'other for which. Shakespeare was equally blithe about his impersonation plots, but, date for date, with better reason, because, in the periods of which he wrote, portraiture was not reproducible in millions for daily breakfast-table inspection, nor was John Aubrey so widely read as Paul Slickey.

Lord Ickenham is a card, a joker ready to stand in for anybody in a full house. He has claimed that the only people he wouldn't be able to impersonate are a circus dwarf and Gina Lollobrigida. In the story 'Uncle Fred Flits By' he was driven to seek shelter from the rain in a suburban house, and he pretended to be (*a*) a vet come to clip the parrot's claws (Pongo was to be his deaf and dumb assistant. 'Tap your teeth with a pencil, and try to smell of iodoform!'), (*b*) a Mr Roddis and (*c*) a Mr Bulstrode – in that order as the plot developed, in the space of about one hour. In *Uncle Dynamite* he went down to the house of an Old School acquaintance, pretending, to one and all, to be Major Brabazon Plank, the famous explorer from Brazil. This worked easily and well until he met (*a*) the policeman who had arrested him at the Dog Races, and who knew him therefore to be George Robinson of East Dulwich, and (*b*) the real Major Brabazon Plank. The Old School acquaintance whom Lord Ickenham, then 'Barmy' Twistleton, had beaten with a fives bat as a boy, for bullying, was too dazed by all this imposture to matter much. Anyway, as so often in later Wodehouse books, the Old School acquaintance was preparing to stand for Parliament, which left him wide open for blackmail to keep his mouth tight shut. On general principles Lord Ickenham doesn't like to meet his Old School contemporaries. They tend to wear beards and be toothless, and this makes Lord Ickenham feel he must be forty if a day.

In *Uncle Fred in the Springtime* Lord Ickenham is not only himself impersonating Sir Roderick Glossop, but he takes with him to Blandings Polly Pott, a bookmaker's daughter, who has to pretend to be his (Lord Ickenham's) daughter, and his nephew Pongo, who has to pretend to be his secretary. In *Cocktail Time* Lord Ickenham becomes Inspector Jarvis of

Scotland Yard. If impersonation fails temporarily, he has a smooth technique with knock-out drops. 'It is madness to come to country houses without one's bottle of Mickey Finns' he says. He used these tranquillizers with effect at Blandings ('Pongo lit a reverent cigarette; he did not approve of his Uncle Fred, but he could not but admire his work'), and wished he had had them handy in *Uncle Dynamite*. He was in the Home Guard round Ickenham in the Second World War, and would probably have been a baffling underground fighter in the English Resistance had the invasion happened.

Lord Ickenham was a younger son who came into the title unexpectedly after twenty years in America, as a soda-jerker and cow-puncher among other pastimes. In a set piece of excellent buzzing dialogue with Sally Painter at Barribault's restaurant, he has told of his early struggles as a mere Hon., and how he later deservedly won through to being a haughty earl. You can't keep a good man down, is his opinion. And he is frank in his further opinion that he is a good man, *capable du tout*, especially in the springtime. He admits that he sometimes feels like a caged skylark at Ickenham, with Lady I. forbidding his sweetness-and-light-spreading excursions. 'There are no limits, literally none, to what I can accomplish in the springtime,' he says. In the noble sentence from the first story, repeated for reminder and emphasis in the later books, a Crumpet at The Drones says to his guest: 'I don't know if you happen to know what the word "excesses" means, but these are what Pongo's Uncle Fred from the country, when in London, invariably commits.' Since Wodehouse demands a country-house setting for most of his novels, Lord Ickenham commits excesses also at Blandings, Ashenden Manor and Hammer Hall.

Lord Ickenham provided the mature Wodehouse with some good new outlets. In his determination to whack amusement out of any situation that could be stood on its head and made to kick its heels in the air, he paralleled the unrepentant frivolity of his senescent author. A lifetime friend of Galahad Threepwood, Lord Ickenham is more of a practical joker than Gally, more of a licensed loony. He is the grown-up-school-boy-slightly-inebriated-undergraduate who inebriates himself especially with the exuberance of his own buzzing verbosity. He is the best buzzer in all Wodehouse. His joy in impersonation, lying and blackmail, his manic generation of muddle and mayhem as a challenge to his own powers of Houdini-like escape – these enabled Wodehouse to ravel his plots into webs apparently hopelessly tangled, and then, in magical dénouement, to shake them out into happy endings, with all the right couples paired off. And, although one must at all times and at all costs avoid accusing Wodehouse of offering us messages, Lord Ickenham in his middle sixties is a high-stepping proof that, for the elderly as for the young, the brow should be worn low and unfurrowed, the hat should be perched on the side of the head and the shirt should not be stuffed.

Also – and perhaps this really was a message – rank is but a penny stamp. I had a feeling that, in *Uncle Fred in the Springtime*, Lord Ickenham's friend 'Mustard' Pott, a real vulgarian in name and nature, was a shade over the odds of credibility, and that, even though he had that charming daughter, happily paired in the end to the boxer-poet, Ricky, nephew of a Duke, 'Mustard' would not in fact have been so democratically accepted at The Drones and at Blandings as Wodehouse asked us to believe. Still, if 'Mustard' Pott was a bit of a strain, he was a strain in the right egalitarian direction. But when, in *Cocktail Time*, Lord Ickenham's ex-ship's steward, now butler, friend Albert Peasemarch won the love of Phoebe Wisdom, sister of the pompous Q.C., and thus half-sister of Lady Ickenham herself, I found myself hardening in my suspicions that this was a sop to the American reading

public. I was inspecting *Cocktail Time* again just when
Behrman's articles on Max Beerbohm were appearing in
The New Yorker. Behrman, the American, comments on
Beerbohm's long-felt unease about servants and servanthood.

> In all times, of course, domestic service has been a demoralising
> state of existence. To belong to one class and to live in close contact
> with another, to 'live hardly' in contemplation of more or less
> luxury and idleness, to dissimulate all your natural feelings be-
> cause you are forbidden to have them, and to simulate other feelings
> because they are expected of you – this has always been an un-
> natural life, breeding always the same bad qualities ... We, during
> the last thirty years, have been smiling over the blessings of
> universal education, and we are just beginning to realise, with
> horror, that we ought to have postponed that system until all menial
> duties could be performed by machinery.

This view isn't exclusive to Beerbohm and Americans,
but self-service and 'do-it-yourself' are philosophies deeper
rooted, and with sanctions stronger than merely pragmatic, in
a land where people's grandfathers were fighting each other
about Slavery.

So my thoughts about *Cocktail Time* ran, and still run, like
this: that after more than fifty Wodehouse books about the
English nobility and gentry, however feeble-witted, with their
butlers and valets, however superior, complaints may have
been levelled by captious American critics that this kind of
English master/man relationship was not only ludicrous but
regrettable: that Wodehouse, who did not, thank heaven,
ride either the tygers of wrath or the horses of instruction,
might conceivably, for *Cocktail Time*, have decided to crack
the pattern that his own books had genially set – just to show
it could be done – and that therefore the butler courts the
chatelaine and wins her, and Lord Ickenham himself, having
given the match his encouragement, ends up by going off on
a toot with the said butler in London, this being the ultimate

proof that the friendship between earl and manservant was a friendship between equals.

I feel no difficulty about Lord Uffenham, the amusing but rather common peer who sets the pace in *Money in the Bank*, and is operative in *Something Fishy*. Lord Uffenham in *Money in the Bank* is an absent-minded, pear-shaped pa-man in reduced circumstances, who lets his ancestral Shipley Hall to a rich tenant and hires himself to her (unknown to her) as a butler. The later Uncle Fred novel, *Cocktail Time*, shows some affiliation to *Money in the Bank* in purlieu, plot and personnel. Compare Johnny Pearce's Guest House with Mrs Cork's Health Colony, the lost letter with the lost diamonds, Oily and Sweetie Carlisle with Soapy and Dolly Molloy, Johnny Pearce's old Nannie with Jeff Miller's housekeeper, Ma Balsam, Lord Ickenham with Lord Uffenham. In both stories awkward customers get locked in cellars. In *Something Fishy* Lord Uffenham, still impoverished, is living in digs in the salubrious London suburb, Valley Fields, tenant and friend of his ex-butler of Shipley Hall days, Keggs. Lord Uffenham says 'Lord-love-a-duck!' and 'Yerss' when he means 'Yes'. Although the sixth Viscount, Lord Uffenham is in no other sense an aristocrat. Lord Ickenham, the fifth Earl, is a total aristocrat, and Peasemarch, though he had come into property and was only being a butler because he liked it, was very much, as Jeeves would say, 'of the people'. As a ship's steward he had a fat part in the earlier novel, *The Luck of the Bodkins*, but it was the part of an amusing (to the reader) bore (to the passengers).

My feeling of disquiet about Lord Ickenham's good fellowship with both 'Mustard' Pott and Albert Peasemarch is the result, not of my own snobbery, but of my great admiration for Lord Ickenham as a wit, *farceur*, *flâneur* and *boulevardier*. I don't think Pott or Peasemarch could really have kept Lord Ickenham amused long enough to make such good fellowship even fictionally valid. But, if Wodehouse wanted occasionally to put in a plug for the classless society, Lord Ickenham was a fine vehicle for his plug.

Finally, and here I am not theorizing, Lord Ickenham gave the autumnal Wodehouse a chance to air a technique of love-making pleasantly at variance with the formulas established hitherto. The Ickenham System, as recommended to the laggard male, is to grab the adored object by the wrist, waggle her about a bit, clasp her to the bosom like a stevedore heaving a sack of coals, breathe hot words of romance into her ear (e.g. 'My mate!') and shower passionate kisses on her upturned face. This, says Lord Ickenham, is what many girls want, and it brings very good results. (Lord Uffenham had much the same ideas, and gave similar advice to Jeff Miller in *Money in the Bank*.) Lord Ickenham's nephew, Pongo, a romantic youth who has been falling in love ever since his boyhood dancing-class days, represents (at least in one book) the technique against which the Ickenham System is a revolt. Pongo yearns to win a girl's love by sacrifice – by saving her from a burning house, by finding opportunity to help her in her troubles – and then to kiss her gently on the forehead and fade off, *preux* to the last drop, into the sunset. In some of the bilge-literature he has been reading, such selflessness is rewarded not only with a saintly feeling of heroism, but with the girl running after him and saying 'Take me, I am yours, my shy king among men!'

Lord Ickenham scorns such goings-on, largely on the grounds that the girl is insensitive to them; what she wants is to be flung across a saddle-bow by an Elinor Glyn or Ethel M. Dell demon lover, and galloped off with into the burning desert. Anyway, though there has been a good deal of Pongo-esque renunciation, with Wodehouse's apparent approval, in some of his earliest heroes, his late-flowering Lord Ickenham firmly insists on the whirlwind embrace, the reckless declaration and the risked slap in the face and angry 'Unhand me, sir!' He successfully eggs Bill Oakshott on to apply the System to Hermione Bostock, and he successfully eggs Peasemarch on to apply it to Phoebe Wisdom. (He less successfully eggs on the diffident policeman to apply it to Johnny Pearce's formidable old Nanny. It gets him a box on the ear, but he wins her in the end.) Did Lord Ickenham himself try it in his youth with Lady Ickenham? She broke off their engagement six times before she married him. Now, in his not-so-sere sixties, he is not given any purposeful courting to do. But he agonizes Pongo with the amount of hand-patting, waist-encircling and easy osculation that he achieves in quick time with the beautiful girls with whom he is so easily on avuncular terms. Pongo automatically falls in love with them, speechlessly, at first sight. Lord Ickenham gets his arm round them, and Pongo resents this.

In one other small way Lord Ickenham may have been a spokesman for his past-middle-aged author more coeval than any of his other characters. Wodehouse gave him a wider background reading, and memory of reading, than he gave even to Jeeves. Lord Ickenham shows familiarity, in reference and quotation, with all the stock Wodehouse sources, the Bible, Shakespeare, Tennyson, Gilbert, *et al*. But he also shows his converse with Pierre Louÿs's *Le Roi Pausole*, Walter Pater, Damon Runyon, Hemingway, the Sitwells, Sinclair Lewis, Fenimore Cooper, Newbolt, Evelyn Waugh, Proust and Kafka. And he once dives into the deep end of *Pickwick* with all the aplomb of a Bernard Darwin and in a way which must have made his current hearers wonder what on earth he was talking about.

We are never exactly told at what public school Lord Ickenham was educated: where he lent 'Bimbo' Brabazon Plank the two shillings that were for so long outstanding, and where he beat 'Muggsy' Bostock with a fives bat. The fives bat suggests Winchester or Rugby, not Eton. But 'Barmy' Twistleton, now Earl of Ickenham, still trails clouds of schoolboy frivolity from whatever prison-house he attended, and if he ever speaks in a debate in the Upper Chamber of the Palace of Westminster, may I be there in the gallery to hear him. I expect there'll be a catapult visible on his hip.

In *Service with a Smile* he meets Lord Emsworth in Moss Bros. Both had been attending the opening of Parliament, and both are now bringing back their suitcases full of hired finery.

'Were you at that thing this morning?' said Lord Emsworth.

'I was indeed,' said Lord Ickenham, 'and looking magnificent. I don't suppose there is a peer in England who presents a posher appearance when wearing the reach-me-downs and comic hat than I do. Just before the procession got under way, I heard Rouge Croix whisper to Bluemantle "Don't look now, but who's that chap over there?", and Bluemantle whispered back, "I haven't the foggiest, but evidently some terrific swell."'

When Peter Fleming wrote fulsomely of Wodehouse's *Louder and Funnier* in the *Spectator*, he received a letter from the Alpes Maritimes:

Dear R.P.F.,

Thanks awfully for your kind review. The local peasants as I pass whisper to one another '*Il me semble que Monsieur Vodehouse est satisfait de lui aujourd'hui.*'

Uncle Fred, Lord Ickenham, was '*satisfait de lui*' all the time. And can one blame him?

IMAGES

There is a strong body of opinion which holds that Lord Ickenham ought to have been certified years ago. I understand he is always getting flattering offers from Colney Hatch and similar establishments.

*

'My dear, you look like Helen of Troy after a good facial.'

*

Jeff felt entitled to be a little severe, as some knight of old might have been, who, preparing to save a damsel from a dragon, found she had already knocked it cold with her distaff.

*

'To one like myself who, living in Hampshire, gets out of the metropolis, when he is fortunate enough to get into it, *via* Waterloo, there is something very soothing in the note of refined calm which Paddington strikes. At Waterloo, all is hustle and bustle, and the society tends to be mixed. Here at Paddington a leisured peace prevails, and you get only the best people – cultured men accustomed to mingling with basset hounds and women in tailored suits who look like horses.'

*

Mr Pott said that lending money always made him feel as if he were rubbing velvet up the wrong way.

*

He felt as if he had been lolling in the electric chair at Sing Sing and some practical joker had suddenly turned on the juice.

*

Images

A man, to use an old-fashioned phrase, of some twenty-eight summers, he gave the impression at the moment of having experienced at least that number of very hard winters.

*

He was either a man of about a hundred and fifty who was rather young for his years or a man of about a hundred and ten who had been aged by trouble.

7

THE LIGHT NOVELS

The Little Nugget (1913), *Uneasy Money* (1917), *Piccadilly Jim* (1918), *A Damsel in Distress* (1919), *The Coming of Bill* (1920), *The Prince and Betty* (1921), *The Indiscretions of Archie* (1920), *A Gentleman of Leisure* (1921), *Jill the Reckless* (1921), *The Girl on the Boat* (1922), *The Adventures of Sally* (1922), *Bill the Conqueror* (1924), *Sam the Sudden* (1925), *The Small Bachelor* (1927), *Money for Nothing* (1928), *Big Money* (1931), *If I Were You* (1931), *Dr Sally* (1932), *Hot Water* (1932), *The Luck of the Bodkins* (1935), *Laughing Gas* (1936), *Summer Moonshine* (1938), *Quick Service* (1940), *Money in the Bank* (1946), *Spring Fever* (1948), *The Old Reliable* (1951), *Barmy in Wonderland* (1952), *French Leave* (1956), *Something Fishy* (1958), *Ice in the Bedroom* (1961), *Frozen Assets* (1964), *Company for Henry* (1967), *Do Butlers Burgle Banks?* (1968), *The Girl in Blue* (1970), *Pearls, Girls and Monty Bodkin* (1972), *Bachelors Anonymous* (1973).

'LIGHT NOVELS' is a category of Wodehouse's output that includes many more than the thirty-six listed above. In fact, short stories, autobiography, plays and essays apart, all Wodehouse's books are light novels. The earliest ones were fairly light, and the subsequent ones became lighter and lighter. In the last forty-five years they were, almost uninterruptedly, farces. This chapter takes a short look at the novels which are not parts of sagas and in which the recurrent characters, if any, are not dominant.

Objection: all Wodehouse's books have all recurrent characters. Objection sustained. But the characters differ in names and in local habitations: the fresh young men and brisk maidens, the willowy young men and intellectual maidens, wrongly paired at the beginning, properly paired at the end of the book; the aunts and uncles, the short-tempered American millionaires, the bossy wives and widows, the hen-pecked husbands, the crooks, the butlers, the policemen, the magistrates, the genial alcoholics, the over-efficient secretaries, the Private Eyes, the poets, the bad artists, the retired colonials, the pimply office boys, the ex-pugilists, the theatrical producers and the impoverished peers. Egregious characters are rare. *Summer Moonshine* contains two, surprising enough to be memorable in an otherwise run-of-the-mill novel. One is the 'plasterer', an American whose job it has been to find absconders from The Law, and to plant summonses on them. His hobby in retirement, just for the excitement of the chase, is to be a plasterer still. The other is Princess Dwornitzchek, a really unpleasant stepmother, almost a villainess. But, to illustrate similarity, compare the young heroes of *Summer Moonshine* with those of the next light novel in date, *Quick Service*. Joe Vanringham and Joss Wetherby are practically identical except in name. Compare their elderly employers, Mr Busby and Mr Duff, practically identical except in name.

Compare *Spring Fever* with its next in date, *The Old Reliable*. The names are changed, sometimes not very much. The local habitation is changed – a country house in England and a big house in Hollywood – but otherwise you might say the two books were the same story. They were.

Wodehouse mined his ore in several seams and often the seams criss-crossed. A play became a novel; a novel became a play. Something that was originally sketched out as a play, but not produced, was skilfully filled out with descriptive narrative and sent to the mint as a novel. *Ring for Jeeves* was the novel Wodehouse wrote from the play written by Guy Bolton for which Wodehouse had loaned him Jeeves as a butler character. In the case of *Spring Fever* and *The Old*

Reliable, one idea produced two novels and one play. The play was never produced, but both novels were.

Wodehouse wrote *Spring Fever* as a novel. It already had the three-act rhythm in its plot. After it had been published Wodehouse heard that the American actor, Edward Everett Horton, was looking for a play with a juicy butler part in it for himself. Horton, Wodehouse and their attendant agents had a transatlantic discussion, and terms were decided. Wodehouse turned *Spring Fever* into a play, but for Horton's American audiences. Characters and settings became American. The local habitation became Hollywood. Spink the butler became Phipps the butler, Lord Shortlands became Smedley Cork. The gorgon, Lady Adela Cobbold, daughter of Lord Shortlands, became the gorgon, Mrs Adela Cork in Hollywood (even the Christian name remained the same there). After Wodehouse had done much tailoring and re-writing of the script for Horton, Horton's other commitments finally made him decide he couldn't put the play on. So now Wodehouse had a play script on his hands, and it was so far from the original novel that he thought he could make it pay further dividends. He made it into a new novel.

Within the meaning of the act, *The Old Reliable* is a new novel. Only a professional ferret would notice the way it rhymes with *Spring Fever*. My advice is simply that, except for purposes of professional analysis, you don't read *Spring Fever* and *The Old Reliable* in that order on the same weekend. That might induce a slight feeling of what the American plasterer in *Summer Moonshine* called 'onwee'.

In a few Wodehouse novels you find characters so far wide off the beaten Wodehouse track of characterization or looks in one way or another that, knowing Wodehouse's preference for typecasting, you feel sure he was describing the people who actually took the parts in a play. In *Barmy in Wonderland* (written from a Kaufmann play) there is a theatrical writer character so meticulously described for appearance that I would be surprised if I could not pick him out from a group photograph of the cast in Kaufmann's play on Broadway.

Wodehouse said that he had never written a serious story and had never wanted to. *The Coming of Bill* (1920) is the nearest he came to it. It's a good book, a study of young married life, with Ruth, a rather spoilt girl, as heroine, and Kirk, a rather bad, impecunious artist, but a perfect physical specimen, as hero. Ruth has a bossy aunt who is a eugenist, and she arranges the marriage and supervises the issue, Bill. (The discovery of Ruth's pregnancy shows as curious an ignorance of the facts of life as the discovery of Sophie Chapin's pregnancy in Kipling's story 'An Habitation Enforced'.) The marriage starts well. Then Ruth comes into money, while Kirk is away trying to make the family's fortunes in some mining venture. Ruth also heads towards an *affaire* with a polo-player (whose father had died thinking himself a teapot). Kirk's mining fails and, when he comes back, Ruth expects him to agree to live on her money. He doesn't like it. She loses her money. But her aunt must still be defied, and young Bill must be rescued from the antiseptic life and nursery that the aunt has arranged for him. Kirk kidnaps his own son and eventually a happy family life is achieved, with Kirk, Ruth and Bill together, poor but self-sufficient. Mrs Sarah Delane Porter, the aunt, is a true-to-type Wodehouse aunt. There is an English butler in Ruth's father's house in New York. That father is a millionaire and a human snapping turtle. There is an ex-pug friend of Kirk's, masseur to the millionaire.

You get, in *The Coming of Bill*, a distinct 'Three Acts — there's a play missing here' feeling. Kirk's studio in New York has a balcony gallery on to which bedrooms and bathroom open. Only an architect who was also a theatrical producer would design a lay-out so handy for the great scene: upstairs the heroine in labour, with her aunt, doctor and nurses scurrying across the balcony; downstairs the husband hero, worrying, discussing life and thinking of death, with his pugilist friend. The two of them put on the boxing gloves for a friendly punch-about. The pugilist decides that the way to stop a husband worrying about becoming a father is to put him down for the count. Collapse of husband to a good straight left to the jaw, the first cry of the new-born infant upstairs, emergence of aunt and doctor to inspect the new patient, the recumbent father. Good stuff. Good theatre. Good Wodehouse. But show me a studio designed that way anywhere off the stage.

The Coming of Bill is set entirely in New York and Connecticut. It is almost an all-American novel. Kirk Winfield has an English manservant of a sort, and Keggs, the millionaire's butler, is, as I say, English. No other Wodehouse light novel (unless you count *The Old Reliable*) is so preponderantly American. The pattern is usually for an even balance of Americans and English in the cast, or for the English to preponderate. Wodehouse the Englishman, living much in America, developed for his novels an Anglo-Americanism which suited his knowledge of people on both sides of the Atlantic, and his double market. Some of his novels have first 'acts' set in one country, second 'acts' on a ship, and third 'acts' in the other country. Wodehouse doesn't bother to make much difference between the dictions of ordinary American and ordinary English characters. Both come out as fairly straightforward English. He has crooks and pugs talking Brooklyn in England, or butlers talking over-stately English in America. These are for comedy. But Mervyn Potter, the American actor in *Barmy in Wonderland*, speaks, in print, pure Wodehouse 'buzzer' English. If you take it that the Canadian accent is much the same as the American, doesn't it strike you as odd that Psmith, in *Leave it to Psmith*, can impersonate Ralston McTodd, the Canadian poet, at Blandings without any specific bother about the accent, and no bother about changing his idiosyncratic Psmith phraseology?

Nowhere in Wodehouse is there a breath of a political message about Anglo-American friendship, and yet his books have probably had a considerable influence in helping the English and the Americans not to be frightened of each other. The eruptive American millionaire, Pop Stoker, finds to his horror that English policemen can't be bribed; he gets talked down by Jeeves; he loses his elder daughter Pauline in marriage to Lord Chuffnell and his younger, Emerald, to Gussie Fink-Nottle. Pop Stoker is a twenty-minute American egg forcibly softened up by the English way of life in the end. Bill Dawlish (William FitzWilliam Delamare Chambers, Lord Dawlish) decides to go to America to make his fortune:

'Hang it,' said Bill to himself in the cab. 'I'll go to America!' The exact words probably which Columbus had used, talking the thing over with his wife.

Bill's knowledge of the great republic across the sea was at this period of his life a little sketchy. He knew that there had been unpleasantness between England and the United States in seventeen-something and again in eighteen-something, but that things had eventually been straightened out by Miss Edna May and her fellow missionaries of the Belle of New York Company, since which time there had been no more trouble. Of American cocktails he had a fair working knowledge, and he appreciated ragtime. But of other great American institutions he was completely ignorant.

(*Uneasy Money*, 1917.)

Wodehouse gives you Chichester Clam, the American shipping tycoon, imprisoned in a potting-shed at Lord Worplesdon's English country house, Steeple Bumpleigh (*Joy in the Morning*), and Lord Emsworth in America doing a nice American girl a good turn by selling encyclopaedias for her. He gets treed by a dog in the process ('Birth of a Salesman'). Lord Havershot goes to Hollywood and marries a nice American girl (*Laughing Gas*). Film star Mike Cardinal comes from Hollywood and marries Lady Teresa (Terry) Cobbold (*Spring Fever*). He is another good Wodehouse 'buzzer' hero. The only thing against him in the Wodehouse Code is that he is too handsome. However, he gets his face bashed crooked in a fracas with a burglar in an English castle, and everybody's happy, Mike included. Americans come to England to learn, and Mike Cardinal has learnt something the hard way, and wouldn't have had it any other way. He gets his Terry, and his impoverished future father-in-law, Lord Shortlands, sells his white-elephant English castle and is all set to go to Hollywood to play butler parts in films. Silly Ass Archie Moffam goes to America (*The Indiscretions of Archie*) and learns to love baseball. He also learns to love (with less difficulty) Lucille, daughter of an American millionaire. In *If I Were You*, the earl marries the American manicurist, Polly Brown. *Hot Water* adds an Old Etonian French viscount to the Anglo-American salad bowl.

Such are the Wodehousian resolutions of the problem of Americans and English being separated by a common language. Put them in some good farcical fights, mix in some pretty girls, and the New World will redress the bank balances of the Old, and have a fine time doing it. Wodehouse is an advocate for more and prettier American chorus girls marrying into the English peerage, and for more and prettier English girls marrying rich Americans – or even poor ones, if they're pleasant. Peers and pugilists, millionaires and chorus girls, butlers and confidence tricksters – mix them up and they'll soon be looking so silly that nationalisms will have disappeared and the Western World will be that much a better place. In *Piccadilly Jim*, written after a long stretch of years in America, Englishman Wodehouse was so relaxed that he had Surrey

playing Kent at cricket at Lord's. This slip might be endearing
to an American, except that no American would know it was a
mistake.

There was poetic justice in Wodehouse adding American
citizenship to his British in his seventies. He had served both
countries well in his books. He had been an honorary American since before the First World War, and he has his constant
readers and cultists there as here. Referring to a date that
would be 1926 or 1927, George Arakian, writing about the
American jazz musician Bix Beiderbecke, says:

> Whenever Bix was in New York, he had a standing invitation to
> play at the Princeton dances. Frank Norris and Squirrel Ashcraft,
> independently of one another and in almost the same words, made
> clear ... that when Bix was around the talk was seldom about
> music. 'Bix had some unusual things in common with us,' says Ash-
> craft. 'We discovered that he could quote long passages from P. G.
> Wodehouse as well as we could, and we could spot the approximate
> page and the exact character who said any chosen line from his
> books – he had written forty-eight.'
>
> ('The Bix Beiderbecke Story' in *The Art of Jazz*,
> edited by Martin Williams.)

Jill the Reckless is one of the best contrived, one of the
fullest of 'something for everybody', one of the longest and
probably the best value for money of all the pre-farce light
novels. Jill Mariner, the English deb, loses her money and is
thrown over by her fiancé, Sir Derek Underhill, 'superb' polo-
player and a fine shot, but pompous and a stickler for good
form. It looks as though Sir Derek has chucked Jill because
of her pennilessness. Actually it is his beastly mother's
machinations, and the fact that Jill has got arrested fighting
about a parrot. (Later, when Sir Derek discovers that Jill
is a chorus girl, he is glad that their engagement is over.)
Jill goes to America, to stay with some dour country cousins
in a bleak area of Long Island. Her dour, mean and morose

uncle thinks she has money and will buy some property from him. When she reveals that she is penniless and doesn't want to buy anybody's property, her uncle and his family stop treating her like a transatlantic cousin guest. They make her work as a nursemaid and a slave. She has to read aloud to them, and fetch in the wood. She decides it is better to be penniless in friendly, noisy New York than out in the country. It is then that she becomes a chorus girl, and she marries the boy out of her childhood in Worcestershire, Wally Mason, now a successful playwright and play-fixer in London and New York. Freddie (you always know the type that is coming when Wodehouse calls a young man Freddie) Rooke, of Winchester and Magdalen, and rich, is something of a Mark Tapley. He comes to New York to try to patch up things between Jill and Derek, and this is where he is going to come out strong. Freddie in New York is petted by a nice American chorus girl, Nelly Bryant, because she thinks he has lost his money, like her friend Jill. Freddie and Nelly marry. Jill has a sympathetic old wastrel of an uncle, Major Selby, an ex-Indian Army, now a well-tailored, kind-hearted, Micawberish semi-crook, a cheque-bouncer and giver of dud IOUs. He had been sole trustee of Jill's money and had lost it for her, gambling for himself on the Stock Exchange. He is, though, determined to pay it back to poor little Jill somehow, even if it means the 'supreme sacrifice' of marrying rich American Mrs Peagrim. (Lord Uffenham is similarly heroic in *Money in the Bank*.)

The gorgon mother (in later books 'mother' becomes 'aunt'): man breaks engagement (bad show!): Anglo-American stage technicalities: gallant little Jill, 'I'm all smashed up inside', but brave and witty (perhaps Derek had been right that 'she was wrong for him. There are men who fear repartee in a wife more keenly than a sword. Derek was one of them'): Bible-quoting butler: a big boost for New

York: Goble, the theatrical manager with a seducer's eye on Jill – he asks her to supper (ooh!): and hero who does early morning physical exercises. The hero is the faithful St Bernard type, 'like a big, friendly dog', amusing, ugly, strong. He had from boyhood kept Jill's photograph, but, when he got the opportunity in New York, he refused to do the cave-man act with her. With Wally Mason, as with many of the early Wodehouse heroes, there is quite a lot of the renunciation principle which gets laughed at in the later, especially Uncle Fred, books. Wodehouse in 1921 is still allowing himself a little sentimentality. And he is still, frankly and seriously, trying to analyse what a girl feels when she is in love. Jill had thought herself genuinely in love with Derek. 'The touch of his body [in a taxi] against hers always gave her a thrill, half pleasurable, half exciting.' This is as near as Wodehouse ever came in print, I think, to suggesting that a nice girl can be physically aroused. I do not know what Wodehouse meant the distinction to be between 'pleasurable' and 'exciting'. But if I had read the book first as an adult in 1921, I would probably not have been troubled by this passage. Wodehouse soon settled for the love-at-first-sight technique for the young man and the (after the first shock) rapid acceptance of this love by the girl. He produced much happier results by formulating young love into hyperboles of devotion, jealousy, wrath, despair and happiness regained than by trying to explain its intermediate processes.

In *Jill the Reckless* there is a loyal girl–girl friendship between Jill and Nelly, of a type that Wodehouse treated fairly seriously in his early books, and used for laughs only (Madeline and her athletic girl friend in *The Mating Season*) in his later farces. At the date of *Jill the Reckless* Wodehouse is still noticing girls' eyes – wistful, dark, weary, restless. And Wally Mason is good at complimenting Jill seriously on her clothes and hats. Editors of popular magazines used to say to authors: 'You've got to describe girls' clothes and describe them seriously.' Wodehouse discarded seriousness, anyway. But the successful author whose books span seventy years learns that descriptions of clothes date an old book almost as blatantly as money-values do. You never find girls' clothes described in terms of fashion in the later Wodehouse books.

The Adventures of Sally is another Anglo-American novel, with some sentimentality and a good deal of theatre in it. Sally Nicholas is the American girl, whose mouth is wide and whose eyes disappear when she laughs, and, says Ginger Kemp, her English adorer (a rugger and boxing blue; he can also stop dog-fights; but he's shy): 'When you talk quick, your nose sort of goes all squiggly. Ripping, it looks.' Sally is small, brave and generous. She is sometimes witty. She is bossy in a nice way with Ginger Kemp. She is often broke. She has a fat, foolish and over-ambitious brother, something like Ukridge, but not funny. She starts by being engaged to a too-good-looking, too-self-pitying English playwright, who fails, drinks and lets her down. Bruce Carmyle, a rich Englishman, pursues Sally with faintly dishonourable intentions, but he eventually proposes marriage and she accepts him because she is at that moment tired, broke and dispirited. Then Carmyle finds that she is a professional partner in a New York dance hall, and this shakes his snobbish English soul. Sally eventually accepts Ginger Kemp, and they go off to the country (in America) and breed dogs. Sally will be the boss there, but Ginger will love it.

A later good one, *The Luck of the Bodkins*, published in 1935, is largely farce, played out on an Atlantic liner. Monty Bodkin, who has appeared before in two positions held open for a succession of characters in a succession of books (editor of a children's magazine for Lord Tilbury, and secretary to Lord Emsworth at Blandings) is a rich, handsome, pleasant Drone, and would be a drone except that his fiancée's father says he can't marry her until he has shown that he can hold down a job for more than a year. His fiancée, Gertrude, a harmless but jealous girl, is travelling to America with the English girls' hockey team, and at first she isn't speaking to Monty because of a photograph of himself that he sent her from Cannes. She noticed a tattoo patch on his chest in this photograph, had it enlarged, and found that it read 'Sue Brown' round the shape of a heart. On the ship most of the play is made by a Hollywood film star, Lotus (Lottie) Blossom, a high-spirited beauty with a pet baby alligator and a penchant for 'larkiness'. (This is the word used by her steward, Albert Peasemarch, later Lord Ickenham's friend in *Cocktail Time*.) Lottie has a fine command of persiflage and repartee. A Hollywood mogul is being made by his wife to smuggle a necklace for her into America, and it scares him stiff. Going to America concurrently, and headed for Hollywood, is Ambrose Tennyson. The mogul had signed him up as a writer, because he thought he was *the* Tennyson whose writings he heard so much praised in England. Lottie keeps getting Monty into trouble with Gertrude, though there is always an explanation of their compromising togetherness as innocent as the explanation of the tattoo-marked 'Sue Brown'. Everything ends happily at a New York hotel, with Monty and Gertrude cooing, Lottie engaged to Ambrose Tennyson, and Ambrose's brother Reggie engaged to the mogul's amiable sister-in-law – one all-English pairing, two Anglo-American.

Ambrose and Reggie Tennyson, brothers and both sympathetic characters, differ radically in their attitudes to jobs and living on other people's money. Wodehouse's uncritical blessing goes out to both of them.

Reggie's views on jobs were peculiar, but definite. There were some men – he himself was one of them – who, he considered, had no need for a job. A fair knowledge of racing form, a natural gift for bridge and poker, an ability to borrow money with an easy charm which made the operation a positive pleasure to the victims – these endowments, he held, were all that a chap like himself required, and it was with a deep sense of injury that he had allowed his loved ones to jockey him into the loathsome commercial enterprise to which he was now on his way. A little patience on their part, a little of the get-together spirit, a temporary opening of the pursestrings to help him over a bad patch, and he could have carried on in such perfect comfort. For Reggie Tennyson was one of those young men whom the ravens feed.

But, and this was the point, the ravens do not feed the Ambroses of this world. The Ambroses need their steady jobs. Here is a conversation between Reggie and Lottie Blossom about Reggie's brother:

'Ambrose and I can't get married now,' said Lottie.

'Oh, come,' said Reggie. 'He may be broke, having given up his job at the Admiralty, but you've enough for two, what?'

'I've enough for twenty. But what good is that? Ambrose won't live on my money. He wouldn't marry me on a bet now.'

'But, dash it, it's no different to marrying an heiress.'

'He wouldn't marry an heiress.'

'What!' cried Reggie, who would have married a dozen, had the law permitted it. 'Why not?'

'Because he's a darned ivory-domed, pig-headed son of an army mule,' cried Miss Blossom, the hot blood of the Hoboken Murphys boiling in her veins. 'Because he isn't human. Because he is like some actor in a play, doing the noble thing with one eye counting the house and the other on the gallery. No he isn't,' she went on, with one of those swift transitions which made her character so interesting and which on the Superba-Llewellyn lot had so often sent over-wrought directors groping blindly for the canteen to pull themselves together with frosted malted milk, 'He isn't anything of the kind. I admire his high principles. I think they're swell. It's a pity there aren't more men with his wonderful sense of honour and self-respect. I'm not going to have you saying a word against Ambrose. He's the finest man in the world, so if you want to sneer and jeer at him for refusing to live on my money, shoot ahead. Only remember that a cauliflower ear goes with it.'

We are beginning to recognize, by 1935 (the date of *The Luck of the Bodkins*), the two recurrent types of Wodehouse heroine or girl friend. There are several more Jills and Sallys to come, under those names or as Joans, Annes, Terrys, Kays and Mollies. They are the splendid girls, generally small, motherly to weak fathers and uncles, inclined to be motherly to the Rickys, Joes, Jeffs, Bills and Sams that they eventually marry. The Lottie strain leads on to the delightful young female mayhem-mongers who appear especially in the Bertie Wooster books. They are offshoots of Psmith, and future Aunt Dahlias: Stiffy Byng, who made her curate fiancé pinch the helmet of her village enemy, Constable Oates; Pauline Stoker who appeared in Bertie Wooster's bed; Corky Pirbright, the Hollywood star; Nobby Hopwood, fiancée of Boko Fittleworth; and Bobbie Wickham who started Bertie puncturing hot water bottles and who addressed the dreaded Rev. Aubrey Upjohn, Bertie's ex-prep-school headmaster, as 'Listen, Buster.'

You notice (Corky, Bobbie, Stiffy, Nobby) how their names could well be masculine. They are literary descendants of the young Middle School raggers of the early Wodehouse school-books. Bobbie Wickham's first introduction (she has been in six short stories and one full-length novel, and she is the most durable of the lot) is: 'The visitor, who walked springily into the room, was a girl of remarkable beauty. She resembled a particularly good-looking schoolboy who had dressed up in his sister's clothes.'

In the same story the description of Bobbie Wickham by Sir Joseph Moresby, the magistrate who had just fined her for speeding in her two-seater is: 'a red-headed hussy who ought to be smacked and sent to bed without her supper'.

These festive young female squirts, androgynous mischief-makers, are a sore trial to their mothers (Bobbie), guardians (Stiffy and Nobby), and their uncles (Corky). They talk expert schoolboy slang. They are charming, unscrupulous, quarrelsome, mettlesome, demanding, jealous, wheedling, quick to tears ('oomph! oomph!'), quick to wrath, especially with their loved ones, and always apt to 'start something'. They are the sort of girls that Uncle Fred particularly admires. In a discussion with Bill Oakshott about his imperious girl friend, Uncle Fred says: 'I don't suppose Hermione Bostock has ever made so much as an apple-pie bed in her life. I'd give her a miss.'

It is particularly the gloomy, Hamlet-like young men of the stamp of his nephew Pongo, Uncle Fred thinks, who should marry the sort of girl who sets booby-traps for bishops. Galahad Threepwood had said to his niece Millicent, herself currently gloomy and Hamlet-like, because crossed in love: 'In my young days a girl of your age would have been upstairs, making an apple-pie bed for somebody instead of lolling in chairs reading books about Theosophy.'

The trouble is that these apple-pie-bed-making girls tend to make their adorers gloomy and Hamlet-like by their very festivity. Tuppy Glossop, always refreshingly, and sometimes dangerously, outspoken, said of his fiancée Angela: 'I'm not saying I don't love the little blighter. I love her passionately. But that doesn't alter the fact that I consider that what she needs most is a swift kick in the pants.'

The Lotties, Stiffys and Bobbies of this world climb down drainpipes, push policemen into ponds, puncture people's hot water bottles and make Bertie drop flower-pots on to the conservatory roofs of girls' schools at night. They may be headaches. They are never bores.

The bores among the Wodehouse girl friends are the Gertrudes, Honorias, Madelines and Florences. Gertrude is a hockey international, Madeline thinks the stars are God's daisy-chain, Florence is literary, and Honoria is the daughter of Sir Roderick Glossop. They are not bores to the reader, but they all represent authority, and that puts them on the Other Side. They are, as the American John Aldridge explains in an introduction to a Wodehouse anthology, trying to push Bertie Wooster and his like up into dreaded adulthood.

Sally's happy-go-lucky girl friend Gladys, in *The Adventures of Sally*, gives Sally a piece of advice which, if you take it as a standard Wodehouse attitude, brings the light novels full circle:

> 'Chumps always make the best husbands. When you marry, Sally, grab a chump. Tap his forehead first, and if it rings solid, don't hesitate. All the unhappy marriages come from the husbands having brains. What good are brains to a man? They only unsettle him.'

'Brains only unsettle a husband,' says Leila Yorke in Wodehouse's 1961 novel, *Ice in the Bedroom*. Wodehouse wrote it when he was seventy-nine, and it is as fizzy as any in the list. It has a spring sprightliness and an autumn benignity. Wodehouse had, till now, been irreverent, just short of unkindness, to our then colonial empire, the people who went there and, particularly, the people who came back. Here he has given a prize Drone to Kenya, and Kenya's gain would be Mayfair's loss. Another act of benignity in this novel is the finally unreserved glorification of the status of best-seller female bilge-novelist. Leila Yorke here is built very much on the lines of Bertie Wooster's excellent Aunt Dahlia. She smokes cigars, likes plenty of champagne, talks good pithy slang, is kind to the young, makes £15,000 a year and finds her long lost husband (a failed actor, mother-ridden and suppressed) performing seedily as a waiter at a Pen and Ink Club luncheon. She rescues him, discovers that his mother has at last done the right thing and passed on, and whisks him off to a life of luxury and sunshine that they will both enjoy.

There is a pleasant reversal of this pleasant rags-to-riches theme for another, less important, couple in the book. The aged, white-bearded Mr Cornelius, a house-agent, lives happily in his little corner of Valley Fields, pottering, playing chess, feeding his rabbits and writing a history of the district. (We met Mr Cornelius before in *Sam the Sudden* and *Big Money*.) It is Mr Cornelius who lends Freddie Widgeon the £3,000, but Freddie mustn't tell Mrs Cornelius. Why? Because Mr Cornelius has just inherited a million pounds or so from a distant brother, and if Mrs Cornelius were to get to hear about it, she would take steps:

'Mr Widgeon, have you any conception of what would happen, were my wife to learn that I was a millionaire? Do you think I should be allowed to go on living in Valley Fields, the place I love, and continue to be a house agent, the work I love? Do you suppose I should be permitted to keep my old friends, like Mr Wrenn of San Rafael, with whom I play chess on Saturdays, and feed rabbits in my shirt-sleeves? No, I should be whistled off to a flat in Mayfair, I should have to spend long months in the South of France, a butler would be engaged and I should have to dress for dinner every night. I should have to join a London Club, take a box at the opera, learn to play polo,' said Mr Cornelius, allowing his morbid fancy to run away with him a little. 'The best of women are not proof against sudden wealth. Mrs Cornelius is perfectly happy and contented in the surroundings to which she has always been accustomed – she was a Miss Bulstrode of Happy Haven at the time of our marriage – and I intend that she shall remain happy and contented.'

Valley Fields is Mr Cornelius's own, his native land. Valley Fields, Wodehouse's fond memory of Dulwich, is south-east of London and the number 3 bus connects it with Piccadilly Circus. Castlewood, Peacehaven and The Nook, the property of Lord Uffenham's retired butler, Keggs, have been adjacent houses there in two previous novels, *Something Fishy* and *Big Money*. (Barry Conway is living at The Nook with his bossy old Nannie in *Big Money*.) It was to Valley Fields that Lord Ickenham brought his nephew Pongo in the 'Uncle Fred Flits By' story. Here, in other stories, have come other Drones Club members, one at least with false beard to escape his creditors, and not a few Old Wrykynians in some of the early novels of the 1920s.

The great thing about Valley Fields for Wodehouse was that it gave him adjacent small houses, with fences between of a decent height for a small bachelor to lean over and see a small, pretty girl. In each garden there is certainly a tree for putting deck-chairs under in the almost perpetual sunshine, and probably a statue of a nude infant with a bit of a tummy on him. If there is a policeman in the offing, he lives at one of the houses and so can be in uniform or mufti as the plot requires. Everything is peaceful. Valley Fields is an island valley of Avilion where a Drone can live on a clerk's salary. The Drone feels like a caged eagle at the office, but in Valley Fields he can sit in the garden in flannels and his Eton Rambler blazer, and he can get to know that pretty girl, who is herself probably in reduced circumstances too. In Valley Fields live the happy lower-middle classes, and burglars only find it a good hunting ground if other burglars have cached 'ice' in a bedroom from a theft at a country house far away. Mr Cornelius won't move from Valley Fields for anybody's money. Keggs has his money invested in property there, but he is a resident alien. He goes on round-the-world cruises. An ex-butler would know that the property values in Valley Fields were sound, but his sophisticated upbringing as a butler would make him hanker to go on long cruises occasionally.

To Valley Fields then, in *Ice in the Bedroom*, comes impoverished Freddie Widgeon to share a small house with his cousin George, the policeman. Here comes Leila Yorke, bilge-novelist supreme, but with the absurd idea currently that she should write a stark, grey novel like George Gissing's for once. She has been cunningly persuaded by Freddie (who is more interested in Sally Foster, Leila Yorke's secretary) that Valley Fields is utterly grey and stark and has lots of squalor, and Leila Yorke forgives him his misrepresentation because he is in love with Sally. Here comes Sally, whose nose twitches like a rabbit when she's excited, just as that earlier Sally's had done in *The Adventures of Sally* and Anne Benedick's had done in *Money in the Bank*. Here comes Soapy and Dolly Molloy, and their rival and enemy, Chimp Twist.

I suspect that Wodehouse, needing a London suburb as a setting for action in *Do Butlers Burgle Banks?* (1968) pencilled in Valley Fields and then said to himself 'No, we can't have Valley Fields getting all the action. I'll change it to Wellingford this time. That'll fool the too constant reader.' If so, he forgot to rub out one pencilled 'Valley Fields', in Chapter 4, part 4, and it has gone through to the book. Even if it is a mistake, it is still a sort of tribute to the London suburb of Wodehouse's fondest memories. It drifts again, gently and this time without error, into *Bachelors Anonymous*, the last novel on the list.

I was saying that *Ice in the Bedroom* had a spring sprightliness and autumn benignity. A book that is all autumn benignity is the aforesaid *Bachelors Anonymous* (1973). It reads as though Wodehouse had been in no hurry with it but was not going to try to flesh out old bones. Twenty years earlier he would have put 15,000 more words into the story, and two more sub-plots. But now the scenario was absolutely sound and would carry the book to a decent end at a decent pace, if without much action or conflict. A group of American males, determined to cure themselves of marriage, are startled when one of their most crippled members, five-times-married-and-divorced Hollywood tycoon Ivor Llewellyn, heads for London on his own. He must be protected, the old fool. Otherwise he will go and ask some girl to marry him just because he can't think of anything else to make conversation. He mustn't be allowed to put his head in the noose again. So his friends put on a crash rescue operation, and, at the end of the book, the friends have found themselves good ladies to marry, and Llewellyn, thanking his stars that he has escaped the predatory film-star, is the only bachelor left.

Even if Wodehouse had lived for another half century I think he would have kept to his formula: that for a man and a girl who find themselves becoming fond of each other it is marriage or nothing. Among the novels of today this gives Wodehouse's a period charm in addition to their other excellences.

IMAGES

Chimp Twist was looking like a monkey that had bitten into a bad nut, and Soapy Molloy like an American Senator who has received an anonymous telegram saying 'All is discovered. Fly at once.'

*

She spoke so quietly, so meekly, her whole air so like that of a good little girl remorseful for having been naughty, that a wiser and more experienced man than Lionel Green would have climbed the wall and pulled it up after him.

*

That song wants a woman to sing it. A woman who could reach out for that last high note and teach it to take a joke. The whole refrain is working up to that. You need Tetrazzini or someone who would just pick that note off the roof and hold it till the janitor came round to lock up the building for the night.

*

He's as jealous as billy-ho. Smear a bit of burnt cork on him, and he could step right on to any stage and play Othello without rehearsal.

*

Her eyes and hair were a browny hazel. The general effect was of a seraph who ate lots of yeast.

*

Hash looked like one who had drained the four-ale of life and found a dead mouse at the bottom of the pewter.

*

On paper Blair Eggleston was bold, cold and ruthless. Like so many of our younger novelists, his whole tone was that of a disillusioned, sardonic philanderer who had drunk the wine cup of illicit love to its dregs but was always ready to fill up again and have another ... Deprived of his fountain-pen, however, Blair was rather timid with women. He had never actually found himself alone in an incense-scented studio with a scantily-clad princess reclining on a tiger-skin, but in such a situation he would most certainly have taken a chair as near to the door as possible and talked about the weather.

8

THE OTHER SHORT STORIES, THE OLDEST MEMBER, MR MULLINER, EGGS, BEANS & CRUMPETS AND YOUNG MEN IN SPATS

The Man Upstairs (1914), *The Man with Two Left Feet* (1917), *The Clicking of Cuthbert* (1922), *The Heart of a Goof* (1926), *Meet Mr Mulliner* (1927), *Mr Mulliner Speaking* (1929), *Mulliner Nights* (1933), *Mulliner Omnibus* (1935), *Blandings Castle* (1935), *Young Men in Spats* (1936), *Lord Emsworth and Others* (1937), *Eggs, Beans and Crumpets* (1940), *Nothing Serious* (1950), *A Few Quick Ones* (1959), *Plum Pie* (1966).

IN THE 1920s and 30s there were many illustrated magazines on both sides of the Atlantic paying high for good humorous short stories, five- to eight-thousand-word episodes, complete with sunny plot, a beginning, middle and end, and the young happily paired off in the fade-out. Wodehouse wrote for this profitable market. He became one of the golden boys of the magazines and, not necessarily the same thing, a master of his craft.

Craft? Or art? Well, it depends how you define your terms. Wodehouse's short stories, from *The Clicking of Cuthbert* onwards, are extremely crafty, and never arty. His plots are always mechanically good and often very funny in themselves. The narrative and dialogue is yeasty. The pace is fast and even, the 'plants' dexterous and the texture creamy. You may not be able to follow all the twists and turns of a Wodehouse novel plot. His short stories are limpid and lucid. (Three long ones, 'The Crime Wave at Blandings', 'Life with Freddie' and 'Jeeves and the Greasy Bird', give some evidence of having started as the First Acts of novels and then having been choked down. And 'The Awakening of Rollo Podmarsh' has several more twists than is good for it.) The level of quality, story by story, is consistent and very high. I know a dozen of the Wodehouse novels that I might call pot-boilers. Of the hundred and fifty or so short stories that he has published since 1920 I would say that one or two are too complicated, one or two are thin, but none is feeble or tired. Everyone has his favourites. Wodehouse had his ('Anselm Gets his Chance', 'Goodbye to All Cats' and 'The Amazing Hat Mystery' are three of them). I have mine. But I have re-read the whole canon recently, and I am sure that my selection largely depends on the circumstances in which I first read them, the people with whom I first laughed about them, and the people at whom I know that I can quote from them.

The *Strand* was paying Wodehouse a peak 500 guineas a story in the 1930s, The *Saturday Evening Post* 4,000 dollars and the *American Magazine* (for one Mulliner series) 6,000 dollars. Twelve short stories could gross Wodehouse the equivalent in dollars and guineas of £20,000 from the magazines before they became a book with its own dollar and sterling royalties to follow.

Television and the logistics of advertising changed the direction of much magazine publishing and greatly diminished competition for the individual Wodehouse short story in America and England. Wodehouse, living in America, preferred to write about England and English people, and he wrote with a totally English accent. Almost all the magazines that used to scramble for Wodehouse short stories died before he did. In England the slack has been taken up because TV and radio have discovered that his stories and books, of whatever vintage, are excellent material for conversion. Up to the time of Wodehouse's death American stations had not been buying Wodehouse enthusiastically.

Wodehouse gave up writing short stories about English public schools as soon as he started to sell to America. His first two subsequent collections, *The Man Upstairs* and *The Man with Two Left Feet*, are of interest now only to remind us that young Wodehouse, though possibly a born writer, had a long period of hack apprenticeship before he found his form and, jettisoning sentimentality and seriousness, came into his birthright. Wodehouse made no apologies for it. In *Performing Flea* and elsewhere he said that, though he worked hard and kept his income rising year by year, he never felt he had more than a toe-hold on the craft of his profession till the 1920s, by which time he was in his personal forties. He always envied, nostalgically, the young who write well virtually from the egg. Perhaps only someone totally established in maturity, and genuinely unsentimental about himself when young, could have allowed 'In Alcala', an early, pulpy item written for the pulps, to survive through and reach Penguin form in *The Man with Two Left Feet*. 'In Alcala' is a strangely untypical Wodehouse story, a collector's item, perhaps, because in it Wodehouse uses seriously a formulaic expression ('showering kisses on her upturned face') that he laughs at as a Rosie M. Banks tripe-type cliché in a dozen contexts in later books. Such saleable sentimentality as he indulged in in the stories which made these two early books, Wodehouse left behind for the forthcoming 'Sappers' of the magazine world.

Mercifully. Far behind. In one of the Bingo Little stories, Bingo's wife Rosie has gone to Droitwich with her mother. Bingo, left with the baby and no money for cocktails and cigarettes, gets a letter from Rosie enclosing £10, with instructions to open a wee savings account for the baby. Another pram-pushing father, who meets Bingo and Son in the Park that day, bets Bingo a tenner that his son is uglier than Bingo's, a passing policeman to be judge. Bingo, holding that his Algernon Aubrey looks like a homicidal fried egg takes the bet with confidence, and loses his baby's tenner with horror. He faces a fearful get-together with Rosie when he goes to Paddington to meet the Droitwich train. What, she will ask, about that wee pass-book?

'I've got to take Mother to the flat,' said Rosie on the platform. 'She's not at all well.'

'No, I noticed she seemed to be looking a bit down among the wines and spirits,' said Bingo, casting a gratified glance at the old object, who was now propping herself up against a passing porter.

Bingo has enormous troubles of his own. His mother-in-law has never raised a finger to harm him in any of the chronicles. She is an elderly invalid, and is now in a bad way after a testing railway journey. But Bingo has time to relish the old object's distress. Nobody sees Bingo's gratified glance except the reader, and the reader is delighted by this gratuitous swipe at old age and invalidism by one who is young and healthy.

If you think that the mature Wodehouse held any subject sacred, point to it in his books. Sex? No, he doesn't hold sex sacred. He simply by-passes it or transmutes it. In his light novels his nice chorus girls easily give the brush-off to theatrical producers who name the price of advancement to an acting part. There would presumably be licentious clubmen at The Drones, but Wodehouse's formula purifies them into the Pongo/Bingo/Barmy/Freddie type of hopisthognathous romantics. They are constantly falling in love, and are not laggard in pursuing the objects of their desires, if that is the right word. But they pursue strictly with flowers, lunches, lushing up the girl's parents, kid brothers and dogs, and with object matrimony. There is no suggestion that either clubman or girl would recognize a double bed except as so much extra sweat to make an apple-pie of.

With the possible exceptions of Percy Pilbeam, marcelled (artificially corrugated) hair in the male, English lecturers in America and phoney young littérateurs generally, Wodehouse seems to have had no strong dislikes. But he was funny and irreverent about practically every sacred cow in the British pasture. Several of the subjects about which he was most irreverent in print were, we know, personal enthusiasms of his own – cricket, rugger, boxing, keep-fit exercises, dogs, cats, Tennyson, Shakespeare, the Old School and, by his own account, golf.

As a writer of light fiction, I have always till now been handicapped by the fact that my disposition was cheerful, my heart intact, and my life unsoured. Handicapped, I say, because the public likes to feel that a writer of farcical stories is piquantly miserable in his private life, and that, if he turns out anything amusing, he does it simply in order to obtain relief from the almost insupportable weight of an existence which he has long since realised to be a wash-out. Well, today I am just like that.

Two years ago, I admit, I was a shallow *farceur*. My work lacked depth. I wrote flippantly simply because I was having a thoroughly good time. Then I took up golf, and now I can smile through the tears and laugh, like Figaro, that I may not weep, and generally hold my head up and feel that I am entitled to respect.

If you find anything in this volume that amuses you, kindly bear in mind that it was probably written on my return home after losing three balls in the gorse and breaking the head off my favourite driver . . .

Wodehouse established The Oldest Member, himself full of reverence for the sacred game, to tell some of the most hilariously irreverent stories about it in all its literature. There is no cricket after *Mike*, except one story in *Nothing Serious* (1952), where the young man and the lovely girl are united in thinking that cricket is a ridiculously boring game. But they cannot marry until the young man manages to get out, with financial allowances intact, from under the thumb of a rich uncle to whom cricket and Lord's are a religion. There is only one game of rugger after the school stories, and that's when Tuppy Glossop insists on playing in a village match in order to impress a girl friend. Bertie Wooster, who tells the story as one to whom the Rugby code is a mystery, makes it an epic of irreverence.

After *The Coming of Bill*, which is unsentimental, but fairly serious, Wodehouse decided to be firmly irreverent about children. At the cot age, they look like mixtures of Edward G. Robinson, Boris Karloff and Winston Churchill, and later they are either fiends or sissies. The child who comes out best in all the books is the slum girl on fête-day at Blandings in 'Lord Emsworth and the Girl Friend'. This girl cops McAllister, Lord Emsworth's gardener, on the shin with a stone and helps Lord Emsworth to defy his sister Connie. The child who comes out worst is the small son of golfing parents who gets into bad Christopher Robin habits and, when saying his prayers, counts the house through the little hands on which he has drooped his little gold head. He also asks his father to write poetry for him. His mother (bless her) says 'Does mother's little chackabiddy want his nose pushed sideways? Very well, then!' We are left with the comfortable certainty that the child reformed.

Wodehouse has been irreverent about magistrates, old nannies, policemen, poets, peers, politicians, aunts, alcohol, uncles, adolescent spots, baronets, invalids, old age, publishers ('Don't kill him, Bill. He's my publisher!'), Christmas, butlers, ex-butlers, millionaires, Chekhov and the other Great Russians, the good grey poets, Colonial ex-Governors, newspaper magnates, popular novelists, amateur dictators (Spode and his Black Shorts) and Hollywood.

He has been irreverent about Royalty and the Church. There are only two passing references to a reigning monarch in the stories, and they are both small gems. Lord Emsworth, worried about his cherished prize pumpkin, has a dream in which he takes the King to see it. When they get to the frame in which it should have been basking in its enormous glory, they find it has shrivelled to the size of a pea, and 'Lord Emsworth woke, sweating, with his sovereign's disappointed screams ringing in his ears'. And the great hatters, Bodmins of Vigo Street, by appointment to His Majesty – that means that 'when the King wants a new topper, he ankles round to Vigo Street and says "Bodmin, we want a new topper."' Though the Prince of Wales wore soft silk shirts with a black tie in France in the evenings, Jeeves would not allow Bertie to wear them in London. Jeeves was conservative, but Jeeves was right.

For sustained innocuous irreverence, without a hint of mockery, towards a subject that popular humorists tend tastelessly to misuse or cravenly to avoid, see Wodehouse on the Church. Perhaps taking his original cue from W. S. Gilbert, but, after that, out on his own, with his own words and music, Wodehouse has given us a succession of splendid men of God, several superb church interiors and many most human predicaments suffered by clergymen in pursuance of their saintly duties. There is an excellent quarrel between a hot-tempered vicar and his bishop (they were at school together and slip easily into schoolboy slang in the heat of argument) about the number of orphreys the vicar is wearing on his chasuble. They are about to come to blows when the curate, Augustine Mulliner, calms them down and makes them shake hands and apologise. The Bishop of Bongo-Bongo is saved by his cat, Webster, from making an ass of himself and marrying an unsuitable widow. A country vicar's daughter, Angelica Briscoe, with whom Barmy Fotheringay Phipps and Pongo Twistleton both fell in love at first sight, turned out to be a competent schemer, well able to put those two city slickers through useful martyrdoms (the School Treat and the Mothers' Outing) and then to ditch them both. The Wodehouse 'message' is that clergymen's daughters know all the responses. Corky Pirbright's uncle in his country cure of souls is plagued by an atheist policeman of the village. When Jeeves has managed, with a good blow to the back of the head with a cosh, to make the copper stop sneering at Jonah and the Whale, the reformed character says to the vicar: 'Can I sing in the choir right away, or must I join the Infants' Bible Class first?' 'The Great Sermon Handicap' provides all the makings of a colossal racecourse gamble for Bertie, his friends and the fiendish Steggles. Stiffy Byng's clumsy fiancé, the Rev. 'Stinker' Pinker, has to steal the village constable's helmet for her. The Rev. 'Beefy' Bingham, full of good intentions and love for Lord Emsworth's niece, gives Lord Emsworth horse-liniment for his twisted ankle; and, when Lord Emsworth, after a restless night, has gone to swim in the lake at Blandings, the Rev. Beefy tries to rescue him from 'drowning' with a good punch on the jaw far from land. The vicar in 'Anselm Gets His Chance' would never let Anselm preach on Sunday evenings, until a burglar blacked his (the vicar's) eye on a Saturday night.

Wodehouse's treatment of the Church of England is frequent, knowledgeable, irreverent, friendly and funny. He had sat on many hard pews through many sermons, at school and in the holidays. All his clergymen are 'gentlemen'. One gets sent to the South of France by his doctor, and his replacement is the nephew and heir of a Liverpool shipping millionaire. Some have been rugger players and boxers of repute. Some have ungovernable tempers, others ungovernable daughters or nieces. It was the bishop catching his teenage daughter reading that shocking book, and attacking it in the pulpit, that started the popularity of *Cocktail Time*. All Wodehouse's clergymen are human. Not a single one is shown in the act of being pious or holy, though it is never suggested that they aren't. 'If they find me out, bim will go my chance of becoming a bishop.'

That was the headmaster when, recovered from his Buck-U-Uppo, he realized that his forgetful friend and companion, the bishop, had left his shovel hat on the scene of their joint midnight crime. I wonder why his publishers have not collected a *Wodehouse Church Omnibus*, with five or six complete short stories and several gobbets from the novels. It would be a popular, and well received, gift book to answer the question 'What shall we give the curate/vicar/dean/bishop/archbishop for Christmas?'

Wodehouse's Mr Mulliner, Oldest Member, Eggs, Beans and Crumpets are narrators chosen to tell whatever stories Wodehouse feels suitable for them. Their phraseologies differ, but they tell stories of roughly similar structure. Compared with the Bertie/Jeeves short stories, these are one twist short; but that's the point of Jeeves. He is a god-like plot-twister. If Jeeves had been operative in the story of the Bishop of Bongo-Bongo and his cat Webster, it would not have been by chance that Webster arrived in a crate at the widow's house and did battle with the beastly Percy. Jeeves would have organized it, knowing that the fight would happen and the bishop would thereby be saved from the widow. Jeeves has saved many of Bertie's friends from unfortunate engagements.

Wodehouse's Oldest Member seems to sit on the terrace at a variety of golf club-houses, in England and in America. But even if he is a type and even if he is virtually interchangeable with Mr Mulliner except for the sorts of stories each tells, he is a comforting old sage, and one settles back to hear his stories with a good deal more pleasure than most of the auditors he nailed for them on the terrace. He himself has not played golf since the rubber-cored ball superseded the old dignified gutty. The course of his Club has a period flavour, too, with cottages round its boundaries which can be rented, with housekeeper, at a moment's notice and its members, old and young, almost entirely untrammelled by jobs. The Oldest Member hears their confidences, watches over their love affairs and philosophizes on all aspects of the great game:

'When I played, I never lost my temper. Sometimes, it is true, I may, after missing a shot, have broken my club across my knees; but I did it in a calm and judicial spirit, because the club was obviously no good and I was going to get another one anyway ...'

Mr Mulliner holds his court in the bar parlour of the Anglers' Rest, drinking hot Scotch and lemon, courteously ordered from, and courteously served by, Miss Postlethwaite, the barmaid. He surveys a wider field than the Oldest Member, but, like the O.M., he dominates his audience and they have to listen. His stories are almost all about his nephews, and he has one in almost every profession – the Church, photography, Hollywood script-writing, detection, poetry, to name a few. Since the locale of his tales can change from Mayfair to Malibu, his audience can check on his statements even less than the Oldest Member's audience can on his. So Mr Mulliner tells 'stretchers'. He was Wodehouse's favourite mouthpiece for the really tall story. He tells his 'stretchers' with determination, grace, ease and solemnity. He has a vocabulary of phrase and situation dredged almost wholesale from popular bilge literature. Some of his characters have lives in stories other than his. Roberta ('Bobbie') Wickham made her first appearance in a Mulliner story, later played lead in 'Mr Potter Takes a Rest Cure' (which Wodehouse related without an intermediate narrator and, one guesses, slightly under the influence of Saki), and later came into Bertie Wooster's orbit, for two short stories and a whole novel. Wodehouse saw saga possibilities in her and let her cause trouble for a succession of young men. Bertie thought he was in love with her and tried to push it along. By the end of *Jeeves in the Offing*, Bobbie seemed destined for the altar with 'Kipper' Herring.

The Young Men in Spats and the Eggs, Beans and Crumpets told their stories mostly in the bar of The Drones. That club deserves a monograph, but will not get it from me. You must look for the Drones in Dover Street when you're next in the district; it is on the east side, and has steps going down to the street. In *Leave it to Psmith* it had Thorpe and Briscoe, coal merchants, opposite it. In *Cocktail Time* it faced The Demosthenes Club. The place where I should put it, from the geographic evidence in the books, is No. 16 Dover Street. It is the club above all that I should like to belong to, and, as Percy Gorringe, a side-whiskered Bloomsburyite from Liverpool, was a member and 'Mustard' Pott acceptable as a guest, I don't see why it need be too exclusive for me. Is there any club so hallowed in English fiction? There 'youth holds carnival' as Wodehouse said in *Leave it to Psmith* in a rather Dornford-Yates-sounding, but prophetic, phrase. And some of those youths, considering their pin-headedness, tell remarkably good stories remarkably well.

Wodehouse gave us other London clubs briefly: The Senior Conservative, to which Lord Emsworth and, in his monied days, Psmith belonged; The Senior Buffers, to which Lord Shortlands and Lord Yaxley belonged. The Morpheus, to which Lord Marshmoreton belonged; the old Pelican, where Galahad Threepwood and his gay friends revelled; The Six Jolly Stretchercases, a club without premises except in the Pump Room at Droitgate Spa; The Senior Bloodstain, where detectives gathered; The Snippers and The Senior Bay-Rum for hairdressers; The Senior Test-Tubes for chemists; The Negative and Solution for photographers; The Junior Lipstick where Mayfair's girlhood laid bets about one another's forthcoming engagements; and The Junior Ganymede in Curzon Street, where butlers and gentlemen's personal gentlemen met and discussed their masters. (Jeeves was taking the chair at one of its recent lunches, and he is doubtless its most eminent member.)

But The Drones is the home from home and water-hole of Bertie Wooster and all Wodehouse's best young men. Wodehouse made The Drones, made its membership and made the language of its dining- and smoking-rooms. If the Spirit of Wodehouse has a single address, it is The Drones Club, Dover Street, London, w.1.

IMAGES

Women are divided broadly into two classes – those who, when jilted, merely drop a silent tear and those who take a niblick from their bag and chase the faithless swain across country with it. It was to this latter section that Agnes Flack belonged. Attila the Hun might have broken off his engagement to her, but nobody except Attila the Hun, and he only on one of his best mornings.

*

When Chester came to the eighteenth tee, the Wrecking Crew foursome were just leaving it, moving up the fairway with their caddies and looking, to Chester's exasperated eye, like one of those great race-migrations of the Middle Ages.

*

Her hair was a deep chestnut, her eyes blue, her nose small and laid back with about as much loft as a light iron.

*

In moments of excitement she had a habit of squeaking like a basketful of puppies.

*

He intensified the silent passion of his dancing, trying to convey the idea of being something South American, which ought to be chained up and muzzled in the interests of pure womanhood.

*

George tells me that when the train stopped, out in the middle of a single empty meadow, entirely devoid of cover, no fewer than twenty-seven distinct rustics suddenly appeared, having undoubtedly shot up through the ground. The rails, which had been completely unoccupied, were now thronged with so dense a crowd of navvies that it seemed absurd to pretend that there was any unemployment in England. Every member of the labouring classes throughout the country was so palpably present. Moreover, the train, which at Ippleton had seemed sparsely occupied, was disgorging passengers from every door. It was the sort of mob scene that would have made David W. Griffith scream with delight; and it looked, George says, like Guest Night at the Royal Automobile Club.

*

A head-shrinker ... one of those fellows who ask you questions about your childhood and gradually dig up the reason why you go about shouting 'Fire!' in crowded theatres. They find it's because somebody took away your all-day sucker when you were six.

*

A conscience as tender as a sunburned neck.

*

It was that strange, almost unearthly light which comes into the eyes of wronged uncles when they see a chance of getting their own back from erring nephews.

*

Breakfast had been prepared by the kitchen maid, an indifferent performer who had used the scorched earth policy on the bacon again.

*

Presently the door opened and his head emerged cautiously, like that of a snail taking a look around after a thunderstorm.

*

It is never difficult to distinguish between a Scotsman with a grievance and a ray of sunshine.

*

'I didn't know poets broke people's necks.'

'Ricky does. He once took on three simultaneous costermongers in Covent Garden and cleaned them up in five minutes. He had gone there to get inspiration for a pastoral, and they started chi-iking him, and he sailed in and knocked them base over apex into a pile of Brussels sprouts.'

'How different from the home life of the late Lord Tennyson.'

*

Professor Binstead picked up a small china figure of delicate workmanship. It represented a warrior of pre-khaki days advancing with a spear upon some adversary who, judging from the contented expression on the warrior's face, was smaller than himself.

9

BERTIE WOOSTER

The story 'Extricating Young Gussie' in *The Man with Two Left Feet* (1917), four stories in a collection of eight entitled *My Man Jeeves* (1919), *The Inimitable Jeeves* (1923), a loosely stitched novel of eighteen chapters which make ten separate stories in *The Jeeves Omnibus*, *Carry On, Jeeves* (1925), a collection of ten stories, four of them from *My Man Jeeves*: a fifth which, in *My Man Jeeves*, had been told by and about Reggie Pepper and is here tailored to make a Bertie/Jeeves story 'Fixing It For Freddie' (in this Aunt Agatha's name is still apparently Miss Wooster: so it should strictly ante-date the lot): one describing Jeeves's arrival from the Agency: and a last one narrated by Jeeves himself, *Very Good, Jeeves* (1930), a collection of eleven stories. *The Jeeves Omnibus* (1931), collects and re-collects thirty-one stories; Wodehouse distinctly edited and tidied the old material for this new collection. In *A Few Quick Ones* (1959) is 'Jeeves Makes an Omelette', a rewrite of another old Reggie Pepper story in *My Man Jeeves*. There is one short story in *Plum Pie* (1966). The first proper novel is *Thank You, Jeeves* (March 1934). *Right Ho, Jeeves* followed the same year (October 1934), *The Code of the Woosters* (1938), *Joy in the Morning* (1947), *The Mating Season* (1949). *Ring for Jeeves* (1953) is the only Jeeves novel not told by Bertie; he is mentioned in it, but does not appear. *Jeeves and the Feudal Spirit* (1954), *Jeeves in the Offing* (1960), *Stiff Upper Lip, Jeeves* (1963), *Much Obliged, Jeeves* (1971) and *Aunts Aren't Gentlemen* (1974).

'PROVIDENCE looks after the chumps of this world; and personally I'm all for it,' said Bertie Wooster in 1925. Providentially he was with us to the end, as delightful a young chump as ever.

In France, some time ago, I read in a local paper one of those horror news-stories that encourage me, when motoring anywhere south of the Loire, to keep to the main roads. In some village in the Mauriac district there had been, in the course of a single weekend and at the time of the full moon, a series of blood-curdling crimes, topped off by the unsuccessful burning down of a cottage – unsuccessful, because its two aged inhabitants escaped. The *coupable* had not yet been found, but the police were looking for an *innocent* of the village, who had disappeared. They seemed to be confident that this *innocent* would, when located, prove to be the *coupable*.

I like this French use of the word *innocent* – the village idiot. My mind was very full of Bertie Wooster at the time. *Mutatis mutandis*, and with all the crimes deodorized, I saw the Gironde village as a Steeple Bumpleigh, Totleigh, Brinkley or Skeldings, with Bertie Wooster, the lunatic innocent, generating 250 pages of alarm and confusion.

A reviewer in the *Times Literary Supplement* once condemned 'the sort of insensitive souls who see nothing but a vapid wastrel in Bertie Wooster, that kind, chivalrous and, on the whole, eminently sensible Englishman'. It seems to me that to call Bertie Wooster eminently sensible is not only wrong; it underrates by a mile Wodehouse's aims and achievements in handling Bertie as a character. Bertie is not a vapid wastrel, agreed (by all except Aunt Agatha). He is kind and chivalrous, agreed. He is an Englishman, agreed. But as far as brain is concerned, he is as near to being null and void as makes very little difference. The *Lit. Supp.* reviewer (*Lit. Supp.* reviewers were anonymous in those days) would presumably have amplified his judgement by saying that Bertie's eminence was that of a half-wit among nit-wits. Well, Wodehouse could have pulled that off easily enough. In fact, though, he pulled off something much more difficult. He made Bertie a nit-wit among half-wits, a super-fool among fools.

He is, to me, one of the most charming innocents in print. My heart aches for him in his enormous agonies and rejoices with him in his puny exaltations. But Jeeves is right – Bertie is mentally negligible.

And Wodehouse made him his medium in more than a dozen books. They are tales told by an idiot, but Bertie proves to be an unselfconsciously brilliant narrator. This has needed very careful handling. As a character in the books, Bertie's only claim to literary achievement (and he is outspokenly proud of it) is the 'piece' he once contributed to his Aunt Dahlia's magazine, on 'What the Well-dressed Man is Wearing'. But as Wodehouse's medium, Bertie has written all those stories and novels, and this fictional dichotomy does not grate for a moment. As a storyteller Bertie is his own central character, and he has to narrate strictly from the first-personal point of view, often writing scenes in such a way that Bertie-the-character must not realise the purport of what Bertie-the-narrator is narrating, but his readers must. Very difficult, and he does it very smoothly. But still Bertie the writer must project his fictional self as a man capable of being mightily proud of a single incursion into print, in *Milady's Boudoir*.

Wodehouse's other recurrent mouthpieces tell their stories with themselves standing on the side-lines, and with narrator's licence. They may start in double quotes, stating the facts from personal experience. But soon the double quotes disappear, the voice of the specified narrator fades out, and narrator Wodehouse takes over. We are told what a man and a girl say, declaring their love, in a golf-bunker or a two-seater, and we do not ask 'How do you know they said that if you were not there?' Author Wodehouse/Oldest Member is a fly on the wall of the bunker; author Wodehouse/Mulliner is a fly on the windscreen of the two-seater. But Bertie is the core of his own stories, and he has to be there throughout, or fill in with reported speech, delivered to himself. One or two other narrators sustain this technique for a single book (Jeremy Garnet for the second edition of *Love among the Chickens* and Reggie Havershot in *Laughing Gas*). Bertie has done it for ten novels and fifty-odd short stories.

At his preparatory school, Bertie was known as 'Bungler' Wooster. This nickname may not have had associations with the Conan Doyle Sherlock Holmes stories ('Scotland Yard bunglers') in the minds of Bertie's masters and friends. It certainly had those associations in Wodehouse's mind. I seem to keep finding, or I keep seeming to find, trace elements of Doyle in the Wodehouse formulations. I sense a distinct similarity, in patterns and rhythms, between the adventures of Jeeves as recorded by Bertie Wooster and the adventures of Sherlock Holmes as recorded by Dr Watson: Holmes and Jeeves the great brains, Watson and Bertie the awed companion-narrators, bungling things if they try to solve the problems themselves; the problems, waiting to be tackled almost always in country houses, almost always presented and discussed at breakfast in London; the departure from London, Holmes and Watson by train, Jeeves and Bertie by two-seater; the gathering of the characters at the country house; the gathering of momentum, Holmes seldom telling Watson what he is up to, Jeeves often working behind Bertie's back; the dénouement; the company fawning on Holmes or Jeeves; the return trip to 'the rooms' in town; possibly Holmes's '... and I pocket my fee' paralleled by Bertie Wooster's 'How much money is there on the dressing-table, Jeeves? ... Collar it all. You've earned it!'

The high incidence of crime in the Wodehouse farces, especially the Bertie/Jeeves ones, may be an echo of the Sherlock Holmes stories, too – blackmail, theft, revolver-shots in the night (*Something Fresh*), airgun-shots by day ('The Crime Wave at Blandings'), butlers in dressing-gowns, people climbing in at bedroom windows, people dropping out of bedroom

windows, people hiding in bedroom cupboards, the searching
of bedrooms for missing manuscripts, cow-creamers and pigs.
I am not accusing Wodehouse of having concocted his stories
deliberately on Doyle's lines; I am saying that, of all the
authors to whom Wodehouse's debt shows itself, Doyle is
second only to W. S. Gilbert. And Wodehouse would gladly
have acknowledged both debts.

On another level you may see Bertie Wooster as a modern
Don Quixote, constantly setting out on adventures to help
his friends and constantly making an endearing ass of himself.
Don Quixote has a wiser *vade mecum* in Sancho Panza; Bertie
has the wiser Jeeves. Bertie, like Don Quixote, has his brain
curdled with romance. Don Quixote's romance came from
books of knight-errantry; Bertie's from Edwardian fiction and
a regular diet of detective novels. Don Quixote's enchanting
books were burnt, but he carried the gist of them always in his
mind; Bertie has an ever-ready memory of the plot-clichés of
the Rosie M. Banks writers of his boyhood. When he tries to
disentangle his friends' problems along Rosie M. Banks's
lines, he gets those lines crossed and the entanglements made
worse. He is a prime bungler. A good-natured romantic, but
a bungler. One comes back to the Doyle word.

The important thing, if you study Bertie, is not so much the
width of his reading of bilge literature as the depth to which he
absorbs the stuff. His little mind keeps a gooey sludge of
words, phrases and concepts from what he has read, and it
gives him a magpie vocabulary of synonyms and quotations.
It contributes largely to his Code. He is a fantasist. Even,
perhaps specially, in moments of tension and peril, his attention seems to wander, and he gets beside himself, watching
himself, aligning himself with the heroes of his reading, adopt-
ing their attitudes, blurting out their clichés of speech. Bertie
shares his escape-route with Mr Pooter, Walter Mitty, Billy
Liar, Catherine Morland, Emma Bovary and other literary

dreamers. So far Bertie has only encountered Sir Roderick Glossop, the loony-doctor, socially. Never in the consulting-room. But Sir Roderick may still be waiting for Bertie fairly confidently as a patient.

In *Right Ho, Jeeves*, Bertie, while nobly, if cautiously and anonymously, pleading Gussie's cause with Madeline Bassett, makes it appear to Madeline that he is brokenly and shyly pleading his own love for her. It was an old Wodehouse plot-shape; indeed much older than Wodehouse. For a brief, climactic moment Bertie finds that Madeline has received his words as a proposal. And his book-bred Code says that no gentleman can break off his engagement to however disastrous a girl. You'd expect, if you didn't know Bertie, that in this crisis his brain would either cease to function or, ice-cold in an emergency, would attend to the matter in hand with single strictness. Not so. Bertie, clenching his fists in agony, is wondering whether his knuckles are, or are not, standing out white under the strain. And when, seconds later, Madeline tells Bertie that she is sorry, the thing's impossible, you'd expect that the relief would clarify Bertie's mind wonderfully, and pinpoint his attention on the facts. Again not so. The relief is great, yes. But Bertie the fantasist lets his mind wander and is instantly beside himself again, seeing the event in homely images:

'I am sorry . . .' said Madeline . . .
The word was like one of Jeeves's pick-me-ups. Just as if a glass-ful of meat sauce, red pepper and the yolk of an egg . . . though, as I say, I am convinced that these are not the sole ingredients . . . had been shot into me, I expanded like some lovely flower blossoming in the sunshine. It was all right, after all. My guardian angel had not been asleep at the switch.

If you say that this is Bertie the narrator, remembering in tranquillity and with a trained literary mind events which allowed no such mental gymnastics at the time, I am not convinced.

Bertie's mind drifted *during the crisis* into mazes of metaphor and meat sauce. He was carried off on a stream of semi-consciousness and free association, with time for a parenthesis stating his doubts about the Jeeves pick-me-up recipe. Then he sees himself in the guise of some lovely flower blossoming in the sunshine. He is back to his books.

Bertie hops through the looking-glass and stands beside himself very often and at slight provocation. His memory is so full of the words and music of heroic action that he can find a phrase to fit almost any situation. His narrative and conversation are larded with second-hand alternatives to direct description. By mixing his soiled metaphors and colliding his clichés, he fabricates a burbling language of evocative innocence. Quite often in narration he drops into the Bertie-beside-himself third person singular:

Those who know Bertram Wooster best are aware that he is a man of sudden, strong enthusiasms and that, when in the grip of one of these, he becomes a remorseless machine, tense, absorbed, single-minded. It was so in the matter of this banjolele-playing of mine . . .

and

'Yes, Jeeves?' I said. And though my voice was suave a close observer in a position to watch my eyes would have noted a steely glint . . .

and

When I wore it (the white mess jacket) at the Casino at Cannes, beautiful women nudged one another and whispered; 'Who is he?'

and

He quivered like a mousse. I suppose it must always be rather a thrilling experience for the novice to watch me taking hold . . .

In his last book of all, Bertie is still watching himself in a
mirror, hearing himself talk and ready with self-applause
when it is earned.

> 'Hullo, old ancestor,' I said, and it was a treat to hear me, so
> full of ginger and loving kindness was my diction.

Bertie laughing down from lazy eyelids and flicking specks
of dust from the irreproachable Mechlin lace at his wrists;
Bertie answering an angry questioner 'with a suavity that became me well'; Bertie inspecting his imagination and finding
that it boggled; Bertie saying 'Oh' and meaning it to sting –
with Bertie, we are dealing with a young man whose boyhood
reading has been wider than a church door, and whose memory of it is deeper than a well. Bertie is a shining example of a
magpie mind cherished whole into adult life.

Shakespeare had a magpie mind, too. It is only the fine,
imaginative, noticing mind, like Shakespeare's and Bertie
Wooster's, that dares wander down the garden path without
losing its way back. Your lawyer and chartered accountant
would feel naked and lost so far from home. If they look wist-
fully out into the garden, and to the perilous seas and faery
lands beyond, they take good care to keep the magic casement
shut, lest they start climbing through. Shakespeare equates the
lunatic, the lover and the poet – types who can't keep their feet
on the ground or their minds on the subject under advisement.
Bertie is three parts lunatic. He sometimes loves. In his wild
imagery he is not far off from being a poet.

Bertie asked Pauline Stoker to marry him. It was in New
York, at the Plaza. Bertie relates the incident only in a flash-
back, as a necessary starting point for *Thank You, Jeeves*;
necessary because it gives an excuse for a good jealousy-teeth-
grinding-let's-see-the-colour-of-his-insides menace to Bertie
from his old friend Chuffy, who is now, three months later, in
love with Pauline. The green-eyed Chuffy questions Bertie

keenly about what went on when he and Pauline were engaged. He grills Bertie into revealing that, during the two days' betrothal, he never kissed the adored object even once:

'I hope you will be very, very happy [says Bertie to Chuffy]. I can honestly say that I always look on Pauline as one of the nicest girls I was ever engaged to.'

'I wish you would stop harping on that engagement.'

'Quite.'

'I'm trying to forget that you were ever engaged to her.'

'Quite, quite.'

'When I think that you were once in a position to . . .'

'But I wasn't. Never lose sight of the fact that the betrothal only lasted two days, during both of which I was in bed with a nasty cold.'

'But when she accepted you, you must have . . .'

'No, I didn't. A waiter came into the room with a tray of beef sandwiches and the moment passed.'

'Then you never . . .?'

'Absolutely never.'

'She must have had a great time, being engaged to you. One round of excitement. I wonder what on earth made her accept you?'

That engagement was broken up by Pop Stoker, abetted by Sir Roderick Glossop. But, although Wodehouse frequently juxtaposed sentiment and food, romance and greediness, as incongruities to make comic bathos, for the moment I want to put the lights on that tray of beef sandwiches at the Plaza in New York.

When Bertie recalls those beef sandwiches, is he babbling the free associations of a mind permanently loose in the socket? Or is he half-way to poetry? Shakespeare, as we know, was all for free association. Take Juliet's nurse, her woolly old mind swithering about trying to pinpoint Juliet's age. She remembers, she remembers . . . yes, she'll get it soon. Yes, she had weaned Juliet . . . yes, she had put the wormwood to her dug,

> Sitting in the sun under the dove house wall;
> My Lord and you were then at Mantua.

Forty years ago I wrote in a note against those two lines in my Temple *Romeo and Juliet*: 'cf. Bertie W's beef sandwiches'. Juliet's Nurse, under Shakespeare's guidance, remembers the sun and the dove house and the wall. Bertie, earthier, remembers the beef sandwiches.

Bertie admits that he has a tendency to babble in moments of tension. In a burst of sympathy for the cloth-headed newt-fancier, Gussie, who, terrified by the arrival of the mood, the moonlight and the expectant Madeline all together, started talking about newts, Bertie remembers how, in the dentist's chair, he had, through sheer nerves, held up the man behind the forceps with a silly story of an Englishman, an Irishman and a Jew. But often in a crisis he repeats sounds without knowing their meaning. He refers to someone in an advanced state of gloom looking like a cat in an adage. When Tuppy Glossop is reaching for Bertie's neck in the garden, to wring it for (as Tuppy believes) having traduced him (Tuppy) to the girl (Angela) whom he (Tuppy) loves, Bertie says:

'I have always regarded you with the utmost esteem. Why, then, if not for the motives I have outlined, should I knock you to Angela? Answer me that. Be very careful.'

'What do you mean, be very careful?'

Well, as a matter of fact, I didn't quite know myself. It was what the magistrate had said to me on the occasion when I stood in the dock as Eustace Plimsoll, of The Laburnums; and as it had impressed me a good deal, at the time, I just brought it in now by way of giving the conversation a tone ...

If Bertie wrenches logic and language into perilous distortions, it is not entirely through vapidity. It is partly a genuine hankering for the *mot juste*, the vivid phrase, the exact image. At another moment of acute crisis he can pause to express his shock at discovering that Uncle Tom's second name is Portarlington, or to ask Jeeves to check a quotation for him. Referring to Aunt Dahlia and her weekly magazine, *Milady's Boudoir*, he writes: 'Seeing it go down the drain would be for her like watching a loved child sink for the third time in some pond or mere . . .'

That 'or mere' comes with the pride of a magpie which has collected a gold ring *and* a silver paper milk-bottle top; it is the poet hoarding an alternative for rhyming; it is the pin-head who lets his feeble mind wander in word-associations when an aunt is in peril. This one may be a Tennysonian evocation. Bertie's sources may be anything from the Psalms (frequently) to Scott's last message from the Antarctic (once). He hasn't the discrimination to be a snob about his sources. To go to the Old Vic with his cousin, Young Thos, at Aunt Agatha's orders, to witness Shakespeare or Chekhov, is torture, to him as to Thos. But once a literary phrase has got tamped down in his memory, it becomes a fiery particle of his vocabulary. In Jeeves he has a walking lexicon and dictionary of quotations, which he adds to his simmering brew of tosh and tag-ends, thin on reason but often producing a sweet poetry.

> Reason has moons, but moons not hers
> lie mirror'd on her sea,
> confounding her astronomers,
> but O! delighting me.

Bertie hardly ever tries to be funny and he is not a bit witty. He will use a piffling phrase for a lofty sentiment or a lofty phrase for a piffling sentiment. He bubbles and burbles, innocent and vulnerable. Fantasist, schizo, duffer, do-gooder, hungry for praise, Bertie has a mind that is a tape-recorder for sounds and rhythms, but has no discipline or control in playing them back. This is the quintessence of the highly disciplined and tightly controlled Wodehouse burble. Bertie is its chief executant. But, make no mistake, 'Bertie Wodehouse' language has power, suppleness and great speed of communication. When Hilaire Belloc wrote that Wodehouse was the best writer of English alive, he was paying tribute not only to his control of schizophrenic imagery, but to his discipline in telling a complicated story quickly and clearly. Wodehouse can, in Bertie's artificial language, get from A to B by the shortest route and still litter all sorts of flowers at your feet as you follow it.

Tuppy Glossop was the fellow, if you remember, who, ignoring a lifelong friendship in the course of which he had frequently eaten my bread and salt, betted me one night at the Drones that I wouldn't swing myself across the swimming bath by the ropes and rings, and then, with almost inconceivable treachery, went and looped back the last ring, causing me to drop into the fluid and ruin one of the nattiest suits of dress-clothes in London.

Try altering or cutting a word in that sentence. You can't. Every *mot* is *juste*. When Bertie describes the warning note of an angry nesting swan as being 'like a tyre bursting in a nest of cobras', it shows Bertie, again at a moment of tension, daydreaming into a poetic image even as his adrenal reflexes (fight or flight) send him skimming up the wall of the summerhouse. But it is a glorious image, expressed in words which themselves, of their structure, menace and explode with sibilants.

Bertie Wooster's age stays put at about twenty-four, but you can spot certain changes in his slang styles as the publishing years advance. He stopped saying 'chappie', 'dear boy' and the parenthetical 'don't you know' in the 1920s. He stopped saying 'rattled' (meaning pleased), and 'rotten' as a universal pejorative, in the 1930s. By the middle 1930s he had virtually made his own language, and it became frozen and timeless to the last. A great number of people have tried to parody the 'Bertie Wodehouse' style in print. Rather fewer have tried to imitate it without parody. None has succeeded. The best parodies of Bertie's style are by Wodehouse himself when he let a page go to the printer without quite the necessary polish. Then you are probably reading the sixth draft, rather than the tenth. At his polished best the burble that Wodehouse put into Bertie's mouth is beautiful stuff.

It is pretty generally recognised in the circles in which he moves that Bertram Wooster is not a man who lightly throws in the towel and admits defeat. Beneath the thingummies of what-d'you-call-it, his head, wind and weather permitting, is as a rule bloody but un-bowed, and if the slings and arrows of outrageous fortune want to crush his proud spirit, they have to pull their socks up and make a special effort.

Nevertheless, I must confess that when, already weakened by having to come down to breakfast, I beheld the spectacle which I have described, I definitely quailed. The heart sank, and, as had happened in the case of Spode, everything went black. Through a murky mist I seemed to be watching a negro butler presenting an inky salver to a Ma Trotter who looked like the end man in a minstrel show.

The floor heaved beneath my feet as if an earthquake had set in with unusual severity. My eye, in fine frenzy rolling, met Aunt Dahlia's, and I saw hers was rolling, too.

Twelve Woosterisms in seventeen lines: the general clash of jargon phrases, the Bertie-beside-himself Third Person Singu-lar of the whole first paragraph, a botched quotation from Henley, and two, less botched, from Shakespeare, the babu interposition of the presumably nautical 'wind and weather permitting' inside the botched Henley, the boxing image, the good old Wodehousian elaboration of the 'everything went black' cliché, the good old Wodehousian 'earthquake had set in with unusual severity' (that's generally ' Judgement Day', not 'earthquake'), the medical use of 'the' heart instead of 'my' heart, the medical 'weakened' to emphasize that Bertie had breakfasted downstairs that day for once, the enforced use of the single eye, forgivable in the first case, because Bertie is quoting Shakespeare, but foolishly cyclopean when transferred to Aunt Dahlia in the second.

Since Wodehouse wrote in his Bertie Wooster voice more, much more, than in any other, it is reasonable to suppose that he put it on more comfortably than any other. Is it also reasonable to suppose that we find more of the Wodehouse personal identity hidden in Bertie than in any other of Wodehouse's puppets? I think so.

The self-derogatory First Person Singular has been a staple of English language humour over the last seventy-five years. If 'He slipped on a banana skin' is funny, 'I slipped on a banana skin' is conceivably funny and charming. This is not the only technique of whimsy, but it is a very frequent factor in whimsy. 'Whimsy' and 'whimsical' are rude words in literary criticism these days. But three-quarters of a century ago, and through the majority of Owen Seaman's years on *Punch*, the value-judgement in the words was for the most part kind and appreciative. Seaman's *Punch* catered for, and then overfed, the taste for whimsy. The magazine of his day was full of self-derogatory First-Person-Singular pieces. Admittedly one's suspension of disbelief in *Punch* was made more unwilling by the magazine's weird habit of having, in an issue containing, say, ten 'I' pieces, three signed by initials, three by pseudonyms and four not signed at all. But the fact remains that the 'I' piece has been, for three-quarters of a century of English humorous writers, a favourite stand-by. Its main laws have remained unaltered since Thackeray and Burnand.

Wodehouse, whose *floruit* spanned much of the whimsy era of *Punch*, wrote very little direct 'I' stuff. In *Louder and Funnier* and *Over Seventy* he showed that he could do it expertly. But if you suppose that any good funny writer with a taste for editorial cheques would use a profitable technique for all it was worth to him, you may be surprised that Wodehouse did not cash in more on his opportunities.

Subliminally, I believe, Bertie Wooster was, and increasingly became, Wodehouse's main surrogate outlet for the self-derogatory First Person Singular mood. The name Wooster is significantly close to Wodehouse. Bertie, in portions of his background and many of his attitudes (though not in his Eton and Oxford status), is the young Wodehouse that the older Wodehouse remembered with amusement, candour, modesty and (a sixth-form tag that Wodehouse himself used in several of his youthful books) *pothos* and *desiderium*. The identification in ages is between Bertie at an eternal twenty-four and Wodehouse in that *annus mirabilis* of mental age at which most Wodehouse farce is played – fifteen.

A doctor has told me that when a patient is coming out from under anaesthetic, the anaesthetist needs some test of the stages of his re-emergence. So the anaesthetist starts saying to the patient 'How old are you?', 'How old are you?' And (the doctor told me), however advanced the age of the patient, his first mumbling answer is frequently 'Nineteen'. He may say 'nineteen' two or three times till adequate consciousness returns, and then he gets it right at fifty-five, or sixty-five or seventy-five.

Belloc wrote of the unchanging place where all we loved is always near, where we meet our morning face to face and find at last our twentieth year. Nineteen is (according to the doctor) the usual *annus mirabilis*. Fifteen was Wodehouse's, and Wodehouse, significantly, often let Bertie take him back to the green pastures of that irresponsible period, the last moment at which he could see himself unselfconsciously.

Bertie's manner of life, his money, his personal servant, his riding, shooting (once), rackets (once), squash, darts and tennis, his clubs, his idleness, his love for Fancy Dress Balls, his contemptible cunning, risible ruses and puny piques, his overweening optimism and his babu burble of clashing clichés and inattentive images – these are creations of Wodehouse the

storyteller. Bertie, the kind, the chivalrous, the greedy, the
aunt-ridden, the Code-ridden, the girl-fearing, the pal-helping,
the tag-quoting, the slug-abed – he is a poetic, middle-voice
throw-back to the dewy, pie-faced schoolboy romantic that
Wodehouse saw himself as having been before he struck out
into the world for himself. Bertie, in two separate senses, is
more of an 'I' character than anyone else in the books. On
some spiritual, astral plane, Bertie Wooster and P. G. Wodehouse, their dross shed, may have now met as twin souls.

Bertie is the only one of Wodehouse's heroes or protagonists for whom the mere release from terror and pain is always
a sufficiently happy ending. This modest sufficiency is very
much in the formula of the technique of 'I' humour. Reggie
Havershot, narrator and hero of Wodehouse's light novel,
Laughing Gas, survives ten chapters of bewilderment, indignity
and bullying by an 'aunt' figure. But he is rewarded in the end
by winning a jackpot and a Wodehouse heroine in marriage.
It is sufficient for the First-Personal Bertie that others get the
jackpots and girls, and that he be simply released from bewilderment, indignity, bullying by aunts and other circum-
ambient menaces. Bertie, indeed, almost always actually pays
for his releases by some kind of atonement-forfeit (Old
Etonian spats) or punishment (the great midnight bicycle ride
from Brinkley and back). It is acceptable to the reader as a
minor, but regular, nemesis for Bertie's earlier hubristic
certainty that he can settle his friends' problems, either better
than Jeeves can, or at all. Wodehouse allows such forces of
misrule as Uncle Fred and Aunt Dahlia to go scot-free from
the debt of their immoralities. But not First-Personal Bertie.
Bertie suffers, and, through suffering, he is kept in place. The
addition of punishment to the massive terrors and embarrass-
ments that Bertie gets into through his desire to please is
artistically supportable, and indeed rewarding, to the reader
only because the story is being told by someone cordially

underwritten by the author whose name appears on the spine of the book.

Wodehouse autobiography, chopped small, drifts like thistledown into Wooster fiction. The novel, *The Mating Season*, published in 1949, contains an interesting collection of the sort of memory-accretions, many of them anachronistic, which give strength to the theory that, consciously or unconsciously, Wodehouse used his own nineteenth-century childhood as a general source of Bertie's twentieth-century youth. Bertie is stuck in a house full of aunts – not his own in the book, but giving him frequent cause to philosophize about aunts. Bertie recalls boyhood dancing-classes, boyhood recitations, boyhood pimples, a boyhood Little-Lord-Fauntleroy suit, and a boyhood nannie. He is made to help at a village concert, and he is wise in the ways of village concerts, as Wodehouse doubtless was when he lived with aunts-married-to-clergymen in his school holidays. Village concerts as a regular threat to country life must have been severely hit by the arrival of radio, and killed stone-dead by television. But there, in 1949, is Bertie in the midst of one. Nobody sings 'The Yeoman's Wedding Song', but Muriel Kegley-Bassington comes across with 'My Hero' from *The Chocolate Soldier* followed by 'Oh, who will o'er the downs with me' as an encore. Except for the Christopher Robin verses, every turn has an 1890-ish date to it. The vicar's niece, who organizes the concert, is Corky Pirbright, now a Hollywood star. Her brother, Catsmeat, though a member of The Drones, is an actor. There is much talk of the low esteem in which the respectable gentry holds members of the acting profession – an Edwardian, not later-Georgian attitude. Bertie in this book is unusually full of stage jargon, and is deft to compose a lyric for the squire (who loves Corky) to sing at the concert. This surely is the young Wodehouse, whose dabbling in, and success at, writing for the theatre must have caused his own flock of aunts to think he was getting into bad company in his twenties, much more dangerous than the friends he would have made if he had stayed in the Bank.

For the length of *The Mating Season*, and the date still being 1949, Bertie stays at Deverill Hall, a house more or less run by these strict aunts, but where champagne is served without question at dinner; a house full of modern conveniences, but where all sudden announcements from the outside are made by telegram, not by telephone; Bertie meets the butler, Silversmith (Jeeves's uncle), and is reminded of the old-fashioned, sixteen-stone butlers who made him feel insignificant and badly dressed as a young man. But Bertie *is*, for the purposes of the story, a young man. Aged twenty-four in 1949, he would have been born in 1925, a good fifty years too late for him to have been bothered by Little-Lord-Fauntleroy suits, childhood recitations of 'Mary Had a Little Lamb' and 'Ben Battle', and the sort of village concert that this one turned out to be. Wodehouse was giving his own stripling memories to Bertie, in spite of a difference of fifty years in period. In another book Bertie remembers his Little-Lord-Fauntleroy suit again, and this time he also remembers that he wore his hair in ringlets to match. I don't know if the boy Wodehouse was made to wear his hair in ringlets. Nor do I know for sure (though I would make a bet) that Bertie was speaking for his ninety-three-year-old author in *Aunts Aren't Gentlemen* when he said 'When I was a child, my nurse told me that there was One who was always beside me, spying out all my ways, and that if I refused to eat my spinach I would hear about it on Judgement Day.'

John Hayward in *The Saturday Book* of 1942 made the point that Wodehouse had 'a wide knowledge of English literature and Shakespeare's plays'. He may have had, but the knowledge that he exhibited is essentially schoolboy stuff. Bertie and Jeeves between them bandy quotations from the poets freely.

But where these are not from Shakespeare and the classical poets (and an A-level schoolboy of today might have the same stock), they are from such minor Victorian sources that a boy might have learnt them for Repetition at school in the late 90s, but not in the 1920s. And a significant number of Bertie's images (the tiger and his breakfast coolie, the Pathan sneaking up on the *sahib* across the *maidan*) seem to jump right out from illustrations in *Chums* and similar magazines of the 1890s. This again is Wodehouse giving his memories to Bertie. Bertie once or twice looks back to the days of Covent Garden Balls, fights with costermongers and nights spent at the hammams, almost like the original, eighteenth-century William Hickey. Bertie is an ageless young man, spanning the ages.

Bertie started life as a type, and he became a character. He remains the Knut, the Piccadilly Johnny and the playboy bachelor. But, because Wodehouse liked him and wrote through his eyes so often, Bertie became more three-dimensional than any other character in these highly artificial books. In *Performing Flea* Wodehouse says: 'I go off the rails unless I stay all the time in a sort of artificial world of my own creation. A real character in one of my books sticks out like a sore thumb.' Bertie comes alive in the sense that he is predictable. He dictates his own terms for plot and characterisation. While other cardboard characters walk into the soup and displace hardly a spoonful, Bertie displaces it in credible waves. We go in there with him and suffer with his suffering. When Freddie Widgeon, Bingo, Ukridge or a Mulliner go into the soup, we stay on the rim of the tureen and laugh. With Bertie we share the agony and the wetness. His mental deficiency is such that our own brains feel powerful. But we love Bertie and identify ourselves with him, as Wodehouse did to the limits of his own very rigid modesty and self-esteem.

Bertie looks back to a childhood and boyhood of normal rowdiness. When, in 'The Love that Purifies', he sees a septuagenarian asleep in the garden in a deck-chair, he tells Jeeves that, in his boyhood, he would certainly have done something drastic to such a septuagenarian, probably with a pea shooter. He stole and smoked one of Lord Worplesdon's cigars at the age of fifteen. He may not have been as fiendish a young gangster as his cousin Thos when he was Thos's age, but he wasn't a prig, like Edwin Craye, or a sissy, like Sebastian Moon. He went through Malvern House, Eton and Oxford at the proper pace. But, somewhere about the age of twenty-four, Bertie stopped ageing.

Very occasionally in the last few publishing decades twenty-four-year-old Bertie indicates that he is not such a young young man as he was. He no longer envies the all-night undergraduate energy of Claude and Eustace. As late as *Jeeves and the Feudal Spirit* (1954) Bertie is saying: 'I'm not much of a lad for the night clubs these days. Age creeping on me, I suppose.' But he is still a member of half a dozen in London. And when, after a night-club raid, the magistrate at Winton Street comes to sentence 'the prisoner Gadsby' (Bertie's alias) he says: 'In consideration of your youth I will exercise clemency.' So Bertie gets only a fine, not the jug. And in the 1960 novel, *Jeeves in the Offing*, Bertie shows signs of age, I think, in that he accepts, for the first time without protest, the two frightening jobs that 'Kipper' Herring and Bobby Wickham push him into in order to advance their own loves. They are both jobs that Bertie has been pushed into before, in earlier books, by other friends. And in those books Bertie entered *nolle prosequis* for several recusant paragraphs before the Code of the Woosters got the upper hand. Now, in *Jeeves in the Offing*, he is told to shove the Rev. Aubrey Upjohn into the lake and, when that fails, to go into the study and call him names so that Kipper can come in and take Upjohn's side against the frightful Wooster, and thus get Upjohn to call off the libel suit etc. etc. Bertie, aged in experience if not in years, does as he is told, without a yip, knowing that resistance has always proved useless in the past and will do so again this time. He is getting trained.

There is some doubt about which college Bertie was in at Oxford. He says Magdalen, but he also says that he bicycled (in the nude, after a Bump Supper) round his college fountain, and that could only mean Christ Church. But there is no doubt that it was in his schooldays, not at Oxford, that he acquired the main commandments of his eternal Code.

The Code of the Woosters is part public-school, part novelette. Its two main commandments are: (1) Thou shalt not let down a pal; and (2) Thou shalt not scorn a woman's love. Most of the plots of Bertie's stories hinge on one or the other, or both, of these commandments. Bertie has a genuinely kind heart, and, though Palmanship forces him to undertake terrible exploits, he really is made happier when he can do a good turn for a friend, and especially for two friends, a man and a girl with a lovers' tiff to be tidied up.

John Aldridge sees Bertie as the eternal adolescent set between the warring factions of mother and father surrogates. Aunt Dahlia and Jeeves are the main mother-surrogates, Aunt Agatha and Sir Roderick Glossop are representative father-surrogates. The menaces of the latter (Aldridge's argument runs) 'demand from Bertie an abandonment of the boyhood state and the prompt assumption of deadly adulthood'. But 'with Jeeves to protect him Bertie is free to pursue a way of life exactly suited to his retarded needs and desires. The boyhood world can be preserved intact.'

This seems to me a just psychological analysis. But it needs expansion. What does Authority mean to someone with a family, social and educational background such as Bertie's? I think it is based in the public-school system. In public schools, both of fiction and of fact, headmasters, housemasters and their lackeys, the prefects, represent Authority in a highly un-

democratic state. The serfs and proles of the Lower and
Middle Schools have no say in who bosses them. Authority is
always elected from above. Prefects are not, in any school that
I know of, chosen by an electorate of juniors saying 'Please
govern us.' The housemaster nominates the prefects, the
headmaster nominates the housemaster and the Governing
Body nominates the headmaster. Young Johnny's parents pay
large sums for young Johnny to live in this hieratic discipline,
subdued until the time comes for him, as a prefect, to subdue.

Bertie Wooster's relationship with Jeeves seems to me a
public-school arrangement, easy for Bertie, though surprisingly accepted by Jeeves. Bertie sometimes berates Jeeves like
a prefect berating a fag, not like a master berating a servant.
And as Bertie is always wrong on these occasions, and Jeeves
knows it, Bertie is extremely lucky to have a servant who
understands his master's Code and forgives it. But in the wider
Wodehouse social set-up, though Authority does not specifically employ the public-school indignification of beating
grown-up people on the 'billowy portions', it does, in the
public-school manner, work to a set of sanctions, checks and
balances of great power, but, almost all of them, non-valid in,
and beyond the reach of, Common Law. You can't have the
law on an aunt when she makes you steal pearl necklaces for
her, but you know that, if you don't comply, the cooking of
the best chef in England will be wiped from your greedy lips
in indefinite punishment. Call it blackmail, but can you tell it
to the magistrate? You can't have the law on a ghastly girl
when she says she's going to marry you, but you'll put yourself in peril of the law by pinching a policeman's uniform in
order to set in motion a series of events which will culminate
(if Jeeves is working them out) in your quasi-honourable
release from the engagement. When Stiffy Byng makes her
fiancé, the sainted Rev. 'Stinker' Pinker, prove his love for
her by bringing her policeman Oates's helmet, he can do

nothing but wail 'If the Infants' Bible Class should hear of this!' When Florence Craye makes her fiancé, Stilton, grow a moustache, he is powerless except to grind a tooth or two. When an ex-London magistrate, a maniac collector of old silver, puts a rival maniac collector out of the running for the acquisition of a rare antique by, with cunning aforethought, feeding him cold lobster at lunch and so confining him to quarters with writhing indigestion, the second maniac's ever-loving wife knows that the law cannot help. Bertie must go and steal the cow-creamer back for its 'rightful' owner. In Wodehouse's farces everybody is playing cops and robbers in a law-free society.

Bertie, the most innocent of do-gooders temperamentally, has no inborn authority of his own. He never uses his money to buy authority and, apart from money, what is he? He has accepted the position of being a 'Hey-you' to aunts, uncles and quite a lot of girls. But Wodehouse was in Bertie's corner, and Wodehouse gave Bertie Jeeves. With certain reservations about white mess jackets, Old Etonian spats and banjoleles, Jeeves is completely and self-effacingly pro-Bertie. All three, Bertie, Jeeves and Wodehouse, are transparently anti-prefect (Aunt Agatha), anti-fag (Edwin) and pro the status of the fifteen-year-old public-school boy.

But watch Bertie when he suddenly does get the moral cosh of authority into his hands. He knows all the prefect's manner of speech. Though he is properly the bossed, the chivvied, the man in the ranks, the man on the receiving end of orders and objurgations, Bertie can snap, with absurd ease, into the jargon of authority. Listen to him come the headmaster over terrible Spode, when he has blessedly remembered the magic word 'Eulalie', and thus has the goods on this pestilential amateur dictator:

'I shall be very sharp on that sort of thing in the future, Spode.'
'Yes, yes, I understand.'

'I have not been at all satisfied with your behaviour since you came to this house. The way you were looking at me during dinner . . . and calling me a miserable worm.'

'I'm sorry I called you a miserable worm, Wooster. I spoke without thinking.'

'Always think, Spode. Well, that is all. You may withdraw.'

Macaulay wrote of the 'arrogant humility' of the younger Pitt. Bertie's humble arrogance is a much more touching thing.

Who was Bertie Wooster, and what was his family background? It has to be pointed out, and then quickly forgotten, that in the first story in which Bertie appeared, 'Extricating Young Gussie' in *The Man with Two Left Feet*, his surname was undoubtedly Mannering-Phipps. Also that in three short stories, which you can find in earlier Wodehouse books, related, and acted in, by one Reggie Pepper, Bertie took over, for later books, with little more than the names changed and Jeeves injected. Perhaps also that when, for the length of a novel (*Ring for Jeeves*, 1953), Wodehouse removed Bertie from the scene and lent Jeeves to Lord Rowcester, Lord Rowcester could, with disturbing accuracy, take over Bertie's lines in the hitherto supposedly sacred stichomyth between master and man.

Make a face-sized oval in white cardboard, put two dark smudges for eyes, and hold it above the cot of a very young baby. Up to the age of seven weeks the baby, if he has started to smile at all, will smile just as regularly at the cardboard face as at his mother's. Bertie has cardboard beginnings.

In a literary sense Bertie and Jeeves were both born in America. 'Extricating Young Gussie' was first published in America. All the four Jeeves stories in *My Man Jeeves* (1919) are set in New York. The original miscue at Bertie's surname was probably caused itself by over-anxiety to please America. In Wodehouse's early New York days the resounding and seemingly aristocratic English name was something of a joke.

Americans liked to think that Courtney de Vere-Vere was a typical English name. We liked to think that Silas Q. Higgs was a typical American name. Wodehouse mentions the business of English names in America in one or two of his essays, and, in 'In Alcala', the somewhat autobiographical English hero in New York gets his name cut down by the American heroine from Rutherford Maxwell to George. Mannering-Phipps was at that period a typical English name for Wodehouse's American purposes and was acceptable without a smile to English readers. Gussie himself says he feels a fearful ass in New York when he has to sign his name as Augustus Mannering-Phipps. He starts calling himself George Wilson.

So Bertie was Mannering-Phipps as a pupa. He had a chrysalis stage as Reggie Pepper. And he finally emerged as Wooster. He seems to have become an orphan at eight or nine. He hardly ever mentions his father, still less his mother. For the period of one story only he has a widowed sister with three daughters, but they are soon forgotten. He has a number of Wooster uncles. One of them surprisingly becomes Lord Yaxley, obviously through no damned merit, since he is fat, idle, foolish and slightly pickled in alcohol. He eventually marries an ex-barmaid. Another Wooster uncle, father of Claude and Eustace, died in some sort of a home, 'more or less off his onion', with rabbits in his bedroom. Another uncle, at the age of seventy-six and under the influence of crusted port, would climb trees. The Wooster family has its full quota of loonies to qualify it for Wodehouse's Upper Classes.

Bertie's aunts are more interesting than his uncles.

'The whole trouble is due to your blasted aunt,' said young Bingo.

'Which blasted aunt? Specify, old thing. I have so many.'

'Mrs Travers. The one who runs that infernal paper.'

'Oh, no, dash it, old man,' I protested. 'She's the only decent aunt I've got ...'

Bertie's Aunts Agatha and Dahlia are sisters. It is difficult to dream up a joint childhood that could have produced two such different types, but there it is. Dahlia used to hunt incessantly in the Shires when young. There is no history of the hunting field, or even of youth, in the Agatha archives. She was engaged at an early stage to Percy Craye who was, or later became, the Earl of Worplesdon. But he got into a disgraceful dust-up after a Covent Garden Ball, and Agatha gave him back his ring when she read his press notices in the evening papers. She married a stockbroker, 'a battered little chappie', whose name is variously given as Spenser, Spenser-Gregson and Spenser Gregson. He had made a fortune in Sumatra rubber. He never made a live appearance, and he died conveniently to allow Aunt Agatha to marry Lord Worplesdon for *Joy in the Morning* (1947).

Aunt Agatha strongly advised Florence Craye not to marry Bertie, because he was a spineless invertebrate. And for exactly the same reason she was most anxious that Honoria Glossop *should* marry him. Aunt Agatha is the only person who has ever suggested that Bertie should have a job. Although Bertie does once crush her ('Pearls Mean Tears') and splendidly defy her (end of *The Mating Season*), he is really terrified of her. She has been his scourge and evil conscience from the first. It is comforting in a way to know that Bertie is not her only target. She makes Lord Worplesdon give up smoking, and his agonies are frightful.

Aunt Agatha was tall, grey and beaky, and must have made a convincing Boadicea in that historical pageant at Woollam Chersey. She once started to go in for politics, but retired hurt when rude fellows heckled her speeches.

Bertie's splendid Aunt Dahlia married Tom Travers 'the year Bluebottle won the Cambridgeshire'. It was her second marriage, her first husband having been a drunk. I think her Angela and Bonzo are both children of the Travers marriage.

In the earliest references Aunt Dahlia was Bertie's aunt only by marriage, and Uncle Tom was described by Bertie as 'between ourselves, a bit of a squirt', and not good enough for his wife. At that period, too, Uncle Tom refused to live in the country, and Aunt Dahlia had to compensate for hunting by running *Milady's Boudoir*, a weekly magazine. But soon Aunt Dahlia becomes established as being sister to Bertie's father, and a true Wooster. (She had saved Bertie's life, to her outspoken regret in later years, when, as a baby, he nearly swallowed his rubber comforter.) Uncle Tom forgets his dislike of the country. He develops into a pleasant old silly, very fond of Dahlia in an income-tax ridden sort of way. And he lives perfectly happily at Brinkley (as in Charles Street) so long as too many poets and other pests don't come to stay. He has a lot of money and a bad liver, both made in the Far East, a good collection of old silver, a yacht, mild insomnia and a face like a walnut. Most first-generation rich men in Wodehouse pay the price in dyspepsia. Uncle Tom's pays dividends in a literary sense, because it heightens the importance of Anatole, the fabulous chef whom Aunt Dahlia lured away from the Bingo Littles. Anatole, and only Anatole, can cook food that soothes Uncle Tom's alimentary tract, and enables him to be a plentiful, if not very willing, provider of cheques for *Milady's Boudoir* (which he always refers to as 'Madame's Nightshirt'). If Anatole were to cease to cook for him, Uncle Tom's digestion would play up again, and it would follow, as the night the day, that he would think taxes were crippling him and that the revolution was setting in. The result would be no money to pay Aunt Dahlia's baccarat debts, and general misery.

Five times, so far as I can count, has Aunt Dahlia been in danger of losing Anatole, once as a gambling debt to Lady Snettisham, twice to Sir Watkyn Bassett, once to the frightful Liverpudlian Trotters, and once when Gussie Fink-Nottle made faces at the skylight of Anatole's bedroom at Brinkley. The possible loss of Anatole has been a good plot-maker. Bertie once offered to take a rap to the tune of thirty days in prison to prevent Aunt Dahlia losing Anatole, and Aunt Dahlia can always bend Bertie to her will by the threat that, if he disobeys her, he will not be asked to her *cordon bleu* table any more.

Brick-red and brazen-voiced from the hunting fields of earlier days, a devout blackmailer, able to slang and chaff an opponent with schoolboy pith and relish, Aunt Dahlia is Bertie's all-time favourite relative of any sort, let alone aunt. Their dialogue is some of the best stuff in Wodehouse. They understand each other very well. Aunt Dahlia is a middle-aged version of Wodehouse's best girls, Stiffy Byng, Nobby Hopwood, Bobbie Wickham *et al*. She is an excellent creation.

There was plenty of money in the Wooster family. Bertie's uncles were all comfortably unemployed. His Aunt Dahlia was intermittently short of cash, but both she (at least once) and Agatha (twice) married 'into trade'. Bertie refers to himself as being 'stagnant with the stuff'. He lives in Berkeley Mansions, and there is enough in the Petty Cash float, to which Jeeves had access, for Jeeves to be able to buy two Round the World Cruise tickets at the end of *The Code of the Woosters*. (Did they ever go on that cruise?) The Wooster class is upper, without being of the county. Its nesting territories are London w.1. and the country. I wonder why Aunt Agatha's son, the tough Young Thos, is down to go to Pevenhurst, not to Eton.

Bertie has still not suffered that 'fate worse then death – *viz*. marriage'. But he has run it pretty fine with eight or nine girls at one time or another. Bertie is no wolf. If Jeeves finds Bertie's bed un-slept-in, he assumes, and correctly, that Bertie has spent the night in jug somewhere, not with any girl. Aunts and friends break in on Bertie's bedroom before breakfast, with never a suspicion that he may have company there.

When Bertie, by mistake, climbs into Florence Craye's bedroom window at Brinkley, Florence, to whom he has been engaged once or twice already, assumes that, still yearning, he has come to kiss her while she sleeps. Bertie (who possibly hasn't read Kipling's 'Brushwood Boy') is pained by such advanced modern thought. When Pauline Stoker, to whom Bertie has also once been engaged, is revealed in Bertie's bed, in Bertie's pyjamas, unchaperoned, in Bertie's little seaside cottage at midnight, Bertie is shocked to his foundations. Bertie is pure as driven snow, if not purer. He refers to himself as a 'reputable bachelor who has never had his licence so much as endorsed'.

But, sucker as he is for getting embroiled with, and engaged to, brainy girls like Honoria Glossop and Florence Craye, soupy girls like Madeline Bassett and festive little squirts like Bobbie Wickham, Bertie does from time to time take positive steps as a lover. He had, at the age of fourteen, written to Marie Lloyd for her autograph. He had, when they were kids, let his cousin Angela call herself his own little sweetheart. He had asked Cynthia Wickhammersley to marry him. (This was rash, because she was full of ideals, and would probably have required Bertie to carve out a career and whatnot. Bertie had distinctly heard her speaking favourably of Napoleon. But it all worked out well. When Bertie proposed, Cynthia nearly laughed herself into permanent hiccups.) Bertie had given Pauline Stoker a rush in New York, and was engaged to her within a matter of days. Bertie had been in love with Corky Pirbright. He was in love with Gwladys Pendlebury, the artist. Then there was Vanessa Cook, the protest-marcher. He twice thought he wanted to marry Bobbie Wickham, and twice Jeeves had to show him what a heartless little red-head she was. Once (*Jeeves in the Offing*) Bobbie announced her engagement to Bertie in *The Times*. But that was only to scare her mother into giving her approval to her (Bobbie's) marrying 'Kipper' Herring. On the evidence of *My Man Jeeves*, but suppressed when the same story was included in *Carry On, Jeeves* and the *Jeeves Omnibus*, Bertie had once 'tried to marry into musical comedy'. The family had objected – Bertie's family, that was.

Pauline Stoker put it well when she said there was a 'woolly-headed duckiness' about Bertie. 'Mentally negligible, but he has a heart of gold,' says Jeeves of the young master. When Bertie is old and grey and full of sleep, he will look back on his romantic youth and probably decide that the greatest compliment he was ever paid was from Pauline's father. Pop Stoker, an incandescent American millionaire, hearing that his daughter had spent the night in Bertie's cottage, captured Bertie in his yacht and proposed to keep him there till he had married the errant girl. Pop Stoker, at any rate, believed Bertie had passions that he could unbridle, and Pop Stoker had a nasty Victorian sense of etiquette to deal with the situation as he guessed it.

Pauline would not have been too bad a wife for Bertie. But, when the smoke has cleared away, we accept Jeeves's judgement that Bertie is one of nature's bachelors. We're glad that Bertie lasted the course in single strictness, with Jeeves to look after him and to bring tea for one to the bedroom in the mornings.

IMAGES

'You're a pig, Bertie!'
'A pig maybe – but a shrewd, level-headed pig.'

*

Bingo swayed like a jelly in a high wind ... His whole aspect was that of a man who has unexpectedly been struck by lightning.

*

Stiffy was one of those girls who enjoy in equal quantities the gall of an army mule and the calm insouciance of a fish on a slab of ice.

*

Aunt Agatha, who eats broken bottles and wears barbed wire next to the skin.

*

'Oh Bertie,' she said in a voice like beer trickling out of a jug ...

*

There was rather more of Stinker Pinker than there had been when I had seen him last. Country butter and the easy life these curates lead had added a pound or two to an always impressive figure. To see the lean, finely trained Stinker of my nonage, I felt that one would have to catch him in Lent.

*

I once got engaged to his daughter Honoria, a ghastly dynamic exhibit who read Nietzsche and had a laugh like waves breaking on a stern and rockbound coast.

*

He looked like a Chinaman with a combination of jaundice and ague.

*

'You know that vicarage that you have in your gift, Uncle Watkyn. Well, Harold and I were thinking that you might give him that, and then we could get married at once. You see, apart from the increased dough, it would start him off on the road to higher things. Up till now, Harold has been working under wraps. As a curate he has had no scope. But slip him a vicarage, and watch him let himself out. There is literally no eminence to which that boy will not rise, once he spits on his hands and starts in.'

She wiggled from the base to apex with girlish enthusiasm.

JEEVES

(The only book in which Jeeves appears without Bertie Wooster is *Ring for Jeeves* (1953).)

The Times obituary of Eric Blore, the film-actor, in 1959, ended:

He made a speciality of that most English of all professions ... the gentleman's gentleman or manservant, the very epitome of Jeeves. Indeed, he and another English actor, Mr Arthur Treacher, may be said to have made a virtual corner in butler parts in Hollywood during the thirties, and no study of an upper-class English or American household was complete without one or other of them. Treacher, tall and thin, was haughty and austere, a man with a permanent smell under his nose. Blore, who was shorter and slightly tubby, was a trifle more eccentric in manner, but equally capable of registering eloquent but unspoken disapproval of any untoward behaviour. But he could yet suggest a taste for a lower life, and it was Blore who introduced into an American film *It's Love I'm After* the eloquent line: 'If I were not such a gentleman's gentleman I could be such a cad's cad.'

It is just tribute to Wodehouse that *The Times* could already use 'Jeeves' like that, without quotation marks and without acknowledgement. To some extent it was due to Wodehouse's glorification of the English manservant that Treacher and Blore could live their prosperous lives in Hollywood. Butlers had always been useful in plays, to come on and explain the set-up, in dialogue with a dusting housemaid or into a telephone while the audience settled down. But Hollywood's cameras could wander around and show direct what a stage butler had to get across in speech. Hollywood used the stately and funny butler because he was a fat part and he paid dividends. Wodehouse had put butlers on the map. Hollywood used them where they stood, and paid Wodehouse scant thanks.

Wodehouse wrote a good deal, for him, about writing about butlers and gentlemen's gentlemen. He told us that his love for the tribe on the other side of the green baize door started when he was a boy and used to be lugged round by aunts and clergymen uncles to call on the great houses. Young Pelham was a bust as a conversationalist in the drawing-rooms over the cucumber sandwiches, so his uncles and aunts often sent him off with the butler to have his tea in the servants' hall. And there young Pelham kidded back and forth with footman and housemaid and everybody was very happy – the boy showing off, the servants encouraging him in a way his uncles and aunts never did.

Doubtless even then Wodehouse was awed by the majesty of the butlers. Ukridge's visual description of Oakshott really stands for all butlers: 'Meeting him in the street and ignoring the foul bowler hat he wore on his walks abroad, you would have put him down as a Bishop in mufti or, at the least, a plenipotentiary at one of the better courts.' The first sentence of 'The Good Angel' in the book of short stories *The Man Upstairs* (1914) is: 'Any man under thirty years of age who tells you he is not afraid of an English butler, lies.' Lord Ickenham, for all his insistence that Earls had a right, and almost a duty, to be haughty, was equally at home in castle and cottage. But, though he was at least sixty, his affection for his butler, Coggs, was tempered by awe. Bertie Wooster himself, who normally treats servants as to the manor born, was overawed by Silversmith, butler at Deverill Hall in *The Mating Season*. This was one of those flickers of Wodehouse-Wooster autobiography.

In an unrepublished *Strand* story, in 1914, 'Creatures of Impulse', Wodehouse told of a perfect servant, Jevons (the name Jeeves may have been taking shape even then), who, on an impulse, put ice down the neck of his Baronet master at the dinner table. The Bart sacked him. But then, later, the Bart got an air-gun in his hands in the country, and, on an impulse, shot a gardener in the trouser-seat with it. He couldn't think what had come over him, but he realised he had wronged Jevons, and he summoned him back by telegram. Obviously bits of this story went into the making of 'The Crime Wave at Blandings'. Wodehouse gives us good butlers and bad butlers. Julia Ukridge's butler Oakshott was called 'inky-souled' by no less a rogue than Ukridge himself. It is pleasant to see Oakshott taking off his coat to cuddle a housemaid on his knee in his pantry. It is pleasant to see Oakshott, in a moment of panic, dive into a wardrobe when he thought the police were after him. Another butler preached Socialism in Hyde Park. Another played the fiddle. Beach of Blandings kept a bullfinch and stole pigs. And what about the bank-burgling butler? These are good grace-notes.

You will find fine Wodehouse butlers in fifty books, Attwater, Barlow, Barter, Bayliss, Baxter, Beach, Benson, Blizzard, Bowles (ex-butler), Bulstrode, Chibnall, Coggs, Ferris, Gascoyne, Keggs, Oakshott, Pollen, Ridgway, Silversmith, Slingsby, Spenser, Sturgis, Swordfish, Vosper and Watson being the names that spring to the mind. Swordfish (the name that Sir Roderick Glossop took when pretending to be the butler at Brinkley in *Jeeves in the Offing*) was indeed a name that sprang to the mind of that scheming young menace, Bobbie Wickham. But there is virtually only one gentleman's personal gentleman in the books, and that's Jeeves. You will find a few other valets or what passed for valets, including Archie Mulliner's Meadowes and that other Meadowes, Jeeves's predecessor in Bertie's service (he sneaked Bertie's socks), and Jeeves's substitute in *Thank You, Jeeves*, who got tight, trolled hymns and went after Bertie with the meat knife. But Jeeves is supreme.

'There is none like you, none, Jeeves,' says Bertie, thereby showing a knowledge of Tennyson's *Maud*, but a number of gaps in his reading. The *débrouillard* manservant was a staple of Greek and Roman comedy. Chesterton described Sam Weller as 'something new – a clever comic servant whose knowledge of the world is more than that of his master, but who is not a rascal'. Barrie's Crichton follows Weller. The stately, orotund manservant, often called Jeames, was in and out of *Punch* as early as the 1860s. John Buchan's Sir Archie Roylance had an encyclopaedic manservant who 'patently educated' him.

In Cynthia Asquith's memoir of Barrie is a description of Barrie's own butler, Thurston, who read Latin and Greek while polishing the silver, and would correct Barrie's literary guests when they got their quotations wrong. Frank Thurston became Barrie's manservant in 1922, at a time when Jeeves was already coming out serially in print. If you read Chapter 4 of Cynthia Asquith's *Portrait of Barrie*, you'll see how the factual Thurston resembled the fictional Jeeves:

Dictionaries and various learned tomes cluttered up the pantry ... I discovered him poring over a Spanish book. 'Is that a difficult language, Thurston?' I asked. 'No, My Lady, it presents little difficulty if one has a fair knowledge of Latin and French.' ... He could supply any forgotten date or quotation ... Barrie would counsel guests that, if they must take a 'thriller' to bed, they had better 'hide it in between a Pliny and the latest theory of Ethics', or they might feel abashed when Thurston came to draw their curtains in the morning ... 'You are inimical to your apparel, Sir,' said Thurston to Barrie, who used to burn his clothes with sparks from his pipe ... 'I still haven't found out,' Barrie said one day, 'what it is that Thurston doesn't know, but I don't give up hope.' ... From

Italy he wrote to me, 'The beauty of Venice is almost appalling, and so was Thurston's knowledge of it as we entered it' ... Thurston, uncommunicative, inscrutable, puma-footed ... no one ever heard him enter or leave a room ... was so unusual, indeed, so mysterious a being that he might almost have been written by his master ... A man who inspired not only instantaneous respect, but – for his heart was as good as his head – growing affection. In the last letter Barrie wrote (it was to Thurston) Barrie said 'I want you besides the monetary bequest to pick for yourself a hundred of my books. Few persons who have entered that loved flat have done more honour to books.'

This is a remarkable consonance with Jeeves. Denis Mackail, a good friend and great admirer of Wodehouse, and author of a fine *Life* of Barrie, said there was no need to think there is any link, in any dimension, between Thurston and Jeeves. Wodehouse didn't know Barrie well and never went to the Adelphi flat. It is probable that Cynthia Asquith, when she came to write about Thurston, had herself come to equate him with Jeeves and unconsciously to use some of the Wodehouse brushwork for her portrait of Thurston.

Bring On the Girls suggests a factual origin for Jeeves, but it post-dates Jeeves's arrival and naming by at least ten years and must be ignored. More likely as germ-carriers for the idea of Jeeves are two fictional manservants in the books of Conan Doyle (once more), Ambrose, the cravat-tying, coffee-making valet to the Regency buck, Sir Charles Tregellis in *Rodney Stone*; and Austin, Professor Challenger's servant in *The Poison Belt* (1913).

'I'm expecting the end of the world today, Austin.'
'Yes sir, what time, sir?'
'I can't say. Before evening.'
'Very good, sir.' The taciturn Austin saluted and withdrew.

Compare with this the Bertie/Jeeves dialogue in the first story of all, 'Extricating Young Gussie':

'Jeeves,' I said, 'we start for America on Saturday.'

'Very good, sir. Which suit will you wear?'

There is a difference between a gentleman's personal gentleman and a butler, but it is only that the former is thin and the latter fat, and they have different spheres of duties. Wodehouse would have claimed no originality for Jeeves as a broad type. What Wodehouse could have claimed as his own patent with Jeeves was his successful use of him as a recurrent, charming, funny and credible agent in plot-making.

The Wodehouse farce plots are highly complicated, and Wodehouse took immense trouble in handling them ingeniously. Other good authors, having achieved plots one stage less involved, would feel perfectly justified in their artistic consciences to allow their dénouements to start through a coincidence or act of God. Wodehouse, in the Jeeves stories, used Jeeves as an extra dimension, a godlike prime mover, a master brain who is found to have engineered the apparent coincidence or coincidences. When Bingo Little was sorely harassed by his wife Rosie's old school chum, it would still have been a good story if the picnic basket had been put in the wrong car in error, and if Bertie's car had run out of petrol in the wilds at tea-time by chance. That would have sufficed to cause the flaming row between Rosie and her chum and to have restored sanity to the way of life of the Little household. But Jeeves had engineered it all. There was no error, no chance.

Jeeves in most stories is the rim of the wheel and the hub, the plotter and the plot. Bertie sometimes insists on handling problems his own way. Jeeves, in his background planning, can not only allow for Bertie's mistakes; he can estimate their extent in advance and make them a positive part of the great web he is himself spinning. And he is so confident of his success that he will often take his reward before his success has actually happened and before his reward has been offered.

'Jeeves, you may give away those plus-fours of mine I dislike so.' 'Thank you, sir, I gave them to the under-gardener yesterday.'

Jeeves has a genuine fondness for Bertie, and enjoys helping him and his friends. He likes them to appeal to him, and is not annoyed to be summoned by telegram back from the middle of his summer seaside holiday to rescue them from their idiocies. He takes their side calmly. He remains perfectly polite, and seems quite impartial to the current opposition. He simply out-generals it. If Bertie, through asininity, sets up an unexpected diversion, Jeeves doesn't let that cramp his style. He envelops it and out-generals Bertie, too. He usually makes Bertie pay a forfeit. But, godlike in this too, Jeeves chastens and still loves, loves and still chastens. He accepts Bertie's sacrifice (in the case of the banjolele, a burnt offering), and the score is settled.

Bertie does not bear his grudges against Jeeves for long. Jeeves does not bear grudges against Bertie at all. There is nothing maudlin about their association, either. Bertie can be demanding and even rude. Jeeves can be cold and non-co-operative. Bertie sacked Jeeves twice in a single story and would be silly enough to do it again if there were a major clash of wills. Jeeves has resigned twice and he would do it again at the drop of a bowler hat if Bertie continued in some absurd course. Jeeves means it when he resigns. Even he could not plot the happy end of Bertie's banjolele. It was a menace and Jeeves would not be in the same cottage with it. So he resigned and was immediately snapped up by Lord Chuffnell. As it happened, Chuffy, thanks largely to Jeeves's machinations, was able to woo and win Pauline Stoker, which meant that Jeeves did not propose to stay on as his servant. In Jeeves's experience, when a wife comes in at the front door, a valet goes out at the back. As it happened, Bertie's cottage went up in flames and the banjolele was burnt.

The *causa belli* between master and man was removed and, on Bertie's assurance that banjolele-playing was a thing of the past for him, Jeeves gladly consented to team up with him again. Honour was preserved on all fronts, though Bertie had had to forfeit a good deal of face (with bootblack on it most of the time) as punishment for his diversionary activities in the middle chapters.

When, in Kipling's *First Jungle Book*, Mowgli is flattered by the *bandar-log* and whisked off by them terrifyingly to the Cold Lairs, Baloo and Bagheera, his fond mentors, have their work cut out to rescue him. But Mowgli had disobeyed their instructions in having anything to do with the *bandar-log* in the first place, and Mowgli has to be punished, when the night's alarms and excursions are over. Baloo and Bagheera give him a beating. The principle of Bertie's punishment (not by any means always inflicted by Jeeves) is the same as the principle of Mowgli's, and of Greek Tragedy, and of the Old Testament. Hubris not only gets its nemesis. It requires it, especially with such a childlike character as Bertie. Otherwise, childlike, he would go on swanking. Childlike, he would not have the sense to understand the small print on the social contract. He would not renounce his silliness without punishment. And, for the readers, he would not start the next story with the required clean-slate innocence. The slate would carry an unsettled score. We wouldn't mind about that with Ukridge, Aunt Dahlia or Uncle Fred. We would mind with Bertie.

Considering the tough eggs that Jeeves has to out-general, it is no small part of his superhumanship that he does it without (except in *Ring for Jeeves*) loss of his impeccable servant status. Sir Roderick Glossop, Aunt Agatha, Sir Watkyn Bassett, Spode, Pop Stoker, Florence and Stilton probably to this day do not realize that Jeeves pulled the strings to nullify their menaces to Bertie. Aunt Agatha and

Honoria objected to Jeeves because Jeeves's influence on Bertie was too strong. Jeeves seemed to them an outward and visible sign of Bertie's inward and spiritual spinelessness. Aunt Agatha and Honoria never knew just how much Bertie's escape from their clutches had been engineered by Jeeves. This is a situation that Jeeves has to handle carefully, because aunts go on for ever, and Honoria is apt to pop up in Bertie's life whenever there's a lull. Many of Bertie's friends (Aunt Dahlia, Gussie, Bingo and Co.) do realise Jeeves's omnipotence, and this makes Bertie temporarily piqued and jealous, so that, to show his own cleverness, he concocts silly plans which complicate the plots, increase the pity and terror and laughter, and add to Jeeves's laurels in the end.

Why Jeeves, with that brain, and that confidence in his own brain, should remain a gentleman's personal gentleman is fairly mysterious. He is a keen and shrewd gambler. He could make a fortune in the City, and have all the time he wanted for fishing, shrimping, sea-travel and reading. You can't suspect Jeeves of snobbish motives in staying in service with the nobility and gentry; nor of timidity in not wanting to better himself. I am sure he has read Karl Marx and has been exposed to all the dialectic that might persuade lesser valets to work only for the Red Dawn, or to try to collar the means of production and thus become a master rather than a serf. Jeeves just isn't a lesser valet. He lets the foolish Bertie pull rank on him and call him an ass. A lesser valet of spirit wouldn't allow that. Jeeves takes it in the spirit (public school) in which it is dished out. Which is pretty superb. But Jeeves is a pretty superb person. Bertie calls him an ass occasionally. Bertie snubs him and tells him to put a sock in his reminiscences and poetic analogies. Bertie tells him his brain is softening. Bertie treats him, in fact, not like a social inferior, but like an equal. And Jeeves calmly goes on treating Bertie like an employer first, and like a mentally negligible favourite child second. It is a delicate balance to maintain. Jeeves maintains it.

Jeeves gets his way, and Bertie pays his forfeits. The forfeit is always necessary for Bertie's atonement, but often it is also part of the way Jeeves gets. As story succeeds story, so do Bertie's young enthusiasms and items of swank. He maintains them as long as he can against Jeeves's disapproval, but in the end he gives them up or hands them over. Jeeves had contributed eleven pages about Bertie to the book at the Junior Ganymede Club in which all members had to file the facts about the gentlemen to whom they are personal gentlemen. Probably one of the eleven pages under WOOSTER B. lists all the things that Bertie has loved and lost. The Old Etonian spats, the purple socks, the loud plus-fours, the Alpine hat, the cummerbund, the white mess jacket as worn at Cannes, the soft silk shirts for evening wear, the banjolele, the vase with dragon designs on it and the two moustaches (be it remembered that the first time Bertie lost his moustache to Jeeves, Jeeves himself shaved it off). The list may also include the things that Jeeves has wanted, Bertie has refused, and Jeeves has finally got, such as the trip on Aunt Dahlia's yacht, the Christmas at Monte Carlo and the round the world cruise (if they ever did go on that cruise).

There must be a lot of entries over Reginald Jeeves's by-line in that book, in addition to the eleven pages on WOOSTER B. Jeeves has served at least nine employers since his first job as page-boy at a girls' school. He was with Lord Worplesdon for nearly a year, and resigned because his master insisted on dining in evening trousers with a flannel shirt and a shooting coat. He was with Mr Digby Thistleton, now Lord Bridgnorth, the financier who marketed a product unsuccessfully as a depilatory, and then changed its name to Hair-O and marketed it successfully as a hair-growing unguent. He was with Mr Montague Todd (is this a subliminal memory of

Dickens's Montague Tigg?), another financier, but who did less well, and was, at the moment of Jeeves's mention of his name, in the second year of his sentence. He was with Lord Brancaster, who fed his lethargic parrot with seed-cake steeped in '84 port, and was bitten in the thumb for his kindness. He was with Lord Frederick Ranelagh, who was swindled in Monte Carlo by a confidence trickster called Soapy Sid, the same man who nearly swindled Bertie and Aunt Agatha at Roville. He was with Lord Rowcester for the length of *Ring for Jeeves*. He was with Lord Chuffnell for a week, and Pop Stoker for less. He was with Gussie Fink-Nottle for a few days in *The Mating Season* (Gussie was pretending to be Bertie). At the end of *Stiff Upper Lip, Jeeves* he accepted service with the ever-predatory Sir Watkyn Bassett, but only as a ruse for getting Bertie released from prison.

Jeeves was such a good servant, so much pursued by poachers, that one wonders how on earth he came to be unemployed and on an agency's books at that happy, star-skipping moment when Bertie's man, Meadowes, had to be fired. Bertie went up to London, contacted the agency, had a night out with the lads, and a hangover when Jeeves rang his bell. Jeeves shimmered in and mixed Bertie his since-famous pick-me-up, and was hired with no further questions asked.

Jeeves's origins were 'of the people', and he seems to have had a pattern of aunt-uncle-cousin-ridden orphanhood that mirrored Bertie's own. There was the aunt who tried Walkinshaw's Supreme Ointment for her swollen limbs and was so jaunty about seeing her photograph in the advertisements. (James, the footman at Blandings in *Something Fresh*, had done the same with the same results.) There was the other aunt who paid someone five shillings to bring a movie actor to tea at her house. There was the third aunt in S.E. London who had a passion for riding in taxi-cabs, often breaking into the children's saving boxes to get the money for such outings. The family used to get the parson to talk her out of this craze when they saw an attack coming on. There was Aunt Annie whom the family invited to stay when there was a family quarrel. The whole family so detested Aunt Annie that they became friends again when they other-directed their hatreds at Annie. There was the aunt who owned nearly all Rosie M. Banks's novels. There was that final aunt at the village of Maiden Eggesford.

Jeeves mentions one uncle, and we meet another. His Uncle Cyril had a favourite story which amused his nephew, but amused Bertie less when Jeeves told it to him just before he set out on that midnight bicycle ride from Brinkley. The story was of two men, called Nicholls and Jackson, who rode a tandem bicycle, ran into a brewer's van and were considerably fragmented. In fact, when the accident squad came to collect the bits, they could only find enough for one person, and they buried this under the name of Nixon. Jeeves's Uncle Charlie Silversmith is butler at Deverill Hall and quite in the whirl of the plot of *The Mating Season*. His daughter, Jeeves's cousin Queenie, marries the local constable Dobbs – a church wedding presumably, because by the happy ending of the book Constable Dobbs has been cured of his atheism.

Jeeves has a cousin who is a constable at Beckley-on-the-Moor in Yorkshire, and another cousin who is a jeweller, who taught Jeeves all (and it is considerable) that he knows about pearls and diamonds. He has a third cousin of whom we know nothing because Bertie made Jeeves dam up a flood of reminiscence that was just starting intempestively. And he has that niece who is now Mrs Biffen. She married Bertie's forgetful friend, and £15,000 a year into the bargain.

Of Jeeves's early love-life we know very little, and he doesn't seem to have one at all in the later books. He had an 'understanding' with the present Lady Bittlesham, the then Jane Watson who was Bingo Little's uncle's cook. But the uncle decided to marry his cook to make sure that nobody lured her away from his kitchen. This was, in the story, something of a relief to Jeeves, because he had already got his eye on a young lady called Mabel whom he had met at a subscription dance in Camberwell. This was the Mabel with whom Bingo Little had for a short while been in love, and to whom Bingo introduced Bertie at that dreadful tea-shop near the Ritz. We do not know what became of Mabel. She does not appear in Jeeves's later life, and he does not seem to be mourning her absence or her loss. Jeeves was kissed by a twelve-year-old schoolgirl, Peggy Mainwaring, who sounded nice, but got Bertie into a lot of trouble at Miss Mapleton's School. Jeeves had read Peggy's father's (Professor Mainwaring) philosophical treatises, but he found the opinions expressed in them somewhat empirical. Stiffy Byng once proposed to kiss Jeeves, but she didn't make contact.

Before we study, and theorize about Jeeves's reading and education (he plays bridge and can type and do shorthand), we should perhaps gather what little else of his history has been revealed. Jeeves says he 'dabbled in' the First World War to a certain extent. It seems generally accepted that he feeds largely on fish, and that fish supplies phosphorus to the giant brain. Himself, he has said that he eats 'little or no' fish, but Bertie keeps forgetting this. (A prep school headmaster whom I knew, a Wodehouse addict, in the summer terms took groups of his top form boys to sit for public school scholarships and, a tribute to Jeeves, it was fish for breakfast at the hotels each morning for all his young hopefuls. That was an order.) Alcohol has a sedative, not a stimulating effect on Jeeves. He says once that he smokes only gaspers, though he has been seen enjoying a cigar and, when Bertie asked him, in *Thank You, Jeeves*, if he had such a thing as a cigarette on his person,

Jeeves offered him a choice of Turkish and Virginian. Bertie describes Jeeves as 'tallish, with one of those dark, shrewd faces' and reiterates that his head sticks out at the back. When he wears a hat, it is a No. 8 bowler. He probably wears it for shrimping at Bognor.

Jeeves gives the impression of never being amused or rattled. When he is disapproving to Bertie, he looks something like a governess, something like an aunt. He has a silent walk and, when attacked about the ankles by a Scottie, can do a smooth high-jump on to a dresser. On the other hand he can deal with an infuriated nesting swan on an island in a rainstorm with total efficiency. Bertie passes on the Jeeves technique to his readers:

Every young man starting life ought to know how to cope with an angry swan, so I will briefly relate the proper procedure. You begin by picking up the raincoat which somebody has dropped: and then, judging the distance to a nicety, you simply shove the raincoat over the bird's head; and, taking the boat-hook which you have prudently brought with you, you insert it underneath the swan and heave. The swan goes into a bush and starts trying to unscramble itself; and you saunter back to your boat, taking with you any friends who may happen at the moment to be sitting on roofs in the vicinity. That was Jeeves's method, and I cannot see how it could have been improved upon.'

Jeeves had said: 'In the presence of the unusual, Mr Wooster is too prone to smile weakly and allow his eyes to protrude.' There has been hardly anything unusual enough to rock Jeeves. When he first saw Boko Fittleworth, Bertie's untidy author friend, Jeeves blenched and retired to the kitchen 'doubtless to pull himself together with cooking sherry'. And he clutched at a table when Bingo Little turned up at the flat wearing a beard. Otherwise he has remained calm and dignified, with an occasional twitch of the lip or eyebrow. No more.

Jeeves's mother had thought him intelligent as a child, and in adult years he reads Spinoza, Nietzsche and Professor Mainwaring. Also Dostoyevsky and the great Russians. I have made a cursory count of the sources from which he has ready quotations, and can establish Lucretius, Pliny the Younger, Whittier, Fitzgerald, Pater, Shelley, Kipling, Keats, Scott, Wordsworth, Emerson, Marcus Aurelius, Shakespeare, Browning, Rosie M. Banks, Moore, Virgil, Horace, Dickens, Tennyson, Milton, Henley, the Bible, Stevenson, Gray, Burns, Byron and whoever it was who wrote 'The Wreck of the Hesperus'. Wodehouse has clearly siphoned off into Jeeves all his tags of sixth-form reading, and Jeeves speaks copperplate *Times* Augustan to Bertie's *Sporting Life* vernacular.

'The scheme I would suggest cannot fail of success, but it has what may seem to you a drawback, sir, in that it requires certain financial outlay.'

'He means,' I translated to Corky, 'that he has got a pippin of an idea, but it's going to cost a bit.'

Bertie's friends, Reggie Foljambe and Alistair Bingham-Reeves, have tried to lure Jeeves away for gold, but he is bribe-proof so long as Bertie behaves, and doesn't marry. He runs his 'big Mayfair consulting practice' from Berkeley Mansions and Bertie is quite used to finding people consulting the oracle direct, without coming to him first. 'Jeeves isn't the only onion in the hash,' says Bertie, piqued. But in his calmer moments Bertie knows that that is just what Jeeves is. Jeeves's motto is 'Resource and Tact', and he knows that employers need managing. He managed Bertie for sixty happy years.

Hilaire Belloc singles Jeeves out as Wodehouse's prime contribution to

that long gallery of living figures which makes up the glory of English fiction ... In his creation of Jeeves he has done something which may respectfully be compared to the work of the Almighty in Michelangelo's painting. He has formed a man filled with the breath of life ... I should like the foreigner or posterity (much the same thing) to steep themselves in the living image of Jeeves and thus comprehend what the English character in action may achieve. Talk of efficiency ... If in, say, fifty years Jeeves and any other of that great company – but in particular Jeeves – shall have faded, then what we have so long called England will no longer be.

I would not put so nationalistic a label on Jeeves as Belloc does in this trumpet-tongued peroration. And I am sure that Bertie Wooster is a greater (and more difficult) creation than his manservant. As a pair they are much more than the sum of their single selves. I see Bertie as a marvellously constructed model ship inside the protecting and encompassing bottle that is Jeeves. And I see Wodehouse less as the Almighty passing life to a single Adam through his finger-tip, more (and equally respectfully) as a microscopic craftsman of highly ingenious *trompe l'oeil* puppets confined in ingenious artificial settings.

Bertie suggested to Jeeves that when he died he should bequeath his brain to the nation. I'd be more interested, if I were the nation, or a brain specialist, in studying Wodehouse's brain: the brain that fabricated Jeeves's great one and Bertie's tiny one.

IMAGES

Jeeves coughed that soft cough of his, the one that sounds like a sheep clearing its throat on a distant mountainside.

*

'You, Jeeves?' I said, and I should rather think Caesar spoke in the same sort of voice on finding Brutus puncturing him with the sharp instrument.

*

Blizzard was of the fine old school of butlers. His appearance suggested that for fifteen years he had not let a day pass without its pint of port. He radiated port and pop-eyed dignity. He had splay feet and three chins, and when he walked his curving waistcoat preceded him like the advance guard of some royal procession.

*

The fishy glitter in his eye became intensified. He looked like a halibut which had just been asked by another halibut to lend it a quid till next Wednesday.

*

Joe Beamish [the ex-burglar] was knitting a sock in the tiny living-room which smelled in equal proportions of mice, ex-burglars, and shag tobacco.

*

He groaned slightly and winced, like Prometheus watching his vulture dropping in for lunch.

*

Smedley leaped like an Ouled Nail dancer who has trodden on a tin-tack.

*

It makes me feel as if I had been chasing rainbows and one of them had turned and bitten me in the leg.

*

Freddie experienced the sort of abysmal soul-sadness which afflicts one of Tolstoi's Russian peasants when, after putting in a heavy day's work strangling his father, beating his wife, and dropping the baby into the city reservoir, he turns to the cupboard, only to find the vodka-bottle empty.

APPENDICES

THE FRENCH FOR WODEHOUSE

I mentioned earlier, when discussing the Knut-language which gave something of their conversational style to Psmith and the early Bertie Wooster, that Wodehouse's Lord Tidmouth, in the play *Good Morning, Bill*, produced six separate slang variations for 'Good-bye'. They ranged, in the course of the play, from 'Teuf-teuf' to 'Tinkerty-tonk'. Wodehouse's books have been translated into hosts of modern languages. But how? What foreign language do you know? Well, do you, in that language, know six separate ways, comparable with 'Teuf-teuf' and 'Tinkerty-tonk', in which a blah young English peer with butter-coloured hair and a receding chin could say 'Good-bye'? And that's only the beginning of the difficulties. The mish-mash of elusive allusion of Wodehouse's buzzers and burblers, the hotch-potch of slangs, the quotations, direct or veiled, the wild imagery . . .

French is the only language in which I might begin to judge a Wodehouse translation. The last time I was in France, I bought *Jeeves, au secours* (Amiot-Dumont, Paris). '*Ce livre paruten langue anglaise sous le titre*: JOY IN THE MORNING.' The translators are Denyse and Benoit de Fonscolombe.

Joy in the Morning is my favourite Bertie/Jeeves novel. *Bref*, as the French say, and in Bertie's own words, it is 'the super-sticky affair of Nobby Hopwood, Stilton Cheesewright, Florence Craye, my Uncle Percy, J. Chichester Clam, Edwin the Boy Scout and old Boko Fittleworth . . . or, as my biographers will probably call it, the Steeple Bumpleigh Horror'. (. . . *cet embrouillamini ou ... pour prendre la définition qu'adopteront probablement mes biographes ... l'horrible drame de Steeple Bumpleigh auquel furent mêlés Nobby Hopwood, Stilton Cheesewright, Florence Craye, mon oncle Percy, J. Chichester Calm* [sic], *Edwin le Boy Scout et ce vieux Boko Fittleworth*).

I knew that my depth-analysis of the translation wouldn't be easy, as soon as I discovered that two of Bertie's ways of saying 'Good-bye' ('toodle-oo' and 'pip-pip' – neither of which was used by Lord Tidmouth) become in French *bye-bye*. And 'Shropshire' becomes *Skropshire*. This word only appears in the book once, so the French rendering may be a misprint. But I must take it as it comes ... e.g. *chez Droves* for 'at the Drones' and variously *Catsmeat Ploter-Pirbright, Potter Pirbright-tête-de-mou* and *Potter Pirbright dit Tête de mou* for 'Catsmeat Potter-Pirbright'. (*Mou* is the French for butcher's lights.) And Lord Worplesdon becomes an armaments, not a shipping magnate.

Let's take slang and imagery first. You might like to paste the following in your Michelin Guide as vocabulary for your next travels in France:

A bucko mate of a tramp steamer	*un bosco de caboteur*
A nice bit of box-fruit, what!	*une belle mélasse*
That will bring home the bacon	*ça rabibochera tout*
A joke salt-shaker	*une salière surprise*
Rollicking	*désopilant*
To render unfit for human consumption	*mettre à mal*
To tear limb from limb	*déchiqueter*
To give the little snurge six of the best with a bludgeon	*flanquer au maudit galopin une volée de martinet*
To mince yourself to hash	*se faire hacher la viande*

Some rout or revel	*quelques parties ou quelques bamboches*
Stinko	*parti*
My dear old soul (Jeeves)	*mon petit vieux*
The beasel (Florence Craye)	*la pécore*
A girl liberally endowed with oomph (Nobby Hopwood)	*une fille amplement pourvue de chien*
To pull someone's leg	*monter un bateau à quelqu'un*
Cookoo (mad)	*toqué*
A flop	*un loupé*
Oofy	*pourvu de galette*
Rannygazoo	*la corrida*
A bloke	*un zèbre*
Acts of kindness (as enjoined to Boy Scouts, daily)	*des B.A. (bonnes actions)*
Nobby and Boko have hitched up, have they?	*ça biche Nobby et Boko?*
Everything is gas and gaiters	*ça gaze à bloc*
To write stinkers (letters)	*écrire des engueulots*
A blunt instrument	*un instrument massif*
Loony to the eyebrows	*complètement dingo*
To go to the mat and start chewing pieces out of each other	*être en bisbille et commencer à se dire des 'vacheries'*
A sterling chap	*un crac*
To dot him one	*lui en coller un dans la figure*
A bottle from the oldest bin	*une bouteille de derrière les fagots*
A bearded bozo (King Edward The Confessor)	*un bonze barbu*
A wet blanket	*un vrai parapluie*
To snitch	*souffler*
To thrash that pie-faced young warthog Fittleworth within an inch of his life	*rosser, à deux doigts d'en crever, cette face de tarte, cette jeune verrue de Fittleworth*

His eyes popped out of his head and waved about on their stalks	*ses yeux étaient hors de la tête et erraient de-ci, de-là au bout de leur tige, le nerf optique sans doute*
He moved, he stirred, he seemed to feel the rush of life along his keel	*il remuait, s'agitait comme si la vie dans sa puissance toujours jeune, lui chatouillait la colonne vertébrale*
He realises that dirty work is afoot at the crossroads and that something swift is being slipped across him	*il se rend compte qu'une vilaine besogne est en train de s'accomplir et qu'une peau de banane va lui être incessamment lachée dans les pattes*
To zoom off immediately (for fear of Aunt Agatha)	*faire un départ à l'anglaise sur le champ*
The bean (head)	*le chef*
The napper (head)	*la cafetière*
The onion (head)	*la caboche*
The old bounder	*le vieux rustre*
You bloodstained (Bertie)	*espèce d'ignoble individu*
You horrible young boll-weevil (Edwin)	*espèce d'horrible graine de charançon*
You fat-headed young faulty reasoner (Edwin)	*espèce de nigaud de raisonneur à l'envers*
You outstanding louse (Bertie)	*espèce de vermine*
You degraded little copper's nark (Edwin)	*infecte petit rabatteur de police*
You blasted object (Bertie)	*espèce de détritus*
To hammer the stuffing out of someone	*étriper quelqu'un*
To spot oompus boompus	*mettre le doigt sur les manigances*
He loved like a thousand of bricks	*il était amoureux comme pas un*

Love's young dream had stubbed its toe	*le rêve de jeunesse et d'amour avait les ailes coupées*
I shall probably play on the old crumb (Lord Worplesdon) as on a stringed instrument	*je jouerai probablement sur les fibres de cette vieille noix comme sur un instrument à cordes*
We Woosters can read between the lines	*nous, Wooster, savons lire entre les lignes*
The menace was null and void	*la menace était nulle et non avenue*
He ground a tooth or two	*il grinça des dents*
Her ladyship (Aunt Agatha)	*Madame la Baronne*
Butler	*maître d'hôtel*
Butler	*valet de chambre*

Quotations are a test for the Fonscolombes.

'Odd's boddikins, Jeeves,' I said, 'I am in rare fettle this a.m. Talk about exulting in my youth I I feel up and doing, with a heart for any fate, as Tennyson says.'

'Longfellow, sir.'

'Or, if you prefer it, Longfellow. I am in no mood to split hairs.'

– *Jeeves, je suis dans une forme rare ce matin. D'une jeunesse triomphante, pourrait-on dire. Je me sens d'attaque; nul arrêt du destin ne saurait étonner mon courage comme dit Tennyson.*

– *Longfellow, Monsieur.*

– *Bon, bon, Longfellow, si vous aimez mieux. Je ne suis pas d'humeur à couper les cheveaux en quatre.*

'It reminded me of those lines in the poem – "See how the little how-does-it-go tum tumty tiddly push." Perhaps you remember the passage?'

' "Alas, regardless of their fate, the little victims play," sir.'

– *Il m'a rappelé ce vers du poème 'Vois jouer les pauvrets, pom, pom, pom, dix, onze, douze'. Peut-être vous rappelez-vous le passage?*

– *Vois jouer les pauvrets sans souci de leur sort, Monsieur.*

'I don't know if you remember the passage? "Ti-tum-ti-tum ti-tumty tum, ti-tumty tumty mist (I think it's mist), and Eugene Aram walked between, with gyves upon his wrist." '

– Je ne sais pas si vous vous rappelez le passage: 'pom, pom, pom, pom, dans la pénombre (je crois que c'est 'pénombre'), Eugene Aram fut emmené, les fers aux pieds, quel drame sombre!'

Even though the French translators put the gyves on Eugene Aram's feet in preference to his wrist, it is nice to see them making up a little poetry of their own.

They are clever in translating a small felicity of orthography, too.

'Did you say "Wee Nooke", Jeeves?'

'Yes, sir.'

'Spelled, I'll warrant, with an "e"?'

'Yes sir.'

I breathed heavily through the nostrils.

'Well, listen to me, Jeeves. The thing's off. You understand? Off. Spelled with an o and two f's. I'm dashed if I'm going to be made a – what's the word?'

'Sir?'

'Catspaw. Though why catspaw? I mean, what have cats got to do with it?'

'The expression derives . . .'

– Comment dites-vous? 'Nostre Nid?'

– Oui, Monsieur.

– Ecrit, je le parie, avec un 's'.

– Oui, Monsieur.

Je soufflai bruyamment.

– Arrêtons là, Jeeves. C'est fini, compris? Fini, f, i, fi, n, i, ni. Je veux bien être pendu si je me fait avoir comme le . . . quoi . . . ?

– Monsieur?

– Comme le chat . . . et pourquoi le chat? Je veux dire qu'est-ce que les chats ont à voir là dedans?

L'expression vient . . .

And the discreet dots:

I have just one thing to say to you, Wooster. Get out!

Je n'ai qu'un mot à te dire, Wooster, f . . . le camp.

On two points (in addition to the wrists–feet switch for Eugene Aram) I am at a loss to know why the translators have changed things. You remember that occasion when Lord W., much to Bertie's surprise, calls for champagne in his study at 10 a.m. and makes Bertie celebrate with him? In Wodehouse's version Lord Worplesdon is brought two *half*-bottles in succession, and the two of them share them to the dregs. In the French it is two *whole* bottles. The thrifty Wodehouse would never waste two bottles of champagne on two people without staging one of his excellent tipsy scenes to follow. And, anyway, Lord W. is going to get royally plastered that very night on dance champagne (the French ignores that important pejorative 'dance', incidentally) at the East Wibley Fancy Dress Ball. And, next morning, when Lord Worplesdon, still dressed as Sinbad the Sailor with red whiskers, comes fuming to Boko's cottage, Boko and Nobby, trying to cool him down with some breakfast, offer him sardines several times. In the French it is always fried eggs that they offer. Here the English and the French are both right. Wodehouse in France (1947) originally wrote 'eggs', not 'sardines'. His publisher had to remind him that eggs were very tightly rationed then in England. So he changed it to 'sardines'. In France eggs (for an English breakfast) sounded right, sardines wrong.

There are times when the translators simply don't do justice to the English, other times when they admit themselves baffled and leave chunks out, other times when they seem to get it palpably wrong, and other times again when, perhaps to make up for their baffled omissions elsewhere, they pad with *jeux d'esprit* of their own. We'll take examples in that order.

Scrambled syntax. I think the Fonscolombes miss tricks in

'You were mere acquaintances?'
'Mere to the core.'

which becomes

— *Vous n'étiez que de simples connaissances?*
— *Aussi vrai qu'il fait jour.*

and

... I said, with an intellectual flick of the umbrella

which becomes

... *dis-je, avec un petit mouvement du parapluie qui sentait son intellectuel.*

and

... buttering a nonchalant slice of toast

which becomes

... *tartinant nonchalamment un morceau de toast.*

When Bertie, remembering Jeeves's first encounter with his friend Boko Fittleworth, a very successful but very badly dressed author, says that Jeeves had winced and retired to the kitchen, 'doubtless to pull himself together with cooking sherry', the French simply says '*avec un petit verre*'. They omit the 'cooking' significance. And they spoil, for me at any rate, my favourite of all Wodehouse images. Bertie had come on that great oaf, Stilton Cheesewright, nervously buying an engagement ring for Lady Florence Craye in a Bond Street jeweller's. Bertie very properly prods Stilton in the behind with his umbrella.

He spun round with a sort of guilty bound, like an adagio dancer surprised while watering the cat's milk.

The French says,

> ... *Il se retourna d'un bond avec l'air coupable d'une danseuse classique surprise à tirer la queue d'un chat.*

Why a feminine dancer? And why pulling *a* cat's tail, not watering *the* cat's milk? One raises the eyebrows and purses the lips.

> Nobby. 'You've known Boko so long.'
> Bertie. 'Virtually from the egg.'

becomes:

> – *Vous connaissez Boko depuis si longtemps!*
> – *Pratiquement, du jour où les flancs de sa mère l'ont porté.*

And:

> 'Oh, hullo, Bertie,' Edwin said, grinning all over his loathsome face.
> 'Hullo, you frightful squirt,' I responded civilly. 'What are you doing here?'

This becomes, a little bleakly:

> – *Bonjour, Bertie! dit-il en grimaçant de tout son visage.*
> – *Qu'est-ce que tu fais ici?*

And,

> 'Well, dash it, already I am practically Uncle Percy's ewe lamb. This will make me still ewer.'

becomes:

> – *Eh bien, diable, je suis déjà pratiquement le favori d'oncle Percy, ça me stabilisera dans la place.*

Two passages where the Fonscolombes retire baffled:

> It was many years since this Cheesewright and I had started what I believe is known as the plucking the gowans fine, and there had

been a time when we had plucked them rather assiduously. But his attitude at the recent get-together had made it plain that the close season for gowans had now set in, and, as I say, it rather saddened me.

They do not attempt those lines at all. And:

. . . He said peevishly that I was just the sort of chap whose car would break down when every moment was precious, adding that it was a lucky thing that it hadn't been me they sent to bring the news from Aix to Ghent, because, if it had been, Ghent would have got it first in the Sunday papers.

becomes only:

– . . . *Il remarqua avec mauvaise humeur que j'étais exactement le genre de type dont le tacot tombait toujours en panne au moment précis où on avait besoin de lui.*

Boko has nothing to add in the French. The Browning allusion disappears.

In one passage, the Fonscolombes not only give up on a sentence, but, in trying to re-hash the sense, get it quite wrong. Bertie had undertaken to plead Boko's cause (as a possible husband for ward, Nobby) with Lord Worplesdon. But Boko, in trying to impress Lord W. with the geniality of his nature, had asked him to lunch and sprung his joke goods on him – the surprise salt-shaker which emitted a spider, amongst others. So Bertie's pleading has to be postponed. Meanwhile Boko has had the awful idea of making Bertie act as a burglar at midnight at Bumpleigh Hall (Lord W. is terrified of burglars), so that Boko can chase him off, save the old home and thus get fawned on by its owner (Lord W.). The idea, which Boko and Nobby have discussed, but haven't yet sprung on Bertie, is that Bertie shall (to make it look a professional job) paste brown paper with treacle on the scullery window, break the window and run away . . . Boko then,

with exact timing, raising the alarm. So this dialogue, between
Nobby and Boko, takes place in Bertie's presence:

Boko.   'We're all right. Don't you worry.'
Nobby.   'But if Bertie can't plead . . .'
Boko.   'Ah, but you're forgetting how versatile he is. What
              you are overlooking is the scullery-window-breaking
              side of his nature. That is what is going to see us
              through.'

This becomes, in French:

   — Tout va bien. Ne vous en faites pas.
   — Mais, si Bertie ne peut pas plaider . . .
   *— Oh! Vous oubliez comme il est changeant. Vous perdez de vue sa
terreur de voleurs, ce véritable complexe de crainte de cambriolage.*

Somehow the French couple (man and wife, or sister and
brother?) have made Bertie the one who is afraid of burglars.
Absolutely wrong.

They're wrong about the Cabinet Ministers, too. Here
Bertie *is* pleading Boko's cause to his Uncle Percy, and trying
to get into Uncle Percy's fat head that Boko makes a packet
of money from his writing, and won't be a drain on Uncle
Percy's pocket if he marries young Nobby.

'It would be an ideal match. You and he may not always have
seen eye to eye in such matters as spiders in salt-cellars, but you
can't get away from it that he is one of the hottest of England's
young *littérateurs*. He earns more per annum than a Cabinet
Minister.'

'He ought to be ashamed of himself if he didn't. Have you ever
met a Cabinet Minister? I know dozens, and not one of them that
wouldn't be grossly overpaid at thirty shillings a week.'

   *— Ce serait un mariage idéal. Vous et lui n'avez peut-être pas la même
façon de voir les choses, comme par exemple les araignées dans les salières,
mais vous ne pouvez nier le fait qu'il est un des jeunes écrivains les plus
dorés d'Angleterre. Il gagne plus qu'un ministre.*

– Il devrait avoir honte s'il n'en était pas ainsi. As-tu jamais rencontré un ministre? J'en connais des douzaines et pas un qui gagne assez pour se payer une croûte décente.

The French says, roughly, that Cabinet Ministers *do* get paid thirty shillings a week.

Here, I feel sure, the Fonscolombes have thought that 'You betcher' is a term of endearment:

'He has long chafed at the rottenness of motion pictures, and is relying on me to raise the standard,' said Boko.

'You will, angel,' said Nobby.

'You betcher,' said Boko, swilling coffee.

In French:

– Il est furieux de l'inanité de leur production là-bas (Hollywood) et il compte sur moi pour en hausser un peu le niveau.

– Et vous réussirez, mon ange, susurra Nobby.

– Poupée de mon cœur, gargouilla Boko, lampant son café.

In the following passage a concealed quotation (Young's 'Night Thoughts') seems to have put the wrong idea into the translators' heads. Lord Worplesdon, tired and tight, had been sitting out from the East Wibley Fancy Dress Ball in Boko's enormous car. Boko, thinking that the old chap had gone home on his bicycle, drove himself with Lord W. in the back, fast asleep. (And he left him there, locked in the garage when he got home to Bumpleigh Hall.) But 'tired Nature's sweet restorer' in Wodehouse's typewriter certainly meant sleep, not drink.

Driving away at the conclusion of the recent festivities, Boko must inadvertently have taken Uncle Percy with him. He had sped homewards with a song on his lips, and all unknown to him, overlooked while getting a spot of tired Nature's sweet restorer in the back of the car, the old relative had come along for the ride.

A l'issue des récentes festivités, Boko avait dû ramener oncle Percy dans sa voiture, sans s'en rendre compte. Une chanson sur les lèvres il avait dû foncer sur la route du retour et oublier complètement celui qui l'accompagnait, grâce aux lampées du généreux cordial qu'il avait toujours dans sa voiture pour donner éventuellement un coup de pouce à la Nature.

And in the following passage 'the raw spirit' certainly means drink, not courage and innocence. (Boko's plan had been for Bertie to go charging into Uncle Percy's study at 10 a.m. and to start ticking him off and calling him names. Boko was then to appear and defend Uncle Percy. And Boko had typed out a sheet of offensive things that Bertie had to say to Uncle Percy at this early-morning interview):

Typewritten, with single spaces, I suppose the stuff ran to about six hundred words, and of all those six hundred words I don't think there were more than half a dozen which I could have brought myself to say to a man of Uncle Percy's calibre, unless primed to the back teeth with the raw spirit. And Boko, you will recall, was expecting me to deliver my harangue at ten o'clock in the morning.

Tapé à la machine à interligne simple, le texte devait faire, je pense, a peu près six cents mots, et sur ces six cents mots, je ne crois pas qu'il y en àit eu plus d'une demi-douzaine que j'aurais pu me forcer à dire à un homme du calibre d'oncle Percy, à moins d'être farci jusqu'aux dents de courage et d'innocence. Et Boko, vous vous le rappellez, attendait que je débite ma harangue sur le coup de dix heures, ce matin-là.

Now for a couple of places where the French puts in embellishments. Here 'authorities' seemed to them a bit tame.

I have never forgotten the time at Oxford when somebody temporarily converted Stilton to Buddhism. It led to a lot of unpleasantness with the authorities, I recall, he immediately starting to cut chapels and go and meditate beneath the nearest thing the neighbourhood could provide to a bo tree.

Je n'avais jamais oublié l'époque où, à Oxford, quelqu'un l'avait, pour un temps, converti au bouddhisme. Cela lui avait causé des tas d'ennuis avec les grosses légumes de la boîte, car il s'était mis illico à couper à la messe et à aller méditer sous le végétal qui, dans le voisinage, ressemblait le plus à l'Arbre de Sagesse.

'The fat vegetables of the joint' forsooth!

Then:

'... No, no, I would have said ... not Bertie, who was not only at school with me but is at this very moment bursting with my meat.'

This was a nasty one. I wasn't actually bursting with Boko's meat, of course, because there hadn't been such a frightful lot of it, but I saw what he meant. For an instant, when he put it like that, I nearly weakened.

– ... *A d'autres, aurais-je dit. Pas Bertie, qui non seulement a été en classe avec moi, mais qui en ce moment même est encore tout gorgé de ma viande.*

Voilà qui était déplaisant. En réalité, je n'étais pas gorgé de sa viande, c'est évident, mais il était exact que j'avais fait une bonne entaille au beefsteak, ce soir en dinant chez lui, pour ne pas mentionner les pommes de terre frites et deux autres légumes.

Un instant quand il exposa ces choses, je faillis faiblir.

What's all that about chips and two other veg?

Here are three longer passages that I would like to see set at the next Foreign Office Exam for those offering French ... in fact everybody. The Fonscolombes' renderings are given as *terminus a quo* for improvements.

Edwin, the Boy Scout, was trying to do one of his much-feared acts of kindness in cleaning up Bertie's cottage, Wee Nooke. He had shoved gunpowder up the chimney to clean it, and then poured paraffin (mistaking it for water) on the flames. The cottage was burning merrily, and 'for about two shakes of a duck's tail' Bertie 'stood watching it with quiet relish'.

... Then, putting a bit of a damper on the festivities, there came floating into my mind a rather disturbing thought ... to wit, that the last I had seen of young Edwin, he had been seeping back into the kitchen. Presumably, therefore, he was still on the premises, and the conclusion to which one was forced was that, unless somebody took proper steps through the proper channels, he was likely ere long to be rendered unfit for human consumption. This was followed by a second and still more disturbing thought that the only person in a position to do the necessary spot of firemen-save-my-child-ing was good old Wooster.

I mused. I suppose you would call me a fairly intrepid man, taken by and large, but I'm bound to admit I wasn't any too keen on the thing. Apart from anything else, my whole attitude towards the stripling who was faced with the prospect of being grilled on both sides had undergone another quick change.

Puis, pour étouffer un peu la vivacité de ce plaisir, vint s'insinuer dans mon esprit une pensée assez troublante: la dernière fois que j'avais vu le jeune Edwin, il s'était retiré en direction de la cuisine. Vraisemblablement par conséquent, il était encore sur place et la conclusion à laquelle on se trouvait amené était la suivante: à moins qu'on n'intervint promptement pour prendre les mesures nécessaires, il était probable qu'avant longtemps il serait mis à mal. Cette pensée fut suivie d'une autre encore plus troublante: La seule personne à même de jouer les sauveteurs, rôle indispensable, était le bon vieux Wooster.

Je méditai. Je suppose que, vu de loin et grosso modo, on me tient pour un brave, mais je dois admettre que je ne me sentais pas trop décidé. Entre autres choses, il s'était opéré dans mes dispositions à l'égard du jeune veau qui risquait de se faire rissoler un second changement rapide.

Edwin emerged, missing only his eyebrows, and went off to get the fire-brigade. Enter Uncle Percy, and Bertie, leaning on the gate watching the flames, says 'Hullo'. But he was not feeling at ease. Uncle Percy's son had started the fire, but Bertie was not feeling at ease.

... The spine, and I do not attempt to conceal the fact, had become soluble in the last degree.

You may wonder at this, arguing that as I was not responsible for the disaster which had come upon us, I had nothing to fear. But a longish experience has taught me that on these occasions innocence pays no dividends. Pure as the driven snow though he may be, or even purer, it is the man on the spot who gets the brick-bats.

Mes os se liquéfiaient littéralement.

Vous pouvez vous en étonner; car n'étant pas responsable de la catastrophe qui nous frappait, je n'avais rien à craindre. Mais une assez longue expérience m'avait appris qu'en ces occasions-là l'innocence ne rapporte pas. Celui qu'on trouve sur les lieux du désastre a beau etre blanc comme neige ou même d'avantage, c'est lui qui paie les pots cassés.

and

'Jeeves,' I said, getting right down to it in the old Wooster way, 'here's a nice state of things!'

'Sir?'

'Hell's foundations have been quivering.'

'Indeed, sir?'

'The curse has come upon me. As I warned you it would if I ever visited Steeple Bumpleigh. You have long been familiar with my views on this leper colony. Have I not repeatedly said that, what though the spicy breezes blow soft o'er Steeple Bumpleigh, the undersigned deemed it wisest to give it the complete miss in baulk?'

– *Jeeves, dis-je, allant droit au fait, en vrai Wooster, nous voilà frais!*

– *Pardon, Monsieur.*

– *L'Enfer en a frémi jusque dans ses abîmes sans fond.*

– *Vraiment, Monsieur?*

– *La malédiction du Seigneur s'est abattue sur moi. Je vous avais bien dit que c'est ce qui arriverait si je mettais jamais les pieds à Steeple Bumpleigh. Vous connaissez depuis longtemps mes idées sur cet asile de lépreux. Ne vous avais-je pas répété cent fois que même si les souffles parfumés de la béatitude flottaient en permanence sur Steeple Bumpleigh, le plus sage, à mon avis, serait d'éviter ces lieux?*

In the hotel where I was staying in France was a Belgian whose English was perfect barring a slight trace of accent. He told me his French was better, so I gave him *Jeeves, au secours* and said: 'Have a look at this and tell me whether it gives the Wodehouse impression in French. And if so, well or very well?' Without opening it, he said: 'I will read it. But it cannot be very good, for two reasons. First, there are no equivalents for the Wodehouse *layers* of slang in French. There is no upper middle class in France comparable to the English public-school type, and French student slang is regional and changes much too quickly. Anyway, French is a Latin language. In German and Dutch you'd possibly find that Wodehouse translations could be good. But not in French. It hasn't got the same *sort* of idioms as English. The second reason is this: I have never heard of the Fonscolombes, which probably means that they are not *littérateurs* in their own right. Translation is such a badly paid profession that, if you do it for a living, you've got to do it quickly. Even if Wodehouse could be done into French at all, he certainly could not be done quickly. The best hope would be to get some rich man who for a hobby would pore and polish, pore and polish for years. If the Fonscolombes were that sort, I would have heard of them, and I haven't. My guess is that this will be a journeyman translation and uninspired.'

He spent half an hour with the English text, and then half an hour with the French. Then he said: 'No, they haven't got the spark. This translation is just a translation. It is what the French call *gris* ... grey, lack-lustre, a journeyman job. And *Skropshire* is a misprint.'

You may be inclined to take the Belgian's word for it. But for a quick test of his guess that Wodehouse might go into German more easily, and in a comparable idiom, I compared the first paragraph of *Leave it to Psmith* with its German translation (*Psmith Macht Alles*, translator Heinrich Fraenkel, published by Kiepenheuer and Witsch). The English reads:

At the open window of the great library of Blandings Castle, drooping like a wet sock, as was his habit when he had nothing to prop his spine against, the Earl of Emsworth, that amiable and boneheaded peer, stood gazing out over his domain.

The German for the *whole* of that sentence reads:

Am offenen Verandofenster in Schloss Blandings stand Lord Emsworth und blickte auf seine weiten Domänen.

Would you say that Herr Fraenkel had wrung the last drop of meaning out of the English?

The opening sentences of Wodehouse's early novel, *The Prince and Betty*, are:

A pretty girl in a blue dress came out of the house, and began to walk slowly across the terrace to where Elsa Keith sat with Martin Rossiter in the shade of a big sycamore. Elsa and Martin had become engaged some four days before, and were generally to be found at this time sitting together in some shaded spot.

The Esperanto version of this (translator G. Badash) is:

Bela junulino en blua vesto eliris el la domo, kaj ekmarŝis malrapide trans la teraso al la loko, kie sidis Elsa Keith kun Martin Rossiter sub la ombro de la granda acerplatano. Elsa kaj Martin fianĉiĝis antaŭ kelkaj tagoj, kaj, ĝenerale oni trovis ilin, je tiu horo, kune sidantaj en iu ombroplena loko.

I don't see how this could be bettered.

IMAGES

He was built on large lines and seemed to fill the room to over-flowing. In physique, indeed, he was not unlike what Primo Carnera would have been, if Carnera had not stunted his growth by smoking cigarettes as a boy.

*

Even in his brief visit to the grounds, Wilfred had noticed fully half a dozen places which seemed incomplete without a cross indicating spot where body was found by police. It was the sort of house where ravens croak in the front garden just before the death of the heir, and shrieks ring out from behind barred windows in the night.

*

'Don't blame me if Lady Constance takes her lorgnette to you. God bless my soul, though, you can't compare the lorgnettes of today with the ones I used to know as a boy. I remember walking one day in Grosvenor Square with my aunt Brenda and her pug dog Jabberwocky, and a policeman came up and said that the latter ought to be wearing a muzzle. My aunt made no verbal reply. She merely whipped her lorgnette from its holster and looked at the man, who gave one choking gasp and fell back against the railings, without a mark on him but with an awful look of horror in his staring eyes, as if he had seen some dreadful sight. A doctor was sent for, and they managed to bring him round, but he was never the same again. He had to leave the Force, and eventually drifted into the grocery business. And that is how Sir Thomas Lipton got his start.'

*

He was loosely and comfortably dressed in a tweed suit which might have been built by Omar the Tent Maker.

*

His brow was dark and his aspect gloomy. Even on his good days he looked a little like something thrown off by Epstein in a particularly sombre mood, and this was not one of his good days.

*

She went out, breathing flame quietly through her nostrils.

*

To dive under the bed was with Sacheverell Mulliner the work of a moment. And there, as the door opened, he lay, holding his breath and trying to keep his ears from rustling in the draught.

PELHAM GRENVILLE
WODEHOUSE

Ecce auctor magicus, quo non expertior alter
delectare animos hominum risusque movere.
Namque novas scaenae personas intulit et res
ridiculas cuique adiunxit. Cui non bene notus
dives opum iuvenis, comisque animique benigni,
nec quod vult fecisse capax, nisi fidus Achates
ipse doli fabricator adest vestisque decentis
arbiter? Aut comes ille loquax et ventre rotundo
cui patruusque neposque agnatorum et domus omnis
miranda in vita – sic narrat – fata obierunt?
Nobilis est etiam Clarens, fundique paterni
et suis eximiae dominus, Psmitheusque 'relicta
cui fac cuncta', Augustus item qui novit amores
ranicularum, aliusque alio sub sidere natus.
Non vitia autem hominum naso suspendit adunco
sed tenera pietate notat, peccataque ridet.
Hoc quoque, lingua etsi repleat plebeia chartas,
non incomposito patitur pede currere verba,
concinnus, lepidus, puri sermonis amator.

Quid multa? Quem novere omnes, testimonio non eget. Praesento vobis
festivum caput – Petroniumne dicam an Terentium nostrum? –
Pelham Grenville Wodehouse, Societatis Regiae Litterarum sodalem,
ut admittatur honoris causa ad gradum Doctoris in litteris.

> Address by the Public Orator,
> the late Doctor Cyril Bailey,
> in the Sheldonian Theatre,
> Oxford, at the Encaenia, 21
> June 1939.

The Vice-Chancellor, George Gordon, President of Magdalen, created Wodehouse an Honorary Doctor of Letters in the following further Latin:

Vir lepidissime, facetissime, venustissime, iocosissime, ridibundissime, te cum turba tua Leporum, Facetiarum, Venustatum, Iocorum, Risuum, ego auctoritate mea et totius Universitatis admitto ad gradum Doctoris in Litteris honoris causa.

BOOKS

1902 September	*The Pothunters*, A. & C. Black
1903 September	*A Prefect's Uncle*, A. & C. Black
1903 November	*Tales of St Austin's*, A. & C. Black
1904 September	*The Gold Bat*, A. & C. Black
1904 November	*William Tell Told Again*, A. & C. Black
1905 October	*The Head of Kay's*, A. & C. Black
1906 June	*Love Among the Chickens*, George Newnes
1907 October	*The White Feather*, A. & C. Black
1907 October	*Not George Washington*, Cassell (with H. Westbrook)
1908 June	*By the Way Book*, Globe (with H. Westbrook)
1909 April	*The Swoop*, Alston Rivers
1909 September	*Mike**, A. & C. Black
1910 September	*Psmith in the City*, A. & C. Black
1910 November	*A Gentleman of Leisure*, Alston Rivers
1911 August	*A Gentleman of Leisure*, George Newnes (reissue)
1912 May	*The Prince and Betty*, Mills & Boon
1913 August	*The Little Nugget*, Methuen
1914 January	*The Man Upstairs*, Methuen
1915 September	*Something Fresh*, Methuen
1915 September	*Psmith, Journalist*, A. & C. Black
1917 March	*The Man with Two Left Feet*, Methuen
1917 October	*Uneasy Money*, Methuen
1918 May	*Piccadilly Jim*, Herbert Jenkins
1919 May	*My Man Jeeves*, George Newnes
1919 October	*A Damsel in Distress*, Herbert Jenkins
1920 July	*The Coming of Bill*, Herbert Jenkins
1921 February	*The Indiscretions of Archie*, Herbert Jenkins

1921	February	*The Prince and Betty*, George Newnes (reissue)
1921	February	*A Gentleman of Leisure*, Herbert Jenkins (reissue)
1921	May	*Love Among the Chickens*, Herbert Jenkins (revised and reissued)
1921	July	*Jill the Reckless*, Herbert Jenkins
1922	February	*The Clicking of Cuthbert*, Herbert Jenkins
1922	June	*The Girl on the Boat*, Herbert Jenkins
1922	October	*The Adventures of Sally*, Herbert Jenkins
1923	May	*The Inimitable Jeeves*, Herbert Jenkins
1923	November	*Leave it to Psmith*, Herbert Jenkins
1924	June	*Ukridge*, Herbert Jenkins
1924	November	*Bill the Conqueror*, Methuen
1925	October	*Carry On, Jeeves*, Herbert Jenkins
1925	October	*Sam the Sudden*, Methuen
1926	April	*The Heart of a Goof*, Herbert Jenkins
1927	April	*The Small Bachelor*, Methuen
1927	September	*Meet Mr Mulliner*, Herbert Jenkins
1928	July	*Money for Nothing*, Herbert Jenkins
1929	April	*Mr Mulliner Speaking*, Herbert Jenkins
1929	July	*Summer Lightning*, Herbert Jenkins
1930	July	*Very Good, Jeeves*, Herbert Jenkins
1931	March	*Big Money*, Herbert Jenkins
1931	September	*If I Were You*, Herbert Jenkins
1932	April	*Dr Sally*, Herbert Jenkins
1932	August	*Hot Water*, Herbert Jenkins
1932	March	*Louder and Funnier*, Faber & Faber
1933	January	*Mulliner Nights*, Herbert Jenkins
1933	August	*Heavy Weather*, Herbert Jenkins
1934	March	*Thank You, Jeeves*, Herbert Jenkins
1934	October	*Right Ho, Jeeves*, Herbert Jenkins
1935	February	*Enter Psmith**, A. & C. Black
1935	April	*Blandings Castle*, Herbert Jenkins
1935	October	*The Luck of the Bodkins*, Herbert Jenkins
1936	April	*Young Men in Spats*, Herbert Jenkins
1936	September	*Laughing Gas*, Herbert Jenkins

1937 March	*Lord Emsworth and Others*, Herbert Jenkins
1938 February	*Summer Moonshine*, Herbert Jenkins
1938 October	*The Code of the Woosters*, Herbert Jenkins
1939 August	*Uncle Fred in the Springtime*, Herbert Jenkins
1940 April	*Eggs, Beans and Crumpets*, Herbert Jenkins
1940 October	*Quick Service*, Herbert Jenkins
1946 May	*Money in the Bank*, Herbert Jenkins
1947 June	*Joy in the Morning*, Herbert Jenkins
1947 October	*Full Moon*, Herbert Jenkins
1948 May	*Spring Fever*, Herbert Jenkins
1948 October	*Uncle Dynamite*, Herbert Jenkins
1949 September	*The Mating Season*, Herbert Jenkins
1950 July	*Nothing Serious*, Herbert Jenkins
1951 April	*The Old Reliable*, Herbert Jenkins
1952 March	*Dr Sally* (reissue), Herbert Jenkins
1952 April	*Barmy in Wonderland*, Herbert Jenkins
1952 October	*Pigs Have Wings*, Herbert Jenkins
1953 February	*Mike at Wrykyn**, Herbert Jenkins
1953 February	*Mike and Psmith**, Herbert Jenkins
1953 April	*Ring for Jeeves*, Herbert Jenkins
1953 October	*Performing Flea*, Herbert Jenkins
1954 May	*Bring on the Girls*, Herbert Jenkins
1954 October	*Jeeves and the Feudal Spirit*, Herbert Jenkins
1956 January	*French Leave*, Herbert Jenkins
1957 January	*Something Fishy*, Herbert Jenkins
1957 October	*Over Seventy*, Herbert Jenkins
1958 June	*Cocktail Time*, Herbert Jenkins
1959 June	*A Few Quick Ones*, Herbert Jenkins
1960 August	*Jeeves in the Offing*, Herbert Jenkins
1961 October	*Ice in the Bedroom*, Herbert Jenkins
1962 August	*Service with a Smile*, Herbert Jenkins
1963 June	*Louder and Funnier* (reissue), Herbert Jenkins
1963 August	*Stiff Upper Lip, Jeeves*, Herbert Jenkins
1964 August	*Frozen Assets*, Herbert Jenkins
1965 August	*Galahad at Blandings*, Herbert Jenkins
1967 October	*Company for Henry*, Herbert Jenkins
1968 September	*Do Butlers Burgle Banks?*, Herbert Jenkins

1969 September   *A Pelican at Blandings*, Barrie & Jenkins
1970 October   *The Girl in Blue*, Barrie & Jenkins
1971 October   *Much Obliged. Jeeves*, Barrie & Jenkins
1972 October   *Pearls, Girls and Monty Bodkin*, Barrie & Jenkins
1973 October   *Bachelors Anonymous*, Barrie & Jenkins
1974 October   *Aunts Aren't Gentlemen*, Barrie & Jenkins

Omnibus volumes

1931 October   *Jeeves Omnibus*, Herbert Jenkins
1935 October   *Mulliner Omnibus*, Herbert Jenkins
1939 May   *Week-end Wodehouse*, Herbert Jenkins
1966 September   *Plum Pie*, Herbert Jenkins
1967 June   *The World of Jeeves*, Herbert Jenkins
1968 September   *A Carnival of Modern Humour*, Herbert Jenkins
                  (with Scott Meredith)
1974 April   *The World of Psmith*, Barrie & Jenkins
1975 October   *The World of Ukridge*, Barrie & Jenkins
1976 March   *The World of Blandings*, Barrie & Jenkins

*Mike (A. & C. Black, 1909). The second half of this book was published in 1935 as a separate volume entitled *Enter Psmith*. When Herbert Jenkins took over the publication of *Mike* they reissued it in two volumes – *Mike at Wrykyn* and *Mike and Psmith* – in 1953. The second title is substantially the same as *Enter Psmith*. It should be noted, however, that the two Jenkins volumes have been slightly revised to bring them up to date.

PLAYS

1911   *A Gentleman of Leisure*, with John Stapleton. In New York Douglas Fairbanks starred as Jimmy and, later, John Barrymore
1913   *A Thief for a Night*, with John Stapleton
1913   *Brother Alfred*, with H. W. Westbrook

1914 *Nuts and Wine*, with C. H. Bovill

1916 *Miss Springtime*, lyrics by P. G. Wodehouse. Score by Kalman

1917 *Have a Heart**, score by Jerome Kern

1917 *Leave it to Jane**, score by Jerome Kern

1917 *Miss 1917**, score by Jerome Kern

1917 *Oh! Boy (Oh! Joy)**, score by Jerome Kern. Beatrice Lillie starred in London production

1917 *The Riviera Girl**, score by Kalman

1917 *Ringtime**

1918 *Ask Dad (Oh! My Dear!)**

1918 *The Girl Behind the Gun (Kissing Time)**, George Grossmith, Leslie Henson, Phyllis Dare, Yvonne Arnaud, Tom Walls and Stanley Holloway played in London production

1918 *Oh! Lady, Lady!**, score by Jerome Kern. P. G. Wodehouse wrote the lyric of 'Bill' for this show but the song was cut out and later used in *Showboat*. The book, *The Small Bachelor*, was based on the play *Oh! Lady, Lady!*

1918 *See You Later**

1919 *The Rose of China**, lyrics by P. G. Wodehouse

1921 *The Golden Moth*, with Fred Thompson. Score by Ivor Novello. Starring Robert Michaelis and W. H. Berry

1922 *The Cabaret Girl*, with George Grossmith. Score by Jerome Kern. Starring Dorothy Dickson and George Grossmith

1923 *The Beauty Prize*, with George Grossmith. Score by Jerome Kern. Starring Dorothy Dickson, Leslie Henson and George Grossmith

1924 *Sitting Pretty**, score by Jerome Kern

1926 *Oh! Kay**, with George and Ira Gershwin. Starring Gertrude Lawrence

1926 *Hearts and Diamonds*, with Laurie Wylie. Starring Lupino Lane

1926 *The Play's the Thing*, from the Hungarian of F. Molnar

1927 *The Nightingale**

1927 *Her Cardboard Lover*, from the French, with Valerie Wyngate. Starring Tallulah Bankhead and Leslie Howard

1927 *Good Morning, Bill*, from the Hungarian of L. Fodor

1928   *Rosalie*, lyrics by P. G. Wodehouse. With George and Ira
        Gershwin, and Sigmund Romberg and Bill McGuire

1928   *The Three Musketeers*, lyrics by P. G. Wodehouse. With
        George Grossmith. Score by Rudy Friml

1928   *A Damsel in Distress*†, with Ian Hay. Starring Basil Foster.
        Ann Todd appeared in this

1929   *Baa, Baa, Black Sheep*, with Ian Hay. Ann Todd appeared in
        this

1929   *Candlelight*, from the French of Siegfried Geyer

1930   *Leave it to Psmith*†, with Ian Hay

1934   *Who's Who? (If I Were You)**, starring Violet Vanbrugh and
        Laurence Grossmith

1934   *Anything Goes**, score by Cole Porter

1935   *The Inside Stand*, starring Ralph Lynn and Olive Blakeney

1956   *Come On Jeeves**

        *With Guy Bolton.   †Books dramatized.

FILMS

1915   *Gentleman of Leisure*

1917   *Uneasy Money*

1919   *Oh, Boy*

1919   *Piccadilly Jim*

1920   *Prince and Betty*, starring William Desmond, Mary Thurman

1920   *A Damsel in Distress*, starring June Caprice, Creighton Hale

1920   *Oh Lady, Lady*, starring Bebe Daniels, Walter Hiers

1920   *Their Mutual Child*

1921   *Stick Around*

1923   *Gentleman of Leisure*, starring Jack Holt

1924   *Rodney Fails to Qualify*

1924   *Chester Forgets Himself*

1924   *The Long Hole*

1924   *The Clicking of Cuthbert*

1924   *Ordeal By Golf*

1928 *Oh Kay*, starring Colleen More

1932 *Brother Alfred*, starring Gene Gerrard, Molly Lamont

1933 *Summer Lightning*, starring Ralph Lynn, Winifred Shotter

1933 *Leave It to Me*, starring Gene Gerrard, Molly Lamont

1935 *Dizzy Dames*, starring Marjorie Rambeau, Lawrence Gray

1936 *Piccadilly Jim*, starring Robert Montgomery, Madge Evans

1936 *Thank You, Jeeves*, starring Arthur Treacher, David Niven, Virginia Fields

1937 *A Damsel in Distress*, starring Fred Astaire, Joan Fontaine

1937 *Step Lively, Jeeves*, starring Arthur Treacher, Patricia Ellis

Metro-Goldwyn-Mayer bought *If I Were You* for $25,000 in 1930, and it has not been produced yet. P.G.W. went to Hollywood first in 1930 on a year's contract with M.G.M. at $2,000 a week. Then again for six months in 1936 at $1,500 a week. In 1930 P.G.W. worked on the script *Rosalie*, which was based on a musical which he, Guy Bolton, Sigmund Romberg, William McGuire and the Gershwins had done for Ziegfeld. Nothing came of it and, when P.G.W. went back to Hollywood six years later, M.G.M. put him back to work on *Rosalie*. It was eventually produced, with music by Cole Porter.

INDEX

MORE ABOUT PENGUINS
AND PELICANS

Penguinews, which appears every month, contains details of all the new books issued by Penguins as they are published. From time to time it is supplemented by our stocklist which includes around 5,000 titles.

A specimen copy of *Penguinews* will be sent to you free on request. Please write to Dept EP, Penguin Books Ltd, Harmondsworth, Middlesex, for your copy.

In the U.S.A.: For a complete list of books available from Penguins in the United States write to Dept CS, Penguin Books, 625 Madison Avenue, New York, New York 10022.

In Canada: For a complete list of books available from Penguins in Canada write to Penguin Books Canada Ltd, 2801 John Street, Markham, Ontario L3R 1B4.